You CAN Raise Decent Children

You CAN Raise

Decent Children

by

BERTHOLD ERIC SCHWARZ, M.D.

Diplomate of the American Board of Psychiatry and Neurology

and

BARTHOLOMEW A. RUGGIERI, M.D.

Diplomate of the American Board of Pediatrics

ARLINGTON HOUSE   *New Rochelle, N.Y.*

FIRST PRINTING, JANUARY 1971
SECOND PRINTING, APRIL 1971

Library of Congress Catalog Card Number 72-143276

ISBN 0-87000-113-2

MANUFACTURED IN THE UNITED STATES OF AMERICA

TO

Adelaide McF. Johnson, M.D., Ph.D. (1905–1960)

A courageous physician whose pioneering work has brought a deeper understanding and new hope to the treatment of the emotional problems of parents and children.

CONTENTS

■-●-■

CHAPTER 1. *Violence—The Most Urgent Problem of Our Day*   *23*

To probe for the underlying causes of today's turmoil challenges specialists in many fields. Medical specialists are uniquely equipped to unravel the complexities and subtleties of parent-child relationships that breed emotional illnesses that in our overpermissive society all too often find expression in acts of violence.

CHAPTER 2. *How Baby Habits Affect Later Behavior*   *28*

The influence on later character structure of early feeding and toilet training—the earliest parent-child relationships —is explored.

CHAPTER 3. *Foundations of Masculinity and Femininity*   *60*

The relationship of the boy or girl with each parent affects later sexual identity, as does the parental punishment the child receives.

Preface

Ten years ago when we wrote a book called *Parent-Child Tensions,* we stressed the role of permissiveness in children's (and parents') antisocial behavior. Today, the emphasis on permissiveness as a causative factor is more timely than ever, for we are living in a society torn by violence and destructiveness. If the values we cherish are to be passed on to our children, then concerned parents and other responsible adults must explore the dimensions of the problem so that action may be based on understanding.

Indeed, a rational approach to today's problems through prevention and treatment must be based on a thorough understanding of causes. Although we are aware of numerous causes—sociological, economic, and political—as physicians our chief concern and competence is with the role of the parent-child relationship in today's social turmoil.

We have, therefore, written this book and filled it with timely new material so that what we previously had presented to the professionally trained expert is now made available to concerned parents, psychologists, social workers, teachers, nurses, clergymen, and others. Together with the physician, they are vitally concerned with the formation or the reformation of the personality structure of our children today.

It is our hope, moreover, that the reader may find this book of value in understanding himself, his family, and the other significant people in his life. We have deliberately used nontechnical language, but we have not avoided presenting sometimes difficult concepts. In our attempt to present as comprehensive a picture as possible, we have included some material that a few readers may find upsetting. But only by recognizing the complete picture in its reality can the reader truly understand the problem and begin to see what course of action to take.

We are grateful to our friend, the late Rev. Timothy V.A. Kennedy, M.D., who encouraged us throughout the preparation of our original manuscript and made many valuable suggestions out of his vast clinical experience as a psychiatrist and his special interest in all the forms of delinquent behavior in children and adults. We are also grateful to the late Dr. Adelaide McF. Johnson, one of the originators of collaborative study, who generously read our manuscript and offered helpful suggestions from her own rich clinical experience. Dr. Johnson was a leading authority on emotional factors in the causes, prevention, and treatment of juvenile delinquency and sexual deviations, and on the role of these factors in the development of criminals.

The inspiration for this book lies in the deep and far-reaching influence of two physicians, teachers, and friends of unusual wisdom and perspective, the late Drs. Samuel W. Hamilton and Louis S. London, whose combined careers spanned almost a century of psychiatric and psychoanalytic experience.

Special mention should also be made of the late Dr. Ralph S. Banay, former chief psychiatrist at Sing Sing, who has dedicated his near half-century career and spirited writings to the problems of youth and the medical aspects of crime.

Also found on these pages are the teachings and

the wide experiences of Drs. Reginald G. Bickford, David A. Boyd, Lawrence C. Kolb, Magnus C. Petersen, and Howard P. Rome, whose diversified interests range from the investigative laboratory to the patient's bedside.

We thank our loyal secretaries, Mrs. Evelyn M. Guldner and Miss Vilma E. Semsey, for their help. We also acknowledge our gratitude to Mrs. Joan W. Jesurun for her thoughtful and expert editing of the manuscript.

BERTHOLD ERIC SCHWARZ
BARTHOLOMEW A. RUGGIERI

July 1970
Montclair, N. J.

Introduction

"I'm not worried, Doctor, about the treatment of Johnny's pneumonia. One shot of medicine and he'll be well. It's the other problems that worry me."

Such a comment by a concerned parent is not unusual. The mother's implication that too often the emotional problems of children are not given their just due is indeed true. But today we know that we cannot separate the child's emotional problems from other manifestations of disease. In fact, the line between the child's emotional and physical makeup is poorly drawn; both these aspects of the total child are inseparably mixed. From experience in diagnosing and treating diseases in children (and adults), the physician knows that both emotional and physical factors are present in the same child (and the adult) and interact to produce the final picture of disease that presents itself.

To attempt to classify symptoms arbitrarily as due to either emotional or to physical causes is scientific folly. Emotional problems may masquerade with symptoms that are entirely suggestive of physical disease. Or, emotional problems may actually lead to a serious physical disability, such as obesity or bedwetting. On the other hand, physical disease may masquerade with symptoms that are entirely suggestive of emotional disease. Examples are brain tumor or an overactive thyroid gland.

To study and understand the child (and his parents) as a whole requires years of training and experience in the practice of medicine. Only the physician can form a clear picture of the individual as a whole from the hodgepodge of apparently isolated findings that make up the child: the difficult delivery and the mother's fears of its effect on the baby; the colic at the age of three months; the age at which the first step was taken; the blood pressure; the heart murmur and the fright that it produced in the child and his parents; the sore throats; the goblins in the nightmares; the polio attack; the taunts of his brother; the battle with his mother during bowel training; the unequal reflexes; and the imitation of his father's swagger.

The following chapters on the interactions of the emotions and the behavior of the child (and his parents) are an outgrowth of many informal discussions during the authors' close friendship during years of specialty training at the Mayo Clinic and subsequently as neighbors in the private practice of their specialties, psychiatry and pediatrics. Through the years the authors have become increasingly aware that a thorough understanding of the patient's emotions is indispensable to the total care of the patient.

Man always has been interested in his emotions, how and why he feels, thinks, and acts as he does. Since shortly before the turn of the century, the pioneering research of many physicians has resulted in the study of man's emotions on a more scientific basis. Mention should be made of Sigmund Freud, Carl Jung, and Alfred Adler. Despite the far-reaching significance of their findings, the importance of the work of these men is not appreciated as widely as it should be.

In 1943, while working together at the Institute for

Juvenile Research in Chicago, A. McF. Johnson, M.D., and S. A. Szurek, M.D., first elaborated the therapeutic technique of intensive bilateral or multilateral treatment. Such collaborative study is a technique in which one physician studies the feelings and the behavior patterns of the child while other physicians study the feelings and behavior patterns of the parents (or parent substitutes) and other children. This is done in hour-long interviews ranging from one to five a week and lasting over a period of a few months to several years. The physicians meet weekly or biweekly to discuss the findings of the preceding hours. By such frequent and continued comparison of all the data obtained from both the child and the parents, the interaction of the emotions of child and parent becomes clear. In almost every case of an emotionally disturbed child, it has been found that the child's specific disturbed feelings stem directly from specific disturbed feelings in the parents. Through collaborative study the physician can pinpoint the source of the child's emotional disturbances. This method has clarified many previously mysterious and difficult problems and promises to clarify more. As an offshoot of the findings of collaborative study, it has also been found that the physician frequently cannot treat the child successfully without also treating the source of the child's problems—the parents.

After their earlier researches in Chicago, Drs. Johnson and Szurek continued their work separately at the Mayo Clinic in Rochester and at the Langley Porter Clinic in San Francisco, and elaborated their original discoveries.* At the present time, this therapeutic approach has become widespread and is, in fact, very much the rule in many of the best clinics in this country.

From the authors' experience with this new technique while in the child psychiatry unit of the Mayo Clinic, they learned certain principles of approaching disease that they then applied and expanded in the private practice of their specialties. From the study of thousands of such cases the authors have found this knowledge to be extremely useful in the management of the usual routine problems that make up a physician's everyday practice, in addition to the unraveling of the tricky, subtle, and rarer problems that find their way to the specialist or the large medical center.

Recognizing how vital is this new information and how it would help to answer the many questions that parents direct to the authors in their private practice, it was felt that there would be distinct value in writing a book on these problems for parents and other concerned adults. This information has been shown to be of great value not only in the physician's treatment of these disorders but also in the prevention of emotional disturbances.

During the writing of this book, the question arose whether or not to include chapters on topics that are usually considered hush-hush and improper to mention, much less discuss. The importance of this ques-

*David B. Robinson, M.D., Professor of Psychiatry, State University of New York (Syracuse), a friend and associate of Adelaide McFadyen Johnson, has compiled and edited her collected papers, *Experience, Affect, and Behavior*, University of Chicago Press, 1969.

tion of including or omitting these subjects from the book was increased by our knowledge that recently developed information on these subjects was of a potentially explosive character. On the other hand, the authors knew that these problems are common in the everyday practice of medicine and have far-reaching and serious effects upon society itself. To dodge a discussion of such important problems when so much is known about them would weaken the purpose of this book. Therefore, these subjects have been included, and an honest discussion has been given.

In studying this book, with its many cases from the authors' own practices, the reader will discern a consistent pattern of approaching emotional problems. The specific details of each case apply only to that particular case. However, the general method of approach to the problems being discussed (e. g., juvenile delinquency) applies to all cases coming to the physician with that problem. No case is presented in its entirety; nor could it be. Of the many facts gained by the physicians after many hours of painstaking study of the patient and the parents only the highlights are given. These examples are offered only to make clear to the reader, through detailed application to an actual patient, the general principles to be learned from a careful study of each type of emotional disturbance. Unfortunately, these disturbances are all too common; one has only to look for them.

This book does not attempt to present all types of emotional disturbances in children, and all the known material. Nor was this book written cookbook style, as a handy reference or manual in which the reader can look up a subject in the index and then read the material on that subject alone without reference to the rest of the book. Much of the material presented lends itself to skimming over, with vague generalizations and honeyed platitudes. However, the newer knowledge about these problems may often be difficult for the lay person, with little medical background, to understand. This book was written, therefore, in such a manner that any one chapter can best be understood only in the light of all that has been presented in each of the previous chapters. *This book can be understood best if it is read from beginning to end without omission.*

Collaborative study has shown how the specific feelings and behavior of the child are dependent upon the specific feelings and behavior of the parents. It has been shown that the child's emotional experiences will determine his emotional makeup as an adult. Thus, this book, which is directed primarily to the problems of the child, should also help to clarify the problems of the adult. In this way, there can be not only help but hope for all of society to benefit.

B.E.S.
B.A.R.

You CAN Raise Decent Children

1

Violence—The Most Urgent Problem of Our Day

Today illegitimacy, welfare, and corruption have become a way of life. Many of our cities are torn by insurrection. Whole groups seem to have gone berserk. Looting and burning go unchecked.

Our streets have become unsafe. To walk through a park is to risk mugging, rape, assault, and perverse acts. National monuments and public buildings are desecrated. Assassinations destroy our leaders. Macabre killings, robberies, and manslaughters soar to all-time records. Bystanders are afraid to intervene as innocents are assaulted. Our policemen and firemen, who are in the front lines of society's defense of law and order, are wantonly attacked. The cry of "police brutality" becomes another excuse for further flouting of the law. Few rise to the defense of our police, who are further hobbled by orders restricting them in carrying out their duty.

College campuses have become battlegrounds of revolution. Academic authorities all too often stand by helplessly and permit the usurpation of private and public property while protesting the rights of the rebels—not all of whom are students.

The clothing young people wear reveals their confusion in sexual identity—or they wear almost no clothing at all. Drugs like LSD, goof balls, STP, marijuana, and narcotics have become an accepted way of life for many. The often lethal combination of alcohol and automobiles is widespread. The Puritan ethic is obsolete. Some theologians proclaim that God is dead. Indeed, we are told we are living in the post-Christian era. Ours is labeled the affluent society, yet our youth lack purpose, direction, and identity. However variously individual and group delinquency manifests itself, it is apparent that delinquency is not limited to any social or economic class.

Television, the movies, the theater, the popular press, and radio are filled with acts of violence, lurid sex, and crime. The public is made eyewitness to the dramatic and often spectacular effects of mayhem.

The news media are noisy with the overpermissive viewpoints of politicians, clergymen, editors, educators, and self-styled reformers. All too often John Q. Public is told about the benefits society owes him but with no mention of his personal responsibility.

The right to dissent is confused with license to destroy and to loot. The public, and particularly the all-too-suggestible youth, can be manipulated into a frenzy without any immediate outlet. Often, under the guise of quelling disorders, the leaders foment trouble. They use the threat of violence by their followers to extort what their group demands from society at large. And some misguided citizens encourage such lawlessness while professing only compassion for their fellowmen.

The so-called have-nots in our society are promised the skies by some of our elected representatives. Such leaders talk about the responsibilities of all citizens, but the programs they offer cater to the irresponsibility of pressure groups. Commissions are appointed, superficial sympathy is shown, and pat rationalizations are offered: "If I were poor I'd revolt too." "Not enough welfare." "The government owes everybody equality." "We must develop the moral and sexual rebellion of youth." And the corruption and decay of our society continues unabated.

Many feel that the courts have turned our system of justice topsy-turvy by tipping the scales in favor of the criminal. In our upsidedown culture, some courts have become more concerned about legal hair-splitting and the rights of the predators than the safety of peace-loving, law-abiding citizens.

All too few authorities have been able forthrightly to set limits to the violence of the destructive few. Such officials have not ensured law and order for the all too silent but peaceful majority. Molders of public opinion seem to have forgotten that the primary purpose of government is to maintain peace and to protect its citizens from the lawless within and without.

Before civic peace and social health can be restored, one must search for deep-rooted causes of the delinquency and violence that disrupts our society and corrupts our youth. Such searching is already producing voluminous material from such disciplines as sociology, psychology, anthropology, law, and theology.

One area that medicine is in a unique position to study intensively is the complex and often subtle parent-child relationships. The physician is professionally equipped to appraise the role of heredity and the physical, physiological, and biochemical aspects of both individual and group life. Furthermore, through his studies of the unconscious minds of parents and their children he is enabled to understand the relationships and tensions between the members of a family. He can discover how the family reacts to the bombardment of its moral values by the social and interpersonal stresses of living today. By studying the members of a family and weaving together all the pertinent facts, he can produce specific and often hidden information that can uncover the causes of parent-child tensions.

To the parent, the causes of emotional illness seem bafflingly complex. He knows that man does not get sick on love. It is doubtful that he ever did. On the contrary, emotional illnesses are bred by hatred, fear, lust, greed, and ignorance. These general, non-specific causes are often tinged with horror and revulsion. Although dealing with such passions is not always a pleasant task, we must go where the facts lead us. Only then can we initiate actions leading to prevention and treatment.

Why is one person or one family more vulnerable than another to all these tensions? How is it that a seemingly stable and affluent family background is no guarantee of emotional health? Why does one child in a family, and not the other children, yield to disabling pressures? And what connection do disturbed parent-child relationships have with other emotional states and psychosomatic ailments? For example, why does one child act out his violence while another child develops bronchial asthma or a fear of going to school? What are the earliest roots of these illnesses? What are the links between such early character traits as difficulty with feeding and bowel training, temper tantrums, lying, and disobedience, and later, more formidable problems such as stealing, fire setting, and sexual difficulties? What should the parent *know* and what can he *do* about these unwelcome manifestations so as to help his child gain a healthier and happier future?

Some answers to these questions are presented in this book. For the parent and for other concerned adults, some measure of understanding may be gained and suggestions accepted for coping with this most urgent problem of our day—violence in all its ugly and crippling forms. The following chapters provide many signposts toward better mental health for both parent and child.

2

How Baby Habits Affect Later Behavior

THE MOUTH STAGE

The child's emotional growth should keep pace with his physical growth. Any adult who has watched children develop knows that the child's body grows most rapidly during the first two years of life, with a second period of rapid growth occurring during adolescence. It is perhaps less well known that by the time a child is two years old his brain has grown to more than three-fourths of its adult size. And it is probably even less well known that in the preschool years the foundations are laid for the child's feelings and attitudes toward people that will direct his behavior throughout life. True, emotional growth continues beyond the preschool years and throughout life, but such growth rests upon this early foundation. The emotional values and feelings that are acquired during the preschool years influence all the emotional values and feelings acquired later in life. Failure to gratify the child's simple needs in these early years sows the seeds for later resentment, insecurity, and anger.

The newborn's first response is the birth cry, but any mother will remember that even in her womb the baby had periods of relative activity and inactivity. It is known that during this period various hormones and chemicals are constantly being interchanged between mother and child. Two examples are German measles occurring early in pregnancy and the recent tragedies associated with use of thalidomide in early pregnancy. The results in many cases have been children with various birth defects. As early as the seventh month, while inside the mother's womb, the baby's brain is discharging electrical impulses that can be detected by a brain-wave machine. These brain waves have been shown to change when the mother alters her position or when she hears a loud noise. Thus, even before birth, things that affect the mother are already being reflected in the child's brain. Someday medical science may further unravel these mysterious changes and reveal other physical, chemical, and even emotional relationships between mother and child before birth. As of now, any attempt to discuss what occurs emotionally between mother and child before birth is pure speculation.

Obviously there is a great gap between the newborn's first cry and the adult's precise muscular coordination and his subtle shades of love and hate. The baby is completely helpless. He is dependent upon his parents. He may cry because he is hungry or uncomfortable. He may be in pain, or he may just need love, the feeling of being warm and physically close to another human being. It cannot be stressed too often that the baby learns to love by receiving love.

Mrs. M. wanted a boy very badly, and when a daughter was born, she had immediate trouble. Nancy was a quiet baby in the hospital. Nursery rounds rarely found the baby awake. But the second day after mother and baby went home from the hospital, Nancy began crying for long periods at a time. Nothing seemed to satisfy her. The entire household was in an understandable turmoil. Mrs. M. frantically telephoned the physician, who came to the house, examined the baby, and found no evidence of disease. However, when he picked up Nancy and held her gently in his arms, she relaxed, closed her eyes, and fell asleep. The astonished mother asked, "Do you mean you're supposed to pick the baby up when she cries?" The physician understood the situation better when Mrs. M., discussing her methods of feeding the baby, said that Nancy was feeding herself with a bottle holder. The baby was lacking the physical and emotional attachment to another human being that she desperately needed.

"But Doctor, are you supposed to pick up a baby every time she cries?" If the baby is crying because the diapers are wet, change them; if the baby is hungry, feed her. Or, the crying may be due to gas pains; but it causes the swallowing of more air and thus increases the pain. Finally, crying may simply be crying—a good way for the growing infant to express her energy and restlessness; she has not yet learned any other means of expressing herself. The older child may jump, sing, or run about with the pure joy of life, but the young baby can only cry and thrash about. From this simple expression of feeling, the infant gradually learns from the parents the innumerable and complex emotional reactions associated with living.

Before the birth of the baby, the doctor usually asks the mother whether or not she plans to feed her baby from the breast or from a bottle. This question has aroused much confusion and emotion, but the answer is really not so difficult. The important point is how the mother feels toward her baby. It does not really matter which method is used. If the mother has adequate breast milk and enjoys breast-feeding, that certainly should be the method of choice. On the other hand, if the mother is unable to breast-feed or does not wish to do so for any one of several reasons, she can substitute a formula without any physical or emotional harm to the baby. If the mother loves her child and the child is healthy, the specific method of feeding is of secondary importance.

The ability to breast-feed depends upon the mother's health, her own feelings of contentment, and her innermost sentiments in this matter. If she really does not want to breast-feed, she will be unable to produce milk no matter what she or the physician may say to the contrary. Sudden fright may stop an already established flow of breast milk. For example, Mrs. B.'s ample supply of milk stopped overnight when her husband was accidentally killed.

The child's development progresses downward,

from head to feet. He first fixes on an object with his eyes. For example, by one month of age, a child will commonly follow a moving light with his eyes through a 90° arc. Next, he will reach for an object, and eventually, by four to five months of age, he will succeed in grasping the object, although extremely awkwardly. By about four months of age the child plays with his hands, and eventually manages to place his thumb in his mouth. Even this simple act, expected for this age, causes many mothers to turn to the physician for advice. Continuing this downward progression, the baby learns to control his back muscles so that he can sit without support and then masters control of the other parts of his body so that he learns to crawl, stand, and finally walk.

Many parents are unnecessarily concerned about thumb-sucking. Mrs. F. surprised her physician one morning when she told him that she had the nurses place mittens on her five-day-old baby girl after she "caught" the baby with thumb in mouth.

When a child's thumb finds its way to the mouth at this early age, it is just plain luck. But Mrs. F. did not want a thumb-sucker; the mittens had to stay.

Actually a mother need not become concerned with persistent thumb-sucking until the child is three to five years of age. If the thumb-sucking persists beyond this age, it may be a symptom of emotional disturbance. The child behaves at a babylike level when he should be progressing to young childhood.

Although the various phases of emotional development are discussed separately in these early chapters, nature does not place each phase in its own niche completely separate from the other phases of development. The mouth phase lasts from birth until the first year of life, it is true, but interests and enjoyments which come from the mouth do not end abruptly at one year of age. After all, many adults still enjoy eating, gum-chewing, smoking, kissing, and the like. At one year of age, a new center of interest and enjoyment normally appears and takes precedence over the earlier interests in the pleasures derived from the mouth (see pages 42–59). We shall see in later chapters that such progress may occur later than expected. Even with the appearance of the next stage of emotional development, the great dependence upon earlier means of enjoyment (for example, the mouth) continues as strongly as before.

Carl, at four years of age, continues to suck his thumb. He also bites his nails and grinds his teeth. His mother has tried every means to stop the thumb-sucking: punishment, cajolery, bribery, and painting the thumb with a bad-tasting liquid. Contrary to the magazine advertisements, Carl apparently does not mind the taste of this liquid. Or, his pleasure from thumb-sucking may be greater than his distaste for the liquid. His mother is now considering placing splints on his arms (so he cannot bend them to place his thumb in his mouth) or attaching a rakelike device to his upper teeth against the hard palate (so that when he tries to suck his thumb, the rake will scrape against his thumb). Such cruel and suppressive devices may only increase Carl's desire to suck his thumb.

From earliest infancy, unfortunately, Carl was not permitted to gratify his natural desire to suck. His mother discouraged all thumb-sucking (at an age when this was normally expected), because she feared it would deform his growing teeth and mouth. She stopped the nipple and the bottle completely when Carl was six months of age, thus depriving him of another indispensable means of enjoying himself through the mouth during the first year of life. Most children want a bottle and nipple, at least at bedtime, until they are two to three years old.

Carl's mother always pulled out of his mouth anything he put there with the rebuke, "Dirty boy!" She was apparently unaware that at a very early age the child learns the shape and feel of an object as well, if not better, with his mouth than with his hands and eyes. The answer to this problem of thumb-sucking is therefore more complex than simply saying, "You must not!" or using suppressive measures.

From what they have read and been told, many mothers fear that thumb-sucking will deform the teeth. This is *not* true. More important than such an unjustified fear should be the justified fear of deforming the child's emotional development by not permitting him to do what is expected for his age. He is thus deprived of one of the chief means of obtaining pleasure appropriate for his age.

Nail-biting, teeth-grinding, gnawing on pencils, gum-chewing (and smoking and drinking in adults), with their emphasis upon the mouth as a means of obtaining pleasure and relieving tension, are all related to the mouth stage of development.

Georgie, six years old, was brought to the physician's office by a nervous, worried mother. Georgie was a persistent thumb-sucker and had numerous other emotional problems. His mother feared the worst—mental deficiency. Her answers to the physician's questions established that, at the expected ages, Georgie held his head up, reached for and grasped objects, crawled, sat up, and walked. Careful examination of Georgie revealed no evidence of any disease. From further questioning, however, it became evident that Georgie's home life was not ideal. His parents were recently divorced, and his mother had begun working to support the family. Georgie spent his days in a nursery. It seemed that he had only one joy in life—thumb-sucking—and for that, he was not dependent upon anyone but himself.

Georgie's mother felt that her marital difficulties could not be related to Georgie's thumb-sucking, because, "We never fought in front of the children." She had never understood that it is not what we say, or what we do not say, but how we say it and what we feel that is important. Although open fighting between parents is to be deplored, the growing and impressionable child immediately senses the existence of fundamental and persistent differences between his parents, even if such differences are not verbalized or acted out. Such parental discords injure the emotional growth of the child.

Like Georgie's mother, many women have to work

to supplement the family income. Irrespective of the cause—widowhood, illness, divorce, finances—it is a fact that the mother's increased struggle and hardships themselves will not harm the child. Rather, the mother's real love for her child and her dedication to his welfare will transcend the increased demands on her time. And the child, sensing all this, will rise to the occasion and help. In addition to such material contributions as washing the dishes and making his own bed, the child will work harder in school and behave himself to make life easier for his mother. The grim reality can become the focus for the development of self-reliance and other good traits of character.

A child will sometimes revert to the behavior of an earlier stage of emotional development (see page 53). An anxious mother brought Marcia to the physician's office. The child, eight years old, had been progressing in a generally healthy manner until about six months earlier when she became very nervous, began to have trouble learning her lessons at school, started fighting with her playmates, had frequent episodes of crying over minor matters, began wetting the bed at night, and started sucking her thumb. The mother was sure that all these complaints were due to Marcia's teacher. Marcia had been assigned to this particular teacher's class six months earlier. "Marcia doesn't want to go to school in the morning, Doctor. She wants to stay home. She doesn't even enjoy going out to play with her friends. When she does play with them, she always seems to get into a fight. I can't understand it. She always liked school.

She had good grades, and now her grades are terrible. I'm ashamed of her. I don't know what to do. I've talked to her teacher. She says Marcia just won't concentrate on her lessons and doesn't get along with others. Marcia was all right until this grade. I don't know what to do, I'm so nervous myself these days . . ."

The physician found that Marcia's mother and father were not getting along well together. Marcia, of course, was aware of this situation. The parents had little time for Marcia, who felt neglected and angry. She took out her anger on her playmates, because it was easier than to do so on her parents. And since Marcia felt unwanted at home, she was afraid to leave home and lose what little love she already had. She also was not sure what might happen at home during her absence. Her mother and father might leave her. Life was no longer fun. But Marcia had been happy when she was younger. One way to escape the tension of the current situation was to get away from the unhappy present to the happier past —to the behavior of an earlier phase of her development. Thumb-sucking reappeared. As in other cases of emotional disturbance, thumb-sucking was only one of many symptoms. It was easier to respond to family tensions by regression than by mastering the situation through healthy growth. It was also much easier for the mother to blame the teacher than the home situation or herself—a not uncommon occurrence.

Another child, Abby, was an only child until her sister was born. Abby, four years old, had not used a bottle for years. When Susie was born, all the adoring relatives brought her gifts, but no one remembered Abby, who was used to receiving all the attention and presents. Now, when her father came home from work, he ran to see Susie and brushed by Abby, who always used to kiss her father immediately upon his arrival home. Abby now began to demand a bottle and she began to wet herself. She was competing with her baby sister for her father's love and attention by behaving like her baby sister.

Any parent is aware of the gratifyingly healthy appetite of the newborn. The child's eating behavior at this stage is a most sensitive indicator of his responses to the outside world. The healthy, happy infant eats well. If his emotional relationships and his physical health are sound, it makes no difference whether he is fed on a strict schedule or by self-demand, by breast or by bottle.

To review a few facts concerning a child's physical growth: the average child weighs seven pounds at birth. Usually he doubles his birth weight at four months of age, but it takes him about eight more months to gain seven more pounds. Therefore, by one year of age, the average child weighs 21 pounds. Then he takes about one whole year to gain another seven pounds, so that at two years of age he weighs an average of 28 pounds. It is evident that the child does not maintain his weight gain. Although he continues to gain, of course, he does so less rapidly as he grows older.

Some mothers do not accept these facts even when they are explained to them. Such mothers often erroneously assume that the child will continue to gain as rapidly as he did at first. This would mean that the child would double his weight every four months. A little simple arithmetic shows that, were this to happen, the child would weigh 448 pounds at two years of age! Therefore, since the child is gaining less as he gets older, his appetite also lessens proportionately. This is not to say that the two-year-old child eats less than the four-month-old baby. But pound for pound of body weight, the two-year-old does eat less. A noticeable decrease of appetite occurs usually at about 12 to 18 months of age. Parents who are not aware of this natural pattern frequently become alarmed and try to force, bribe, or coax the child to eat. It is at this stage that feeding problems often first appear.

Mr. and Mrs. H., extremely nervous, brought their six-year-old Clarence to the physician's office. "We need help, Doctor. We've taken Clarence all over. He's been examined thoroughly. He's had all the tests, and he's even been put in the hospital for observation. But no one has been able to make him eat. He never has any appetite. He doesn't eat enough to keep a bird alive." Of course, the child had eaten well until about two years of age, but after that his appetite fell off, and troubles appeared. The mother had tried everything, including vitamins, to no avail. It was evident that the mother had had excellent advice but, possibly because of her own emotional problems, she could not accept the explanations. Little Clarence was, therefore, admitted to the hospital for study. The nurses were ordered to offer him a regular diet for his age three times a day, to make sure that he had no candy between meals, and to make no special point about whether he ate or not. He was permitted full play activity. His problem was clarified in part when a distraught nurse phoned the physician saying, "What can we do about Mrs. H.? She insists on staying with Clarence to make sure he eats and has even brought in baskets of fruit and boxes of candy 'to keep up his strength.' " Mrs. H. was, of course, extremely confused, and a simple explanation could not satisfy her.

Mothers with similar feeding problems usually benefit from a simple explanation. "Doctor, Jane is really much better since I was here two weeks ago. We did what you told us. We offered her food at mealtimes. If she wanted it, she took it. If she didn't want to eat, we made no fuss over it."

Byron presented another problem. He was irritable and, as his mother said, "lazy like his father." In his short life span of fourteen months he had had a succession of infections. "I give him his vitamins, Doctor," said his mother; "still he has no resistance. But look at how fat he is; he looks healthy." Byron was obese, but he did not look healthy. His skin had a pronounced pallor. Upon further questioning about Byron's eating habits, the mother revealed that she was feeding him only milk. He drank as much as 2½ quarts of milk a day, but he was not offered any solid foods. The mother had tried some solid foods when Byron was three months old; he had refused, and she had pressed no further. Since milk lacks adequate quantities of iron, Byron was suffering from severe anemia; this was the cause of his pale and pasty appearance and his poor resistance to infections.

Except for the rare cases of true food allergy, the likes and dislikes that a child has for any particular food are reflections of his parents' tastes. "My David won't look at eggs, and I know they're good for him." "Do you eat eggs, Mrs. S.?" A grimace of extreme distaste, "I can't stand the sight of them! But, Doctor, I tell him they're good for him, and I don't tell him I don't like them." A child senses the parents' feelings in this as in other matters, whether the parent talks of his feelings or not. The father's eating habits also influence the child's likes and dislikes for particular foods. This is especially so of boys who tend to imitate their fathers.

Preschool children often go through phases during which they demand a certain food (for example, macaroni and cheese or peanut butter and jelly sandwiches) or resolutely refuse a certain food or group of foods. This situation usually disappears of its own accord if the parents do not focus undue attention on the problem.

The child quickly senses the great value and interest that his parents place on eating. He finds he can use eating as a means of getting back at his parents. Thus, food can become a weapon in the conflicts between parent and child that occur in the natural course of growing up. When a child does develop eating problems, they usually indicate parent-child tensions. A child who is happy in the knowledge that he is loved and wanted will get over eating problems very quickly.

THE BOWEL STAGE—AND LOVE OF SELF

By the time the child is a year old, he has learned to react in many ways to the world around him: he crawls, stands, perhaps walks; he reaches for and grasps objects, coos, and recognizes familiar persons. In short, he becomes fun for his proud parents. But as he learns to respond more and more to people and objects around him, society, through the parents and other family members, begins to make demands upon him. Soon, usually by one and a half to two years of age, the child begins bowel-training. Later, he must also be bladder-trained. The child must learn to keep himself clean, feed himself, make his wants known, and, finally, he must learn to talk. The acquisition of all this new knowledge takes time, and it cannot all be done at once. When one considers how difficult it is for an adult to learn a foreign language, one begins to realize how much the parents and society demand from the young child. But the child accomplishes his tasks remarkably well. How easily he does so depends upon his intelligence, and even more on how much the parents demand of him. They too would rebel if more were asked of them than they can reasonably be expected to do.

Bowel-training may lead to an early conflict between parent and child. Sometimes a fond mother may boast that her baby was bowel-trained at six months of age. At that stage it is not the baby who is trained but the mother! She has learned that the baby has a bowel movement after a certain meal or at a certain time of the day. She then places the baby on the toilet at that time. But the baby is not trained! One cannot expect the brain to send messages to the bowel when the nerve tracts between the brain and the bowel are not even completely developed until about two years of age. It is as if one were to expect a lamp to turn on without first plugging it into the wall socket and connecting it with the source of electricity. Bowel-training involves a complicated process of learning. The child must have the capacity to recognize the urge to have a bowel movement, to refrain from having it on the spot, and to let the mother know that he must move his bowels. Bowel-training usually cannot be accomplished in a few weeks or even in a month or two.

Many emotional factors are also involved in this process. At this time the baby normally develops a great interest in his own body and its products, particularly the bowel movement, or stool. Every parent will remember the expression of satisfaction and even pleasure on the baby's face as he grunts while having a bowel movement. When the child first learns to speak, he calls the mother and proudly points to his bowel movement, "Mommy, look!" The mother may turn her head away in disgust. Her reaction is understandable to herself but can only be a mystery to the child who is proud of what he has done and has not yet learned the adult point of view.

Like giving up the bottle or the breast, learning to have a bowel movement at a definite time and place is an important step forward in the child's development. The mother in reality confronts the child with the necessity of making another major decision in life. He can gain his mother's love by learning to control elimination as she desires and thus surrendering an early pleasure, or he may feel that his mother's censure is less important to him than the continued pleasure of having a bowel movement wherever and whenever he wishes.

If the feelings exchanged between parents and child are healthy, each will love and respect the other's needs, and neither will have the compulsion to use the bowel-training situation as a means of establishing dominance over the other. Each—parent and child—enters this situation from a position of strength. The parents are big and strong, and the child is dependent on them for his needs; but the bowel movements are the child's own and he will pass them where and when he chooses. Therefore, it is not a question of the parents' "breaking the child in" but of their being patient and understanding, and respecting his individuality. Sensing these feelings, the child in turn will willingly give up the pleasures from his own body in return for his parents' love. He will learn to get greater pleasure by sharing feelings with people than by depending on his own body. In the process of learning bowel control in this way, the child will also acquire the same healthy love, patience, understanding, and respect for his parents (and other people) that his parents showed him.

During the bowel stage of development, as we have seen, any child shows extreme interest in and gets profound enjoyment from bowel movements and from anything which may remind him of them. In the second year of life the child enjoys having bowel movements, making mud pies, getting smeared with dirt, and playing in the sand. Giving daily enemas or otherwise directing undue attention to this part or function of his body will increase his awareness of and indelibly impress on his memory interests which are already uppermost in his mind. As a result of such experiences, emotional remnants from this early time may persist in later life in the form of preoccupation with bowel movements, bowel regularity, enemas, cathartics, odors, and cleanliness, and even such dangerous transient fads as sniffing glue, hair spray, and gasoline. Saying that the individual may retain some of the interests and enjoyments common to the bowel stage of development does not mean that he fails to advance intellectually or in other spheres of emotional development (e.g., sexual). For example, a man and a woman can enjoy marriage and children and be of above average intelligence and still be preoccupied with their own bowel movements and those of their children.

The child who has just become bowel-trained has given up something pleasurable in return for his mother's continued acceptance and love; but the need for this early elemental pleasure derived from the body and its products often continues and must be satisfied. As seen through his parents' attitudes and feelings, society discourages his soiling himself. He, therefore, will seek and find substitutes which are acceptable to society but which afford him pleasures similar to those he has had to give up. The two-year-old makes mud pies and the four-year-old fingerpaints, models clay, and likes to get into the dough that his mother is kneading for the apple pie. Some children just "can never stay clean."

The early interest of the young child in his products of elimination may be transferred to collecting stones, seashells, and leaves of different shapes and colors. In the older child and adult this early tendency may develop into various hobbies: collections of coins and stamps, minerals, butterflies, books, and jewelry. As the child grows older, the original simple activity becomes a thousandfold more complex, and the original connection with bowel-training becomes completely and forever forgotten. Such substitution of constructive and commendable behavior for behavior upon which society frowns is seen in all the various stages of a child's emotional development (see also pages 33, 34, 35).

In the face of his great pleasure from soiling, the young child may respond to his parents' excessive demands for cleanliness (stemming from the attitudes of their own parents in this matter) by overcorrection. He will acquire the same values in such matters as his parents. He will be obsessed with the same overwhelming need for cleanliness and for pleasant odors. Overcorrection may occur in many other areas of the child's emotional development throughout life. By overcorrection he may solve the problem posed by a forbidden need or desire. Thus, one who hates might overly protest his love. One who is envious might overly proclaim his joy at another's good fortune. One who is very sensitive about bad odors might chew mints or gum for his breath and use deodorants and perfume to excess.

Let us return briefly to the very young child and trace the origins of one other important feature of the bowel stage of development. Any mother who has watched her baby grow will remember that during the first few months of life the child seemed to be perfectly satisfied with being fed, having his diapers changed, and being put back in his crib. Gradually, his interest in the world about him awakened so that by four or five months of age, he enjoyed being propped up on pillows so that he could view what went on around him. Gradually, as he developed the abilities to crawl, walk, and handle objects with some degree of skill, he was able to satisfy this curiosity in the world around him without the help of adults. "He's always in the way." "He's always into something." "He's full of mischief." Actually, he is only satisfying his curiosity. But, many of his explorations and discoveries are ill-fated. In the process of learning he makes many mistakes and may even injure himself. The accident rate (injury, swallowing poisons, etc.) at this age is particularly high. It should be stressed that this is a normal stage of development and differs from the problems of the accident-prone person in later life.

With this increasing ability to get about by himself and obtain what he wants, the child becomes very confident of his own abilities. He slowly masters bowel control, the ability to express himself verbally, and the ability to feed himself. He becomes increasingly independent and wants to do everything for himself. With this extreme confidence in his own abilities and with this growing tendency to depend upon himself to get what he wants, he becomes very self-centered and develops a strong love of self. For example, in a room full of two-year-olds, there is much independent activity but little group activity. As the child grows older, it is normal that his center of interest slowly shifts from himself to other people. The three-year-old, who is leaving the bowel stage of his development, is much more gregarious.

THE RELATIONSHIP BETWEEN EMOTIONAL HEALTH AND TOILET TRAINING

Why do people worry so much about their bowels? Why do people attach so much significance to their functioning? The frequent use of enemas, suppositories, and laxatives to initiate bowel movements is taken as an unquestioned part of life's routine. Pick up any newspaper or magazine in any language, and one will find an advertisement for a laxative.

"Doctor, my child does not have a bowel movement every day." "Doctor, my child's bowel movements are too hard." Even nine-year-old Johnny can give a detailed description of his bowel habits. And Grandmother, who feels that there is a direct relationship between her own health and bowel regularity, is also frequently worried about her grandchildren's bowel movements.

Bowel habits vary from person to person within a wide range of normal. That a child must have a bowel movement every day on schedule is a complete fallacy. A child (or an adult) may have a bowel movement every other day, twice a day, or every three days and be completely normal in this respect. The consistency of the bowel movement and not its frequency is the important thing. If the stool stays in the bowel too long before being passed, the body absorbs more and more water from the stool, and the stool becomes harder and harder. Constipation results. If a child (or an adult) has only one bowel movement every three days and the stool is of normal consistency, it should be no matter for concern for that particular person. Another individual, however, may pass a "stony" hard, constipated stool with difficulty and often with discomfort, every two or three days (or even every day). That is not normal. A physician often sees the child whose parent (or grandparent) insists that the child is constipated when, in fact, there is no constipation or bowel disturbance of any sort. Many people mistake a normal, easily passed stool for constipation only because it is firm and formed. The consistency of the stool is determined by the type of food one eats, the amount of fluid one drinks, and one's activities and bowel habits. When food of high bulk content is eaten, the stool becomes bulkier; it acts like a sponge, "holds on" to water, and remains soft. Naturally, drinking much fluid increases the bulk and the softness of the stool.

Mrs. K. knows that her little cocker spaniel will have a bowel movement after eating. She would not dare leave him in the house after a feeding until he has had a chance to run about outside and do his business. However, Mrs. K. does not know what to do about her eight-year-old Jimmy. He eats, runs outside to play, has a normal desire to move his bowels —but he is too busy playing to go back into the house to heed nature's call. He holds back; the desire passes; the stool remains in the bowel; fluid is absorbed from the stool; the stool becomes very hard and firm—constipation results. Mrs. K. apparently does not realize that after eating, the child, like the dog, has a normal desire to move his bowels; the particular meal, breakfast, lunch, or supper, after which this desire occurs, varies from person to person. In dealing with her child, the mother should take advantage of this natural timing.

Enemas, laxatives, and suppositories are artificial aids to be used on rare occasions, not as a matter of routine. If a person's bowel habits suddenly change or if he continually depends on artificial aids, including various patent medicines, a physician should be consulted. If the child has true constipation that persists, then the physician will prescribe treatment— if his examination reveals that the constipation is due to bad habits and not to disease.

"Brenda has been irritable all day. Let's give her some 'magnesia.' That always works!" Newspaper advertisements and old wives' tales to the contrary, when a person feels fatigued, irritable, and sluggish, it may be due to disease or what is going on around him but not because of bowel trouble. The medical facts are exactly the opposite of the popular concepts. For example, if Brenda becomes irritable, her stools may in turn become constipated. On the other hand, Ralph's loose bowel movements may be a physical expression of his concern over some coming tests in school. Constipation or diarrhea may follow various states of emotional unrest. The newspaper and magazine advertisements that imply that sluggish bowels cause a sluggish mind, and emphasize bowel regularity as a prerequisite to health, merely exploit popular misconceptions and half-truths. That such remedies relieve the complaint does not mean that the constipation causes the complaint. Returning to Brenda, her irritability may respond to the "magnesia," but her problem is as effectively—and deplorably—handled by her grandmother who slaps her on the face and tells her to get busy with her play and stop getting in the way. In many cases, laxatives, suppositories, and especially enemas amount to nothing more than punishment. Brenda is frightened out of her complaints. If she does complain, she'll be slapped again—or given another enema.

Although many children are repulsed by laxatives, suppositories, and enemas or the threat of them, other children have completely different associations from such interference with their bowel function. Such children look forward to the laxatives, the suppositories, and the enemas. Incredibly, they may even request them, but they do not know why they do so. They will offer, in all earnestness, what they believe to be the reasons, but they are not the real reasons. These strange ideas do not arise from the child himself but are acquired from the grownups around him.

On his own, the child always will attempt to go forward with his emotional (as with his physical) growth. As he matures, he will meet new feelings and experiences. In some instances, these will come up against unhealthy attitudes or touchy areas in his parents' emotional makeup, and will prevent the child from progressing in a fully healthy manner. As a result, he may be confronted with unhealthy solutions. By behavior and feelings, the parents can influence the child to advance in a totally unhealthy manner consistent with their own warped needs. Or, the child may be allowed to retreat to safer feelings and modes of behavior associated with earlier stages of emotional development when the parent-child relationship was less threatening. But, at the same time, the child's unfolding personality will also meet parental attitudes that are quite healthy. In these areas, the child will acquire the healthy aspects of his parents' personality. As he advances to the next stage of development, he will thus acquire in some areas the healthy aspects of his parents' personality while in other areas he will be forced to make an unhealthy adjustment with his parents' unhealthy feelings. Both parents and child, of course, are only dimly aware of why they really act as they do.

When the first-romance stage appears, with all its accompanying emotional values and pleasures (see Chap. 3), the child becomes more interested in other people of the same and of the opposite sex. He outgrows his earlier interest in himself and his body (i.e., mouth, bowels). He need no longer depend chiefly on his own body and its functions to gratify his needs. But if the child's parents, for reasons of their own, attach unnaturally important values to the functions and the pleasures of the bowel stage, for example, the child will acquire similar values.

If at any time in later life, in his relations with other people, the child is confronted with a frightening or an intolerable situation that defies solution, tension builds up. Without even being aware of it, he will remember the great pleasures and comforts originally derived from his own body at the mouth or bowel stages of development. He will show an increased interest in the needs and the pleasures of these stages (his own body) for relief of tensions. But the relief is not complete. The fears and the disappointments which he had experienced at the more advanced stage of emotional development will continue to haunt him even after his return, for example, to the bowel stage. Instead of difficulties with people, he may have difficulties with his own bowels: constipation, diarrhea, and numerous aches and pains in this region of the body.

Development is a continuous process, with overtones of the past continually seeping into the present. These processes of fixation at or regression to earlier stages of development are seldom complete. They are a patchwork of variable changes. The feelings of both the earlier and the later stages of development are inextricably mixed and determine the child's feelings and modes of behavior as well as his ways of obtaining pleasure. Therefore, the child may show many feelings derived from the first-romance stage of development (see Chap. 3), while also maintaining a keen interest and deriving much pleasure from his bowel function. When such a child grows up, marries, and becomes a parent, his children may in turn acquire the same interest and pleasure in bowel function. The wheel has completed another turn; the attitudes of one generation have been passed on to the next.

As any mother remembers, the young infant is not disgusted by soiling himself. In fact, if she is not quick enough, the child, through his own natural curiosity, will touch and handle his stools. The mother may become excited at the mess the child makes, but the child is only showing his natural interest in his body and its products. Watch the one-year-old having a bowel movement, and, provided there is no associated pain, he may grunt and smile. There is relief of the urge to move his bowels and actual pleasure in the act. But it is not socially acceptable to soil oneself whenever and wherever one wishes to do so. The growing child must, therefore, learn to conform to the dictates of the culture in which he lives. In the child's narrow world, the parents represent this culture. Their demands and wishes should mirror the demands and wishes of society. By obeying his parents, the child learns to act so as to become an acceptable member of society. This process of learning, then, consists of two factors: the child must curb his natural desire for pleasure when it conflicts with his parents' habits, and he must remember what his parents said he should and should not do. He is developing a conscience, which is based, however, on his parents' own consciences. If the child's conscience is to develop properly, his parents' consciences must be sound.

If a mother is gentle and understanding in training her child, he will surrender the childish pleasure of moving his bowels where and when he wishes, in return for her love. He will surrender comfortably and go forward without ill effects in his development. But if there is any emotional undercurrent between mother and child, it is at this stage of acquiring independence that the child finds a strong weapon with which to strike back at his mother. He can soil in the wrong places and at the wrong times; he can refuse to move his bowels at all (and constipation results). By these methods, the child can exert real power over his mother. In the final analysis, despite all the mother's wishes, pleadings, and commands, the child's bowel movements are his, to be passed when and where he chooses to do so. Here is an excellent way for him to show his anger and punish his mother by not doing what she wishes.

Recognizing the values atached to bowel movements by the parents and the child, it can be seen why the child, previously bowel-trained, may begin to soil. Four-year-old Libby began to soil herself shortly after her newborn baby sister was brought home. With all the attention paid to the baby by the parents and the visitors, Libby, previously the only child, and the recipient of all the attention, feared the loss of parental love. Gradually, as she became aware that her parents sincerely loved both her and the new baby, soiling disappeared. She had no further need to depend upon the pleasures of the earlier bowel stage. This is a common example of the way a child may return to the pleasures of an earlier stage for relief of intolerable tension.

Five-year-old Tommy's parents were both killed in an automobile accident, and Tommy had to be placed in an orphanage. Suddenly and tragically robbed of his parents and their love upon which he depended, Tommy began to soil himself. It was only after Tommy learned that he was not alone, that even in an orphanage someone cared for and loved him, that the soiling gradually ceased.

There are, of course, other specific causes for soiling. From what has already been said in this chapter, some cases of soiling, as in the above examples of Libby and Tommy, are temporary and of minor importance; they will disappear with time. Other cases, however, are more persistent and depend upon deep-seated and serious emotional disturbances between parent and child and frequently require treatment for both. In extremely rare instances, factors other than emotional may be the cause of soiling; they can be recognized by the physician.

When the child learns bowel control only after serious conflicts with his mother, he may develop personality scars. These early upsetting experiences may have several results. The child's early disturbing experience with his first person in authority, his mother, may influence his relationships with all other people in authority (teacher, preacher, physician, employer, policeman, judge, and lawyer) whom he meets later in life. Toward them he will show the same attitudes that he originally had toward his mother: either stubborn, active defiance or passive acquiescence and noncompliance.

The exchange of feelings between mother and child at the bowel stage, as at other periods of development, is all-important. No one would doubt that cleanliness is learned, as is bowel-training. The mother's rigid insistence that the child be bowel-trained, that the child "stay clean," and this as perfectly as possible and at as early an age as possible, reflects the mother's rigid, uncompromising, and perfectionist standards. There can be no deviation. The child learns that he can get along with his mother only by strict obedience to her rigid standards. This insistence on early and perfect cleanliness can become a fixed ever-present idea—an obsession (in this case, an obsession for cleanliness). In addition to the child's obsession, he is bound by the memory of his mother's perfectionism and orderliness. This perfectionism spills over and taints related character traits which develop as the child grows older.

The doting relatives think it is wonderful that Mary is so fussy and insists that everything "must be just so," like her mother. Mary repeats and practices endlessly, but she has such unrealistic standards of perfection that she can seldom finish what she starts. Mary is scrupulously clean in her grooming, clothing, and the care of her room. She is always on time and very proper in her speech. Everything follows a definite schedule which may not be changed. What appears so efficient is really a ritual. If her daily pattern becomes interrupted in any way, she "goes to pieces" and does not know what to do in the new situation. She cannot adapt herself to changing conditions. She is unsure of herself and asks endless questions to make certain that she does things exactly right. These countless and repeated questions enrage her mother. Yet, Mary's questions are really the same sort of "right or wrong." "yes or no," "good or bad" questions that her mother continually asks her. "Did you close the window in your room? . . . are you sure? . . . did you brush your teeth? . . . are you sure? . . . there is still a smell on your breath . . . did you have a bowel movement yet this morning? . . . was it constipated? . . . did you wash your hands before dinner . . . ?"

It should be noted that Mary's mother worried about the odor of Mary's breath. Insofar as the mother's concern is within reason, the question is natural, but giving undue attention to the problem is unnatural. People who are obsessed with cleanliness also make a point of odors. Odors are a manifestation of cleanliness or uncleanliness. Such people cannot stand bad odors and will go to extremes to eliminate them. And they take exceptional delight in pleasant odors. Their reactions in this as in other behavior traits (cleanliness, punctuality, perfectionism, orderliness) are exaggerations of the concern seen in the healthy individual.

All these character traits, which have apparently so little in common and which occur in all individuals to a greater or lesser extent, appear during the bowel stage of development as a result of the example and the attitudes of grownups. The parent's example and attitudes at this time will determine whether the child will grow up a healthy individual who constructively uses these traits or whether he will be victimized by them.

Complaints of the digestive tract (which includes the bowel) may be due to emotional problems, to physical disease of the bowels or other organs, or to some of the many physical diseases that are influenced by the emotions. Two of the diseases of the digestive tract that are influenced by the emotions are peptic ulcer and chronic ulcerative colitis.

Peptic ulcer is a condition in which the stomach or the first portion of the small intestine (duodenum) has a punched-out, raw area of varying size in its lining. This disease which is so common in grownups is, fortunately, very rare in children. However, in recent years, more cases have been recognized in children. Like the grownup, the child with this disease has many emotional problems that either contribute to the cause or aggravate the disease. In treating this disease, together with diet, drugs, and surgery, the emotional needs of the patient must also be given attention.

Chronic ulcerative colitis is a serious disease of the large intestine that is found in adults much more frequently than in children. This condition is characterized by frequent, painful, loose bowel movements and many tiny bleeding areas in the large intestine. This disease of unknown cause is commonly associated, in the child, as in the adult, with serious emotional problems. In many cases it is felt that early parent-child problems are important factors that must be considered in the treatment of a person suffering from this disease.

3

Foundations of Masculinity and Femininity

THE FIRST-ROMANCE STAGE

"Daddy! Daddy! Read me the funnies! You promised last night. Come on, Daddy! Joanie's daddy does it every Sunday." With his Sunday morning sleep shattered, Mr. Jones broke into a smile, took little Laurie in his arms, gave her a kiss, and said, "You are really Daddy's girl. I think you're better than Mommy." Indulgently, Mother left the room to start Sunday breakfast, leaving five-year-old Laurie snuggled next to Daddy in bed. . . .

Mr. Thomas, who was on vacation, awakened to hear the patter of his three-year-old daughter's feet along the hallway from her room to her parents'. "Honey," said his wife, "what will we do? Here she comes again. This is the second time." "Well, I know what I'm going to do. She can't sleep with us. That I know." Mr. Thomas reluctantly but gamely got out of bed, met his daughter at the door, gently but firmly grasped her shoulders, turned her around and said, "Back to your own bed, Honey. . . ."

Four-year-old Sue's father always finds her waiting for him when he comes home at night. She is at the door, ready to grab him around the knees, begging to be picked up. In fact, it is very difficult for him to kiss his wife. "No, Daddy, don't kiss Mommy. Kiss me first. . . ."

Both Edith and her twin brother, Tommy, now three years of age, sit at their own small table and feed themselves, with little help from grownups. They can even dress themselves if their mother helps with the buttons and the shoelaces. They no longer soil or wet themselves and usually remain dry through the night. With these necessary tasks in the process of growing up accomplished, they now turn to other interests. Edith wonders why Mommy and Daddy sleep in their own room and why she must sleep apart. Can't she sleep with Daddy too? After all, she is a girl just like Mommy. "When I grow up, I want to be as pretty as you, Mommy. Then I can marry Daddy." Tommy asks, "Mommy, will you wait for me until I grow up and marry you, just like Daddy?" Adoringly, his mother promises, then asks, "But what will we do with Daddy?" "Oh, he's always busy at the office anyway, Mommy; he's never home." But, later in the day, Tommy says, "When I grow up, I want to be a lawyer, just like Daddy. Daddy can do anything!. . . "

To Mrs. W., her physician put this direct question, "Even though your husband is often away on business trips, why do you sleep with your five-year-old son, Chuck?" "But, Doctor, aren't you supposed to love your son? All my friends sleep with their children! After all, what can there be between a mother and her five-year-old son? I dress in front of Chuck, take showers with him, and let him come into bed with me. I suppose you're going to say that isn't good for him. I can see nothing wrong in it."

"Well, Mrs. W., the problem is easy to understand on the one hand but difficult to grasp on the other. If you watched your children and your neighbor's children, you might begin to see how some of this behavior which seems so innocent to you can badly confuse and disturb your child. You see, from the age of three until about six, little boys and girls develop attitudes in their feelings for their parents that will guide them through all their lives in their relationships with other people of the same and the opposite sex. These early feelings are the blueprint for all their later feelings and behavior, be it their choice of husband or wife, or how they get along with other people, their employer, friends, and wife or husband. These feelings depend on the way you treat your child and the way you feel toward your child."

The physician then explained, from the child's viewpoint, this "first-romance" stage of his development somewhat as follows: At this period little boys begin to turn their interests from their own bodies to other people. And the people in whom they are most interested are those who have been closest to them and have done the most to care for their needs in the past—their parents. Boys begin to notice that they are made differently from girls. This may come from seeing their sister, little friends, a new baby, or their mother. An alert parent will note manifestations of this new curiosity in his own child. It is at this age that little boys and girls may examine each other's bodies, first play "doctor" or "house," and show great interest when their mother changes the diapers or bathes the new baby.

The boy directs this new curiosity toward the most important person of the opposite sex in his life, his mother. He has always been close to his mother, closer than to his father, but only because she has done more to take care of him than his father. She has fed him, bathed him, kept him warm, dressed him, cuddled him, guided his first steps, taught him his first words, and, all through her love for him, she has taught him how to control elimination. He has been close to her, because he has been greatly dependent upon her. But now, at about three to four years of age, he first becomes aware that she is made differently and must be treated differently from his father and himself. He knows that men and women go together, and he notices that his father, who is built like himself, is close to his mother, closer than even the boy can be and possibly in a different way. Much goes on between them from which he is excluded, which he does not even understand. The little boy wonders why he cannot be as close to his mother as his father is. He begins to wish that he could be grown up like his father and thus also become as close to his mother as his father is. The little boy cherishes the secret hope that he may grow up to have his mother for himself. He may even ask the mother to wait for him.

But this same little boy has also been close to his father and depended upon him. Recognizing that he is built like the father, the little boy hopes that some day he can be just like his father who is so much bigger and stronger than he is and is so loved and respected by Mommy. To achieve this goal, he will imitate his father. He may ape his father's walk or manner of speech; he may work by the father's side in the tool shed or garden, or he may say he wants to go into the same vocation as his father. He may even want to excel his father.

The little boy is confronted with an upsetting dilemma. In wanting his mother for himself, he must compete with his father who is so much bigger and stronger. The son loves and respects him and depends upon him, but in spite of this he often feels angry toward his father when he sees the father close to his mother in a way that he cannot be.

How this dilemma is resolved depends upon the attitudes of the mother and the father in dealing with the child. The mother should realize that this is a natural and healthy stage through which her son is passing and that, through the feelings exchanged between them, he will establish a blueprint for all his later successes and failures with the opposite sex. The mother should accept her son's affections realistically, in a mother-son fashion. She should be honest with him about her feelings for him. She should do everything possible to sustain his healthy son-to-mother affection for her rather than confuse his growing up by giving him any reason to believe that his yearnings to supplant his father and have his mother all for himself may some day come true. She must not treat her son in any manner suggestive of a husband-wife relationship. This would only confuse the little boy and cruelly distort his future feelings and behavior toward his mother and the opposite sex. For example, taking a shower with her son will not enhance his emotional growth any more than sleeping with him.

If the mother is unwise in her attitudes and actions toward her son at this stage of his earliest manhood, when he grows up he may not be able to sever these unnatural ties to his mother. He may be unable to enter into a mature husband-wife relationship of his own. He may always search for his mother or someone who reminds him of her. He will never be satisfied. Never having had a comfortable and healthy parent-child relationship he may be unable to develop a comfortable parent-child relationship as a father.

It cannot be too much stressed that these unnatural activities can be very frustrating to a little boy, because he is permitted, even encouraged, to do certain things with his mother. Then without apparent reason that he can see, it is stopped. Seeing his mother undress only serves to overstimulate the healthy curiosity of this stage of development in an unnatural and unhealthy way. Such behavior causes the boy to assume a role too much like that of his father who lives in the same room with his mother and undresses with her. The reverse situation in the father-girl relationship has similar implications.

Similarly, when a mother breast-feeds the baby,

little is gained by allowing the older child to watch. Like undressing in front of the older child, this may only serve to confuse him. Witnessing such an intimate situation in which the baby is sustained solely via the breast may lead Johnny to feel, "Why can the baby be so close to Mommy and get this when I can't." This situation mobilizes all the still recent longings and feelings in the young child who is just beginning to assume some degree of independence. The mother may say, "Johnny never said a word when I breast-fed Lucy." Was it that Johnny did not care or was it really that Johnny was flustered and could not discuss the subject, especially since he was getting older and knew that grownups had strange ideas and values attached to this part of the body? Any parental feelings or behavior that serve to remind the child of his recent complete dependence and that discourage or thwart his budding independence will keep the child immature and mar his character development. Such feelings and behavior, by their effects, can only be considered unfriendly.

An extreme example, with definite overtones of a highly disturbed mother-son relationship, was that of Mrs. L. and her son, David. While preparing to breast-feed the baby, she teasingly turned to her five-year-old son, "Come on, David, it's time for your breakfast." Such a cruel taunt cannot fail to imprint on a young and impressionable mind an unnatural alliance of sex and hate.

To return to the story of Mrs. W. and her son Chuck: Mrs. W.'s physician was concerned to help her recognize the basis for her actions, and also her husband's part in the situation.

"Unfortunately, the other side of the coin is perhaps even more important and almost invariably never noticed. For example, Mrs. W., you tell me your husband is a salesman, always away during the week, and, for that reason, you take Chuck to bed with you. Would it not seem to you that this perhaps gratifies your own needs rather than his? Would it not seem a very unusual way of showing mother-son love?

"Now, Mrs. W., although we have so far talked of you, this certainly does not mean it is all a mother's responsibility at this period. For example, is your husband bored and tired when he does come home? Does he sit down and read the paper and watch TV while ignoring his son? Is he patient and understanding when his son plays baseball as a five-year-old might instead of like a Babe Ruth? When he plays with his son, does he do so for the pleasure that he and his son can get out of it together or does he do so only to show off his own superior strength and skill in competition with his son? The boy will recognize such actions for what they really are—confusing and unfriendly. In fact, some fathers are keenly aware of their son's strivings in relation to the mother and frankly resent them. The parent may unwittingly use the young son (or daughter) as the most readily available means by which he can show his jealousy and anger at the other parent? The innocent young child is totally unable to defend himself from being so used. But if the father is comfortable in his feelings toward his son, he will try to put himself in his son's shoes, and accept with a friendly smile and without rancor his son's natural competition with him for his wife."

On the other hand, a boy is not helped if his father is a passive "jellyfish" while his mother "wears the pants" in the family. Little Donald G.'s mother is president of several school and social organizations. She was successful in business before her marriage and had more formal education than her husband. She is now busy organizing the women of her town to back their own candidates for the next election. Donald's father works in a bank but returns home in time to cook and serve the evening meal. Mrs. G. always has an ingenious excuse to have her husband do the family wash and the housecleaning. She even boasts that her son makes his own bed every morning. Mr. G's associates claim he has not made his Maine fishing trip in 15 years of marriage because his wife was always too ill or had "allergies" at the time the trip was scheduled. Mrs. G. boasts to her friends about her husband, "If he weren't so good, I'd divorce him in a minute!" Like any other boy, Donald imitates his father. However, he is imitating an easygoing, passive, effeminate person.

We have seen, then, that neither the husband nor the wife should take advantage (merely to solve his or her own problems and to gratify his or her own warped desires) of these natural feelings of competition and love which the child shows at this first-romance stage of his emotional development. If the parents manage these problems in a healthy manner, the child will pass successfully through the first-romance stage strengthened by his parents' love and their genuine respect for him, rather than weakened and confused by being made the scapegoat for their own problems. In this way, the parents will have helped him lay strong and healthy foundations for his future relations with his own and the opposite sex.

The same can be said for the little girl and her curiosity about and closeness to the father. She may wonder why she is not made like her brother or if something happened to make her different. This curiosity, as in the boy, may be unnecessarily stimulated by unhealthy situations in the home. For instance five-year-old Wanda is not helped by taking Sunday morning showers with her father or by his playing hobbyhorse with her. Nor is it healthy, even on a warm day, for 14-year-old Diane to parade around the living room in her brassière and panties. Her mother proudly explains, "This doesn't go on in front of everybody . . . just with the immediate family and friends." This same mother also added confidentially, "Isn't Diane cute; she's only 14, but she walks like a chorus girl!"

Lynn's father was very close to her. Even when she was in her teens he would hold her on his lap, snuggle her to him, and whisper that he loved her. She had always been "Daddy's girl" and went about with her father. He enjoyed helping her bathe and washing her back (even into her teens). There was a complete open-door policy in this "modern" home where "old fogey notions" were not allowed. As in bathing, there was neither modesty nor privacy in the family dressing habits and conversation. But one wondered how much such behavior represented the father's love for Lynn and how much a distortion of his own needs.

Lynn's father and mother did not get along well. They frequently argued and often would not speak to each other for hours or even days. For as long as Lynn could remember, her parents had had separate bedrooms, ostensibly because her father liked a cold room and her mother said he snored so loudly that she could not sleep. From watching her parents, Lynn had many distorted ideas about marriage and the roles of a father, a mother, and a daughter. As a result of her unnatural closeness to her father, Lynn had reason to believe that she was truly her Daddy's girl friend. But Mother still lurked in the shadows. Lynn felt that her Daddy wanted her very much. As she grew older, his attentions posed serious problems. Instead of advancing to later stages of emotional development, Lynn remained fixed emotionally at the first-romance stage. She continued to compete with her mother for her father's affections long after such competition should have been resolved. This competition brought with it heavy burdens of guilt toward her mother. In time, these specific feelings extended to affect her attitudes in general. Her feelings of competition with her mother slowly extended so that she felt she had to compete with all women in all fields. As a result she could not be friendly or comfortable with members of her own sex. Her feelings toward her father extended to affect her attitudes toward all men. She could not give of herself fully to any man without a similar feeling of guilt. Her later conceptions of love were limited almost solely to the early physical expressions and whisperings shared with her father. She could only function at the immature level of the first-romance stage of emotional development.

Lynn grew up to be an intelligent and beautiful woman. She had many boy friends and was courted as the "belle of the ball." After many heartbreaking false starts, Lynn married. Knowing how unhappy her father and mother had been together, she had been afraid of marriage, but she finally entered it determined to make a success of it. In this, too, she was doomed to unhappiness because of the unhealthy feelings toward men which had become indelibly impressed on her character. She had expensive clothes, a home, a maid, an automobile, and everything material that a young woman might want, but she was dissatisfied and unhappy. She envied her friends who were happily married. She knew that life must have more to offer, but that for some reason it had passed her by. And she never knew why. Her life became a constant search for this elusive goal: parties, travel, repeated divorces and marriages. . . .

QUESTIONS ABOUT THE FACTS OF LIFE

Parents need to recognize that their young daughter or son will acquire, without either the parents or the child necessarily being aware of what is happening, all the feelings and the attitudes of the parents. The child will acquire the same ideals and prejudices and the same virtues and vices of the parents. In many subtle ways the child will keenly sense the underlying feelings, attitudes and values, the deep loves, hates, needs, and forbidden wishes that motivate the parents. And the child will make these feelings his own. These strong undercurrents that determine the parents' own feelings and behavior will similarly determine the feelings and the behavior of the child. When the parent's feelings and what he professes to feel are different, the child learns what the parent actually feels. The parent and the child may not even be aware of this divergence.

"Where do babies come from, Mommy?" This natural question often embarrasses the parent or sends her scurrying to the nearest bookshelf for help on what to say. If the mother is flustered and tries to pass it off, the child senses that this subject is taboo and will not touch on it again. Thus, parents often say, "My child has never asked me that, Doctor. I guess she's not interested." It is less a matter of the child's lack of interest than of parental attitude toward the subject. Most parents are embarrassed because they themselves were brought up to consider the entire subject taboo for discussion. But if the parents are comfortable in discussing this subject, the child will sense the parents' poised and relaxed attitude.

What the child wants is a simple direct answer to her question. She is not interested in an elaborate explanation nor does she need one. "Where do little babies come from, Mommy?" The answer might be, "From inside Mommy's body." If the child has any further questions then she will ask them, and the answer should be just as direct and simple. Usually no further questions will be asked then.

After mulling over this problem for days or weeks or months, the child usually asks, "How do babies get into Mommy's body?" Again the answer should be simple and direct, "By a seed planted there by Daddy." How do they get out? "Through a birth canal that mommies have." It is seldom that more questions are asked, but the same literal answers should be given. It is unnecessary and inadvisable to demonstrate the anatomy to the child.

Bobby H., aged four and a half, was getting along quite well until his baby sister was born. Mother had prepared Bobby for his sister's arrival by telling him that the family would soon have a new baby in the house and that, since Bobby was such a big boy, Mommy would need his help. Realizing that a four-and-a-half-year-old cannot remember things for long periods of time, his mother told him this only shortly before the expected time of birth, and a few times thereafter in response to his questions about her "big tummy." Bobby was bowel-trained, remained dry during the day, only rarely wet at night, fed himself, and had not used a bottle for about two and a half years. Ten days after she returned home from the hospital with baby Irene, Mrs. H. called the physician: "Doctor, Bobby keeps pestering me all the time. He wants attention, and I don't have that much time. He has started soiling and wetting himself again. And now he even wants a bottle. The other day he said he wanted to hold the baby, and he squeezed so tightly I was afraid he would hurt her. This morning he hit the baby with his teddy bear. I know he's jealous of the baby. What can I do?"

Bobby's reaction to his sister's arrival was predictable. Until now he had been the only child in the home; his little world had revolved about him. When Daddy came home at night, he used to speak to Bobby first. Mother always had been with Bobby. When the grandparents visited the house, they had looked for Bobby first and brought presents for him, and only for him. After the baby arrived, things were different. On coming home at night, Daddy would head straight for the nursery to look at Irene. Now, when the grandparents visited, they brought presents only for the baby and virtually ignored Bobby. His mother seemed always busy feeding or dressing Irene, changing her diapers—or just admiring her. It was natural for Bobby to feel that the baby had displaced him in the affections of his parents. Equally naturally, he felt jealousy and anger toward the new baby. Perhaps, if he were to act like a baby, exactly like Irene, he could be loved again. Since Bobby's babyhood had been a happy and comfortable time, he tended, without even being aware of it, to revert in his behavior to that period in his life when things had been less complicated and more pleasant. (This reaction is common to many children and adults when faced with an intolerable situation.) It is not difficult to see why Bobby reverted to soiling, wetting, wanting a bottle, sucking his thumb, and constantly asking to be picked up. After the arrival of a new baby a certain degree of temporary return to babylike behavior by the older child is no cause for concern.

What is important is for Bobby's mother to show him she still loves him. She might say something like this to him, "Bobby, I know you feel that since we have to spend so much time in caring for the baby, we love the baby more than we do you. That is not true. We love you and the baby the same. It is only that since the baby is so small, she cannot take care of herself, just as you could not take care of yourself when you were small. Now you are big and you can take care of yourself and help Mommy. But we still love you."

Even more important than what the mother says is how she says it. You can tell a child many things. You can say "I love you" in such a firm, cold, and nasty manner as to frighten the child. You can also say "I love you" in such a gentle, sincere way that the child will sense immediately that you do love him. Or, you can say nothing and just love him!

It is also important that Bobby's mother and father show him love in many little ways. While the baby is asleep, Mother can take time to read to Bobby, play with him, and show him attention. There is no reason why his father cannot first speak to Bobby when he arrives home at night before going to see the baby. Father can spend time with Bobby before bedtime. And the grandparents and other visitors might bring a present for Bobby whenever they bring a gift for the baby. If the doting grandparents bring a gift only for Irene, the parents might have small toys or knickknacks that can be given to Bobby at the same time. The mother might have Bobby help with the care of the baby when he can. She might have him carry diapers for her. She will not make an issue of this but be guided by Bobby's own feelings.

Her physician pointed out something else to Bobby's mother. "When you said you were afraid that Bobby squeezed the baby too hard even though he was only wanting to show the baby love, you may have been correct. He probably did squeeze too hard. Bobby would understandably feel angry with Irene, his apparently successful competitor for your affections. It is ironic—Bobby has learned many things, yet he sees that although the baby is helpless, squalling, spitting, soiling, and even somewhat smelly, she gets the presents and the attention while Bobby feels frozen out of the family circle. Show Bobby that you still love him. If you do this he will gradually get over this babylike behavior, since the need to behave in that manner will no longer exist. Above all, do not make fun of him and do not punish him for his babylike behavior. If you do, it will only prove to him that he is right in fearing that he has lost your affection. If you react correctly to the situation, these symptoms (which many children show to varying degrees with the arrival of a new baby) will gradually disappear. If you, the mother (and the father), react poorly to this situation, these symptoms, which should last only a short time, may persist, become fixed to some degree, and may influence Bobby's future feelings toward the baby, toward you, the parents, and toward other significant people with whom he may feel he is in competition in later life. This is the first time that a brother and a sister compete for their parents' affection. Such competition will recur over and over again in the future. Whether it is resolved with or without ill effects is determined by your, the parents', attitude toward your children—which in turn is dependent upon the feelings and the experiences from your own childhoods."

Here is another actual call from an upset mother. "This is Mrs. M. I need help. This morning I caught Eloise—she's four years old, you know—being undressed by a five-year-old neighbor boy. I talked to his mother, and she is just as upset and surprised as I am. We don't know what to do or where to turn. Could he hurt Eloise? Can you examine her and see? I want to come down to the office with Eloise and Johnny's mother right now. What should I do? I didn't think she'd ever do this to me!"

Eloise's mother needs to know that during the period from three to six years of age, children are becoming more aware of their bodies and of the differences between the sexes. They are naturally curious. This mother's extreme apprehensiveness and her readiness to assume that Eloise was hurt may indicate that she has problems in this emotional sphere. Her fears may be a symptom of her own insecure feelings toward men; she may fear that men only hurt women.

Returning now to the situation that brings Mrs. M. to the office with Eloise, the physician explains to Mrs. M. the child's natural curiosity at this age. It is not an abnormality and should shortly disappear of its own accord. The child should be told that the grown-ups know that she is curious, and they understand how she feels, but boys and girls should not undress together, because it is not how grown-ups should act.

Since society has certain rules of conduct, these rules should be applied to the child as well as to the adult. The child will accept an explanation if it is presented in this way. The adult should avoid undue attention to the problem or any threats of dire punishment. Such exaggerated reactions could only communicate to the child the parents' own warped emotions and distorted values toward the subject of sex. "But, Doctor, if I don't punish her and emphasize how terrible it is, I'm afraid she might do it again!" If the parents' feelings toward the opposite sex are healthy, they will accept the situation for what it is —the expression of the normal curiosity seen in children at this stage of development. Healthy parents, whose own feelings toward the opposite sex are appropriate, will not fear that such a situation will lead to later elaborations and repetitions. Nor will they fear that their child will get into any trouble because of sex, because he will already have acquired the same healthy attitudes and will continue to develop in the same healthy manner.

It is good for parents to set limits to the child's activity and for the child to know definitely from the parent's feelings and behavior what he can and cannot do. This advice is applicable throughout the child's growing years and adolescence.

ONGOING CHARACTER FORMATION: AGES SIX TO TWELVE

At approximately six years of age, Tom and Diane have good-naturedly accepted the fact that growing up means that the love they have for their mother and father and the love their parents have for them is different from the way their parents love each other. Partly as a result of this realization that Tom cannot have Mommy for himself nor Diane, Daddy, they claim that they really never wanted them anyway. Each seeks out companions of his or his own sex. As a result, from about six years of age until puberty, boys commonly organize into clubs of their own and girls play together. Each group practically ignores the existence of the other. That this is really not the case is shown by the way boys and girls often tease each other and by the way boys pull girls' pigtails and groups of boys playfully interfere with girls' activities. "Mommy, make Tom and Sam leave us alone!" "We're not doing anything, Mother, we're just looking." In fact, little boys commonly feel very fond of little girls (and, similarly, the girls are fond of the boys) but are very embarrassed about admitting it. In imitation of their parents and with genuine affection, they occasionally like to kiss and hug little girls of their choice. It is best for parents to accept such actions at their face value. They are entirely appropriate, and such tender feelings should be recognized.

The parent should not offer any comments that ridicule the child or might instill highly suggestive insinuations that the child will understand poorly— ideas that would be applicable only to adult situations. As Mrs. Brown walked over to the house with her daughter, Dickie jumped off the swing, ran to little Cynthia and kissed her on the cheek. Mrs. Brown laughed and said, trying to impress Dickie's mother and father with her own sophistication, "These modern kids are really precocious, aren't they? No telling what they'll do when they grow up." Another mother's reaction in a similar situation was, "We let our children do what they like, there are no secrets in our house." Mrs. V. gushed, "Francis, you're just like your father. He always had a weakness for pretty girls, and from the looks of his new secretary, he hasn't lost his touch. But, boys will be boys."

"These modern kids are really precocious, aren't they? No telling what they'll do when they grow up." Every good salesman knows that a potential customer may be influenced by repeated exposure to the enthusiasm of the salesman for his own product. The salesman must believe in his own product to sell it. Everyone will also agree that anyone intimately and sufficiently long exposed to a contagious disease has a good chance of getting the disease. Therefore, quarantines, isolation procedures, sterilization, and the washing of hands are all accepted without question. Yet, some will doubt the physician's suggestion that certain ideas and feelings, repeated often enough, may inoculate the patient with an emotion which may be either healthy or unhealthy. These ideas and feelings may be presented directly by words and actions, by verbal insinuation, or more deviously but as effectively by tone of voice, facial expression, half smiles, and failures to comment when indicated. The parent may even verbally forbid repetition of the act, but may show rapt and consuming interest when the child relates his story. Or, the parent may misinterpret and give a completely distorted meaning to a child's innocent remark or behavior. Then the child will make this distortion his own as in the above example.

"These modern kids are really precocious, aren't they? No telling what they'll do when they grow up." Why should a parent with a sound conscience insinuate that the child will show unhealthy interests and reactions when he grows up? Should there be any doubt that the child will be anything but a happy, stable, emotionally healthy, law-abiding citizen? If the child has been raised properly, emotionally and morally as well as physically (diet, vitamins, immunizations, and so forth), these things will take care of themselves. If such doubts are expressed often enough and if the parent sincerely feels that such doubts exist, it serves only to inoculate the child with a sick emotion. The effects of such inoculation can be more far-reaching and permanent than the effects of exposure to the germs of many serious diseases. With modern medicines many infectious diseases respond readily and completely to treatment. On the other hand, repeated or prolonged exposure to a sick emotion often leads to an emotionally and morally sick individual who will find it extremely difficult to make any healthy and happy adjustment to life.

Such a person's symptoms of emotional illness may masquerade or actually be manifested as a physical illness. People feel and act as they do because of their ability to perceive and judge what is going on around them and because of their memories of past feelings and experiences. These abilities to perceive, judge, and remember are functions of the brain. Nerve fibers go from the brain to every organ and tissue of the body. Any disturbance of the brain, physical or emotional or a combination of the two, may affect the function of the brain, and, secondarily, the ability of other organs and tissues to perform their tasks. For instance, some illnesses which are often related to emotional factors are stomach ulcers, asthma, headaches, itching, nervous indigestion, chronic ulcerative colitis, high blood pressure, fatigue, and heart palpitations.

The physician can question the parents directly, and from their description of and reactions to specific situations in their lives he can determine fairly accurately their emotional makeup. With this information he can often predict how they will react in different situations. Special technics must be used, however, to determine the emotional makeup of the child.

It is a well-recognized fact that the child (and the adult) expresses his feelings through his play and dreams. These are two methods by which the physician can often find out how the child really feels and why he acts as he does. The physician participates in the child's games but lets the child direct their course.

For example, the child may identify several dolls with the members of his own household. By letting the child determine what the dolls will do and what will happen to the dolls in play, the physician can determine how the child feels toward the other members of his family and how the child believes that the other members of his family feel toward each other and toward him. Instead of dolls, the child may have a family of toy animals which behave like their human counterparts. The kinds of toys that the child chooses of his own free will represent the feelings that he has in relation to significant people in his life. These feelings interact with his current stage of emotional development, his past experiences, and his hopes and fears concerning the future. The little girl may want to play with soldiers. The little boy may tenderly feed a baby doll with a toy bottle of milk. The little boy may repeatedly shoot a toy gun at every male animal in sight. He may want to place every block so perfectly in position that he never can complete his toy house. The little girl may repeatedly have the mother doll and the father doll getting hurt in toy automobile crashes. All these children are telling the physician, in their own way, how they really feel, although they may be seldom if ever aware of the relationships of their play and dreams to real-life situations.

By playing the game of "let's pretend" with the child, the physician can uncover further information. He may ask the child to make up stories about specific pictures that the physician shows him. The child may draw pictures which he explains to the physician with stories. Or, the child may play "telephone" with the physician. Each—child and physician—takes the part of a member of the child's family (or someone else who is important to the child); the child, of course, is asked to supply the thoughts and the words for both sides of the conversation. Other helpful techniques include the use of a tape recorder, a one-way screen, and television.

From the examples given it can be seen how the physician can obtain a good insight into the family situation as the child sees it, and the child's attitudes toward the various members of his family.

One of nature's safety valves in dealing with feelings is dreams. They can express wishes that are frequently unattainable in everyday life or, more to the point, wishes that are forbidden. Because of the frequently upsetting content of these wishes, they often cannot even be admitted, much less fulfilled, in the everyday life of wakefulness. Nature may protect the individual by permitting him to fulfill these wishes in the dream state. In other words, dreams disguise what would otherwise be upsetting by permitting the dreamer to do in dreams what he cannot do in his everyday life. Through dreams the emotional tension of these unfulfilled wishes is relieved. By understanding the patient's dreams, the physician can become aware of those feelings and desires that the patient not only hides from the world but also, often, from himself.

The physician does not attempt to determine the meaning of any one dream on the basis of that dream alone. Dreams are an attempt at communication. Interestingly, they can even on occasion transcend the limitations of time and space. Dreams can be telepathic or prophetic. The full implications of this on communications between parent and child (or between any other individuals) are only beginning to dawn. Nor does the physician attempt to determine the meaning of even a recurrent dream without knowing thoroughly the patient's emotional and physical background. Recurrent dreams, are, of course, more significant than isolated ones.

The recurrent nightmare strongly suggests that the child is having great emotional difficulties. As with every other kind of dream, the nightmare can be understood only by the physician who completely knows the child, his background, and his environment.

BECOMING A YOUNG MAN
OR A YOUNG WOMAN

Marilyn, aged eleven, has learned from her friends that at about this time of her life her body will change and she will begin to enter womanhood. Her friends have told her that her breasts will enlarge, and hair will appear under her arms and on the sexual parts of her body. However, the most mysterious thing is the appearance of monthly bleeding. Once, a few years before, Marilyn had seen a box of sanitary napkins and had asked her mother about them. Her mother, without embarrassment and without attempting a lengthy explanation at that time, said that when a girl grows up, she bleeds from below each month. This, she told Marilyn was a sign of healthy growing up, and she did not insinuate that there was any uncleanliness, curse, or cause for shame in menstruation.

Through the years Marilyn's mother honestly answered her daughter's questions about the other manifestations of womanhood. Fortunately, Marilyn was not forced to rely solely upon the misinformation of her friends. Because of some mothers' false modesty or even ignorance, however, too many girls are left to learn about womanhood from the storehouse of old wives' tales and superstitions. But Marilyn looked forward to adolescence and the appearance of womanhood as another phase in growing up.

The earliest visible evidence of sexual development in the girl is enlargement of the breasts. By the time most girls are ten to eleven years of age, the small nipples of childhood become raised and the breasts begin to increase in size. The next evidence of sexual development is the appearance of hair on the sexual areas. At about this time the bones of the hips widen, hair appears under the arms, and, finally, menstrual periods begin. These visible surface changes are related to the chemical and hormonal changes within the body. Usually a girl will be able to conceive and bear children within approximately a year of her first period, which appears in the average girl at thirteen and a half years of age. With the completion of all these changes, the girl becomes a woman so far as nature is concerned.

But the girl's emotional growth continues beyond

this period—in fact, throughout life. Her emotional attitudes and values during this period are related, it is true, to the physical signs of womanhood, but they are even more dependent upon the emotional attitudes and values of her parents, for it is they who have the greatest influence upon her developing personality.

John presented an extreme example, on the one hand, of the questionable relationship between hormones and a child's developing personality; and on the other, of the more definite relationship between parental attitudes and the child's developing personality. Although the patient had been seen by numerous physicians through the years, they had been unable to determine his true sex. Alternately he had been called John, had his hair cut short, and been dressed in boy's clothes; or he had been called Janet, his hair had been allowed to grow long, and he had worn dresses. He was seen by the physician at fifteen years of age, when examination revealed that John *should* have been named Janet since "he" had a known congenital defect that made the external female organs superficially resemble those of a male. Interestingly enough, during the physician's study of John's emotions, it was confirmed that "he" had all the feelings and values of a healthy boy his age. John had been brought up like a boy, thought like a boy, and acted like a boy, because the parents had believed that indeed he was a boy. Surgery and appropriate medical treatment corrected John's condition so that "he" could develop normally as a girl. This is a very rare case, but it does emphasize the importance of feelings rather than anatomy.

There have been widely publicized individuals who have had the anatomy and hormones of a male, but who wanted to become female because of emotional illness. Surgical removal of the penis and testicles and the creation of an artificial vagina and breasts have been combined with the administration of female hormones. Although such unfortunate persons receive freaklike notoriety in nightclubs and elsewhere, it remains to be shown that they are not still seriously disturbed (see Chapter 7). Obviously incapable of having children, they are, in fact, modern eunuchs, and grotesque examples of *psychopathia sexualis.* Their life span may be shortened by an increased risk of hardening of the arteries and complications such as the development of cancer.

Frequently, a mother may complain to her physician that her daughter is late in beginning her menstrual periods. Although rare conditions may account for this, in the overwhelming majority of cases, the problem is the mother's lack of knowledge of what is really normal. Actually, there is always a wide range of normal. No two people are exactly alike. Thus, the age at which the various manifestations of approaching womanhood appear are really the average ages. For instance, the average age at which menstruation first appears is thirteen and a half, but it may appear several years earlier or later. The same applies to the initial appearance of breast enlargement, body hair, and every other change in the growing child.

LAURA—OUT OF STEP

Laura had a problem. All her girl friends wore brassières and had the general body configuration of young women. Laura had not yet begun to change, and she keenly sensed the humiliating comparison that some of the boys were making between her and her girl friends. When the physician examined Laura he found her to be normal and healthy. He explained that there is a wide range of normal, and that some girls develop later than others.

Although none of the women in Laura's family were noted for their figures, they were all good mothers and homemakers. Laura's father and mother were happy, well-adjusted parents who would understand their daughter through her growing-up period. The first-romance period of Laura's development had been handled well by her parents. Given the correct understanding and support by her father and mother, evidenced through genuine feeling rather than empty words and vain hopes, Laura had a better chance to achieve a truly full and happy life as a woman and mother than some of her friends who had better figures but a disturbed home life.

SHIRLEY—COMPULSIVE COQUETTE

Shirley was a patient whom the physician had first seen many years earlier when she was a highly disturbed fifteen-year-old adolescent. Shirley always had been physically attractive. She had been a "cute little tomboy," but she missed many days of school due to severe pain during her monthly periods and frequent incapacitating headaches. Her parents never had been able to manage her. Despite all their pleas and commands, she continued to go to wild parties and to remain out until the early hours of the morning. It had been an open secret that Shirley had been seeing a man much older than herself off and on through the years.

Now Shirley was a very beautiful woman. She flaunted her beauty and had the deserved reputation of being a coquette. She had no close friends of her own sex and lamented the fact that she was a girl and that boys had all the advantages. Despite the Hollywoodlike glamor that her teenage friends attached to her "affair," and the superficial appearance of maturity, sophistication, and happiness, Shirley was really very immature and unhappy.

Her obvious troubles with men and her difficulty in accepting her own role emotionally as a woman led to many disappointments in love. Countless courses of hormone treatments and repeated surgery never relieved her many physical complaints, which centered around the internal sex organs. Various treatments changed the nature of her complaints but never relieved her of them. The physician felt that Shirley's early experiences with her father were responsible for her later inability to establish a mature relationship with any man. The physician knew that Shirley's parents never had been able to adjust to each other as husband and wife. The father always had been very close to Shirley. He had helped bathe her until she was 11 years old. This unnaturally close physical contact extended to other activities: tucking Shirley into bed at night until well into her 'teens; napping together; bursting into each other's room while the other was dressing; and frequent kissing, cuddling, and hugging. The father always commented on how pretty Shirley was and how beautiful her clothes looked on her. As Shirley entered adolescence, the father began to compliment her on her figure and always wondered aloud how the boys could resist her. But in all the healthy spheres of a father-daughter relationship, he showed no interest whatever. He cared not at all about her friends, her progress in school, or her everyday successes and failures. Shirley could not turn to him for any genuine support and guidance in dealing with the many problems of her childhood. The father's relationship with Shirley was based not on his "great love" for his daughter (as the father honestly believed and protested) but rather on his own sick needs. By such behavior, the father encouraged Shirley's natural feelings of competition with her mother for her father's affection during the first-romance stage. He held tantalizingly before his daughter the prospect of her succeeding in competition with her mother to win her father for herself. By such behavior, he kept her at this stage of development long after she should have progressed beyond it. These early unresolved feelings were further ignited as she entered adolescence and new and stronger longings appeared. In this way, the early attitudes remained to influence her feelings and behavior toward men and women throughout life.

Shirley's early experiences with her father made impossible a mature relationship with any man in later life. Her concept of love with men was derived from her early experiences with her father. Love meant the same superficial expressions unaccompanied by any genuine feelings. Her father's tantalizing behavior toward her was repeated in her coquettish behavior toward men. She became the coquette who, knowing nothing else, never could really give of herself.

In the presence of other women Shirley felt tense and uncomfortable, as she had with her mother. As a result of the prolonged unresolved competition with her mother, Shirley always felt angry and therefore guilty toward her. These early feelings of guilt and anger and the need to compete became indelibly stamped on Shirley's character. They influenced all her later feelings and behavior toward her mother and all other women.

Laura and Shirley show us how important are the feelings of the parents in molding the character of the child. But these examples should not be considered as further evidence for the popular misconception that "all pretty girls get into trouble." This statement implies that it is the girl's beauty that gets her into trouble. But what this misconception really tells the girl who knows she is pretty is that she might be permitted to do things that the other girls must not do. Standards of conduct should be the same for all girls and women, regardless of their beauty. The comeliness of the girl, in itself a desirable characteristic, easily lends itself to distortion in this way by society, the parents, and the girl herself. With her beauty and her physical attractiveness to men, the means for carrying out such behavior are more readily available to her. Through the girl's beauty, her parents might find a more readily excusable and available outlet for their own distorted needs than if she were less beautiful. But, if such excuses or means were not available, others would be found, because such behavior originates from the parents' attitudes, which do not depend upon the physical appearance of the child.

Joe's sister, Betty, had been gradually prepared for the change to womanhood by a healthy, honest relationship with her mother. In contrast, Joe was supposed to learn things for himself. After all, he was a boy. This was not a subject he would or should have discussed with his mother. And his father was either too busy or unapproachable. Yet, Joe was growing up. He had the same problems in general that Betty had. Joe was getting taller and heavier, his external genitals were enlarging, hair was appearing on his body and face, his shoulders were getting broader, and his voice was getting deeper. These were the visible changes, but Joe was also beginning to show an interest in girls, and he began to take greater pride in his physical appearance. As a matter of fact, he seldom spent less time combing his hair in front of the mirror than did his sister. He showed the same attention to the clothes he wore and the way he wore them.

Finally, Mr. and Mrs. Brown decided that their son, Joe, was sufficiently grown up for Mr. Brown systematically to review the subject of sex with him.

"Come into the living room with me, Joe; I want to tell you some things you should know!" Mother was conspicuously absent, as though by prearranged signal. Joe sensed that his father was flustered and did not know quite how to begin. Mr. Brown finally cleared his throat and with a sheepish look began, "Joe, your mother tells me you've been thinking of girls lately. Is there anything about them you'd like to know?" Mr. Brown approached this problem with his son with the same bluntness and clockwork precision that he used in his work as an accountant. He was embarrassed; so was his son. Joe had many questions; he had had them for years; but he never would ask them of his parents. The son clearly sensed, as he had all along, that his father would prefer to leave the topic alone. But, acting as though it were a chore to be completed as quickly as possible, Mr. Brown fumbled his way through a discourse on sex. Joe kept his eyes on the floor; he was too upset to understand what was said. He asked no questions. At the end of the monologue, Mr. Brown picked up a book and handed it to his son, "Here, read this! It told me all I needed to know. If you have any questions after you've read it, you can always come to me."

It is just as important for a boy as it is for a girl to have the parent of the same sex instruct him on the subject. Both boys and girls have these questions as they grow up. If they feel comfortable with their parents and if they sense that their parents will answer these questions honestly and without embarrassment or punishment, the children will ask questions when they occur to them. The parents' honesty and lack of embarrassment encourage future questions. Sex will be viewed in its proper perspective as another phase of the process of growing up. It will not be shunned as a topic of shame nor will it receive the undue interest accorded to that which is expressly forbidden. Joe sensed his parents' feelings that sex is a shameful and unclean subject that should not be discussed. Subjected to these values throughout his formative years, Joe had long since accepted them as his own. But his curiosity demanded satisfaction. Unable to turn to his parents, he had to depend upon his friends for information all too often distorted by half-knowledge, superstition, and sensationalism. If the parent feels uncomfortable about answering a child's question about sex (and this is common), he should turn to the physician for help, in this matter.

With the help of experienced teachers, nurses (or physicians), films, pamphlets, and so forth, the schools can become another excellent source of information on sex. In some instances such lectures have been given to groups of boys or girls accompanied by their parents of the same sex. At the end of the formal presentations the meetings are thrown open to questions from the boys or girls. Experience has shown that the interest was there—if the instructor approached the material matter-of-factly.

The nocturnal emission (wet dream) represents the male sexual discharge, which leaves a slightly discolored starchy area on the bed sheet, and with a definite odor. Like the appearance of menstruation in a girl, the wet dream is a healthy sign of approaching physical maturity in the boy. So far as nature is concerned, the boy is then approaching manhood and soon will be capable of becoming a father.

Mothers often mistakenly believe that their sons must be having this discharge as a result of handling the external genitals. A mother may often recall that as a young child the boy used to place his hands in the region of his external genitals whenever he was tense. She may have scolded him for doing so and warned him that he would hurt himself or suffer other harm if he persisted in such activity. However, boys and girls often handle their genitals during childhood. When a boy does so before three years of age, it has the same meaning to him as handling his ears, nose, or any other part of his body. It is at this time that he is curious about his own body and is busy exploring it. From three to six years of age, such handling may be accompanied by vague pleasurable physical sensations (masturbation) that he does not understand, which do not have the same relationship, in thoughts and feelings, toward the opposite sex that similar behavior has in puberty and later life. If such extremely unhealthy erotic associations occur at this early age, they could only have been learned from the parents. The same is true of girls during these age periods. After six years of age, such activity can occur occasionally and should cause no undue alarm. However, when it is noted almost incessantly, it suggests that the child has some tension with which he cannot cope directly. He must then revert to an earlier mode of behavior for pleasure and relief of such tension (see p. 36). If he is getting what he should out of life in his relations with other people (especially with his mother and father), tension does not build up, and he need not look for relief by masturbation or other outlets (for example, thumb-sucking, nail-biting, and temper tantrums). The same general rule holds for adolescents. However, at puberty the boy can also relieve his tension through masturbation, but in a more complex way. At this time, the tension is often in the sexual sphere, and the boy can have frank fantasies of different women and of situations that stimulate him during masturbation. Such behavior at this time of life is more consciously related to the boy's sexual interests. Such behavior may persist off and on until marriage. Again, the same is true of girls during this age period.

While adolescence is a prelude to that which will follow, the attitudes of this stage of development are, in turn, wholly dependent upon the attitudes of the earlier stages: the mouth, the bowel, and the first-romance stages.

PUNISHMENT AND DISCIPLINE

Much is said and written about love—and rightfully so. Love lends itself easily to discussion and tramples on the feelings of very few people. However, before one can love, one must first have received love. People just do not get sick from "too much love." But one can give love freely and fully only if one has not been tragically wounded by experiences that lead only to hate. In such a sick indi-

vidual, love can only follow a purging of this preexisting hate. This cannot be done merely by saying
to oneself, "I will not hate; I will love." One must first
learn to recognize hate. Why does he hate? What are
the manifestations of this hate? Only then, when he
understands the meaning of hate, can he rid himself
of it and be ready to receive and give love.

Stubbornness is a way of showing anger. By refusing to do what another person wishes, one effectively
combats him and without violence. For example,
children of a perfectionistic mother, who makes
strict demands that must be obeyed immediately and
to the letter, are angry whether they show anger or
not. This anger may be shown as stubbornness. The
stubbornness may become established as a pattern of
behavior and become directed toward people and
situations that have nothing to do with the mother.
In this manner, the original anger toward the
mother becomes redirected toward others. The child
may not even be aware that he is angry nor will he
remember the people or the situations against which
the anger was originally directed. He is merely stubborn. Such spilling over of anger onto other individuals and situations is not unusual.

Only after his uncontrollable outbursts of anger
have passed and he has calmed down, does he realize
that he has allowed his anger against one person or
situation to spill over against someone else. He may
even feel ashamed that he did so or, rarely, may
grudgingly apologize to the innocent victim of his
anger. He may excuse himself by saying that he was
so angry he did not know what he was doing. And the

wronged person probably will forgive him, remembering all too well that he himself has acted similarly in the past. This common example from everyday life shows how a person's behavior is determined by a passion that he has bottled up within himself and that now seeks an outlet. At the same time, during the act he is often only dimly aware of the existence of this underlying passion or the real reason that he is behaving as he does. People who show long-standing, deep-rooted anger by stubbornness, frequently appear weak, ingratiating, and submissive, as if in an effort to conceal their anger, not only from others but also from themselves.

Instead of showing anger by a stubborn refusal to comply, a child may also show anger by active hostility. He may strike at the mother, the teacher, or others who may or may not be the original cause of his anger. Or he may become critical, sarcastic, and foul-mouthed. The child may also develop a permanent "chip on his shoulder" and become suspicious of everyone. In certain specific situations, to be discussed later, he may resort to fire-setting and stealing.

Most angry children, it should be emphasized, are harboring a long-smoldering rage in response to a specific home situation of one of the many unhealthy types previously described. This rage affects a child's attitudes toward situations and people outside the home and is an ever-present part of him. Such a child never forgets his anger (though he may forget its original cause) or his desire for revenge. Rarely is he or the parent aware of the long-standing emotional disturbances between them that bred the anger. The constantly angry child might be the mean little girl in nursery school who pushes her playmates off the chair, takes their toys, and leaves them crying. He might be the school bully who constantly baits smaller boys and torments girls, not in play but in malice. He might be the adult who enjoys throwing his weight around and delights in punishing his family, friends, and everyone with whom he comes in contact. He might be the tyrant of the home, the office, or the factory. Or she might be the matriarch in the home, the highly competitive career woman, or the prima donna. Such a person's anger is constantly boiling over, and the only relief is in finding a subject for the anger, someone who can be punished. These people derive no real pleasure in inflicting their cruelties; they derive only a temporary and partial relief of the inner turmoil caused by their anger. They are, indeed, possessed of a devil!

On the other hand, the child or the adult who repeatedly suffers at the hands of the bully or the tyrant is commonly the object of much pity. Yet careful evaluation reveals that such a person often finds himself in the position to receive punishment. He may change his school, playmates, job, wife (or husband), but seemingly, as if by accident, the punishment and the suffering continue. This is not chance. To the casual observer and to the long-suffering person himself, the hard-luck story is accepted at face value. But pitiful and tragic as the actual situation may seem to be, there is no mystery, and there is no accident.

The individual who must constantly mete out punishment and the individual who must constantly receive punishment are both "driven by a devil." The receiving of punishment satisfies a definite need, although the sufferer is usually unaware of this fact. There is the child (or the adult) who is always falling and being cut, bruised, and banged up. Some children always have accidents, and when they grow up the same story continues. They are called "accident-prone." One feels pity (and sometimes a little exasperation) as he listens to 12-year-old Sally describe in great detail and with apparent relish her numerous aches and pains and her countless trips to the doctor. This happens each time one sees her; one expects it. As her mother says, "Sally has never been afraid of doctors. Even when she was only six years old, she'd march into the office like a little soldier to receive her injections. Though I know she suffered terribly, she always smiled . . . never a peep out of her. I know she was very miserable and suffered a great deal of pain when her tonsils were taken out six years ago. But she was a perfect lady and never cried. Sally has always acted years older than her age, and she can take punishment!"

Sally's mother has also suffered much and always has had countless ailments. Although she never complains, even a child can look at her face and know how much she is suffering. "Don't worry about me. You people go out and enjoy yourselves. I'll be all right. If it gets worse, I can call the doctor." Her dresser drawer overflows with patent medicines. Every new newspaper advertisement sends her scurrying to the druggist with new hope. She always knows exactly what is wrong with her: "acid stomach; chronic constipation with rundown nerves; acute nervous exhaustion; several dislocated vertebrae with pressure on the pain nerves causing headache; abdominal cramps; lumbago; high blood pressure headache; fatigue from low blood pressure; blood anemia and vitamin deficiency; and monthly cramps from hormone deficiency." When the physician finds nothing physically wrong with her after careful examination, including full laboratory studies, she remains unconvinced. "I know there must be something wrong. Can't you operate? I don't mind if you think it will help me. I can stand the pain." The physician says in a friendly manner, "Mrs. A., I understand how badly you feel, but your problem is terrible nervous tension and emotion. Surgery will not help." . . .

Johnny continues to play with the neighborhood bully in spite of his repeated bloody noses and black eyes. Mr. D. remains on the job in spite of a tyrannical employer, and he even refuses offers of better jobs elsewhere. Mrs. J. "has sacrificed herself all her life for her family," and, strangely enough, her children show no gratitude. If a child truly receives love without any strings attached, one would expect the child to show gratitude and love in return. Mrs. F., following the death of her alcoholic and brutal husband, marries Tom who drinks and beats her every Saturday night. All these people are receiving punishment either from other people or from themselves.

Both the people who give and those who receive punishment are suffering from the same basic mental disorder. One cannot exist without the other. If one has the need to punish, there must also be the one who has the need to be punished. In fact, both these needs often coexist in the same individual. In some persons one need may be stronger and therefore more obvious than the other. Those who must punish are known as sadists, and those who must be punished are known as masochists.

Why this need to punish and be punished? These people frequently have no inkling that such a need exists. It is their way of life. They have forgotten how they got that way and would be surprised and offended if asked, "Why is it that you're always causing trouble?" or "Why is it that you always find yourself in trouble?"

These complex and highly individual problems are for the most part derived from the bowel period. As we have seen, it is at this time that one of the early major contests between parent and child can take place, and it is during this stage that many other learning problems are encountered as the child is taught to conform to the rules of society. The manner in which the parent, who is more powerful than the child, manages the contest over bowel training is often an indication of the way he has managed previous teaching-learning problems and the way he probably will manage innumerable future learning problems. The attitudes in such situations determine the child's later attitudes toward people: he gets along well, fights them, or gives in. The later struggles can reinforce the child's responses to the earlier struggle; or these later struggles, if handled in a healthy manner, can modify the results of any earlier unhealthy ones into socially acceptable channels.

In oversimplified terms, a child or an adult may have the need to punish as a result of deep-lying anger caused by unhealthy feelings from early parent-child experiences. It is more difficult to understand why the child or the adult needs punishment. One reason is shown by the parent who behaves in such a manner as to invite punishment, as did Sally's mother, Mrs. A. Such a parent, by her own example, may instill into the child similar values for determining behavior.

This exceedingly complex need for punishment has many other poorly understood causes. A second reason is shown by the child or the adult who is angry and consequently might feel guilty; he then may need some form of punishment to assuage his deep-lying guilt. A third possible reason for needing punishment is provided by the example of the child who is kept unnaturally dependent upon his parents (see p. 110). Although he may not be aware of it, such a child is understandably angry at being kept in continuous servitude. As a result of his long-standing dependency, he is completely helpless, afraid, and unable to act independently; he always must seek out someone who will demand his complete submission and tell him what to do and when to do it. He must accept this dependency (punishment) in order to acquire the false security that he buys dearly at the sacrifice of his freedom and the containment of his resultant rage. His parents have completely blocked his development to a happy and full emotional maturity. By doing so, they have shown not the love that they profess, but hate. And the child, with his unhealthy extreme dependency, has not the love that this dependency superficially appears to demonstrate, but rather deep-lying hate. Neither parent nor child is ever quite aware of this fundamental hate.

A nondestructive expression of legitimate anger is a healthy response to a specific situation of which the child is fully aware. He is sticking up for his rights in a realistic fashion, and it is healthy and right that he do so. It is important that his larger and stronger parents be fair and permit the child to express his anger in this manner when anger is justified. If they are wrong and the child is justifiably angry, the parents should not deny their wrongdoing but should be honest and admit to the child that they were wrong, that they are sorry, and that his anger is perfectly understandable. This bond of honesty between parents and child cannot be emphasized too strongly. No matter how small, helpless, and inarticulate the child may be, he is a human being with all a human being's rights, feelings, and emotions. These should be respected by those adults near to him who are entrusted with protecting and guiding him to a healthy maturity. Permitting the child to express anger, however, does not mean that he should be allowed to strike his parents or commit any openly destructive acts as an expression of his anger. Such means of expressing anger never should be permitted under any circumstances.

There is equal reason for concern over the child who never shows anger or is not permitted by his parents to show it. From previous and future examples in this book, one can see the results of the bottling up of justified anger.

Many parents, because of unhappy experiences with their own parents, are unable to accept responsibility for their own actions. When unpleasant situations develop for which they really are responsible, they may blame other people or situations. They are forever falling into the trap created by their own past experiences of excusing themselves and blaming others. With parents who are too ready to shift the blame elsewhere, the innocent and defenseless child is as vulnerable as his unfortunate parents were before him. Neither has ever known any other type of behavior from those close to him. In each instance, the child is offered no choice; he must accept the blame; he must not protest. Often, in such warped home situations it is too easy for a parent to vent his pent-up emotions on the child who is defenseless rather than on someone else who may really be responsible for the parent's difficulty but who can fight back. The child will resent being blamed unfairly and being forced to accept the parent's wrath for things that he did not do. Unable to show his anger against his parents, the child must accept their blame, and the resultant anger can only be turned against himself. He becomes depressed. Or, he may copy his parent's solution by blaming others as the parent blamed him. In addition to the anger and the depression which often follow, such unhealthy parental attitudes also breed distrust and suspicion. Unable to trust his parents whose feelings and actions determine his own feelings and behavior, how can the child ever learn to trust anyone else? These changes occur so subtly and gradually that the victim hardly senses that they are present or that they are acting upon him. The effects are cumulative and, if progressive, very corrosive.

If this tendency to distrust and hate others becomes extreme, how can the child ever become friendly with other people? He distrusts and hates them, and they in turn are aware of and react to his underlying hostility with mistrust and anger. The child has the perfect answer. He will think, "No one trusts me! They don't like me! I will not trust or like them!" Cause and effect have been reversed. Thus the child may blame others for situations that his own underlying attitudes have initiated and fostered. With time and progression of this emotional distortion, the child might become the patient who believes that people persecute him and accuse him of various misdeeds. With still further distortion, the patient might have hallucinations during which he hears voices accusing him of various misdeeds. He "knows" that someone is unduly influencing him with electrical machines and that his mind is being read. He is paranoid.

There is, of course, quite a span between the angry child and the patient just described. For this extremely disturbed paranoid state to develop, there must be progression of the symptoms and repeated contact over the years with disturbing influences. However, in paranoid patients who have been thoroughly studied, the trail always leads back to an unhealthy parent-child relationship of the type described. It should be emphasized, however, that lies shared between parents and children do not invariably lead to a paranoid state.

Although discipline of the child, when justified, is necessary, it should never be a distortion of the parents' own difficulties. For instance, the parent might give punishment out of all proportion to the misdeed of the child or without any infraction at all by the child. In this instance, it is the parent who must take his own tension out on someone. The child who cannot fight back is the victim. The rage of the alcoholic father who comes home drunk and whips both mother and child is a common example.

Less obvious but as far-reaching in its effects is the case of the unfortunate, high-strung, tense mother who gets along poorly with her husband and must work to help support her family. She needs an escape valve for her tension. So she is continually yelling at her young son, sending him to his room, putting him to bed early, and depriving him of desserts and movies for numerous minor and fancied misdeeds.

From what has been said, there certainly is a time, a place, and a way for the child to show justified anger and for the parent to scold or even "whack" the child when justified. It is not the physical injury of the slap or the child's anguish at being scolded but the feelings exchanged between parent and child that are all-important.

Physical punishment is seldom necessary for a child who has a healthy relationship with his parents. In such a relationship the child knows what he should and should not do. He knows that when his parents tell him something, they mean exactly that. The child respects his parents and is sure of their love; they in turn respect his needs and feelings as a human being. Their discipline is a simple, direct, appropriate response to a specific childish misdeed of which the child is fully aware. Such an honest parent will seldom have need to punish the child, but when punishment is necessary the parent will feel quite comfortable about it. Punishment is given for the child's sake and not for the sake of the parents.

■—●—●—●—●—●—●—●—●—●—●—●—●—●—●—■

4

Perils of Overattachment to a Parent

THE CHILD WHO IS TOO DEPENDENT

Mrs. Smith was married, less because of any warm feelings toward Mr. Smith than because it was the "thing to do." When Mr. Smith was offered a good job in another city, Mrs. Smith tearfully pleaded with him not to move away from her mother. Mr. Smith, usually very gruff and busy, yielded as was his custom to his wife's tears and pleas.

Perhaps even more than the tears and pleas, Mr. Smith was influenced by the memory of the last time he was offered a better job in another city. Mrs. Smith had agreed that it was a fine opportunity they should not miss, but she kept repeating, "What will Mother do? She'll be all alone. I hate to leave her. She's always so good to us. I don't see how I can get along without her. What will little Eddie do? He's so used to having his grandmother around."

Nevertheless, the plans were all made. But the day before the family was to move, Mrs. Smith's mother tearfully gave a farewell party for them. The next morning, Mrs. Smith awoke with diarrhea, abdominal cramps, breathlessness, cold sweat, racing of the heart, shakiness, and snapping pains in the back of the head and the neck. She was terrified and insisted that her mother be called immediately to her bedside, for she was convinced she was about to die.

After a thorough examination, the physician concluded that all of these complaints were due to acute nervous exhaustion. It was a whole week before Mrs. Smith could get out of bed. During all this time her mother remained at her bedside and ran the household. The planned move was canceled. Hat in hand, Mr. Smith went to his recent employer and asked for his old job back.

The extreme dependency that Mrs. Smith showed toward her mother was mirrored in her young son's feelings toward her. Eddie had been very close to his mother from the beginning. Mrs. Smith never could leave him with someone, not even for five minutes while she went on an errand, without his becoming very upset. He wanted his Mommy! Even at play, Eddie always had to remain close to his mother. The other children did not like to play with him because he was a poor loser; he wanted his own way just as he was used to having it at home.

Mrs. Smith and her husband often said that they might have trouble getting Eddie to go to school. Their fears were fulfilled. The same problem arose when the father wanted to send the son to summer camp. Mrs. Smith thought it was "terrible for Eddie to go with all those little roughnecks; I know he'd rather stay home. He'll get homesick." Again, her fears were fulfilled.

The Smiths boasted that Eddie was a perfect son except for one thing: he always had to have his own way. "I guess he is just too independent," his mother would say; "he wants to assert himself. But that won't be any disadvantage when he grows up." When he did not get his way immediately, Eddie would kick, scream, and scratch his mother and father. In spite of their slapping him and threatening worse punishment, Eddie's outbursts would not stop until he had had his way.

The forces underneath Eddie's extreme dependency on his mother were quite unfriendly. Eddie kicked and bit his mother, and she struck back. She felt that letting Eddie have his own way and keeping him tied to her apron strings were proof of her great love. Her own dependency on her mother was reflected in her inability to cope with Eddie's rage—biting and kicking—as well as by her response at the same physical level—striking back.

Children should never be allowed to hit their parents. And parents whose relationship with their children is healthy need not depend on continuous spankings for discipline. This does not mean that there is not a time and a place for occasional discipline. The child must be taught what he can and cannot do. He should never be permitted to do whatever he wishes at all times under the popular, but utterly false, notion that this is best for his developing personality. If the mother and father are sure of themselves in managing the child, they will have little or no difficulty in setting limits that he will obey and about which he will be comfortable. Such limits should be well understood by the child and should be consistent from day to day; not changing with the vacillating mood of the parent. Setting limits makes the child understand that what is asked is to be done.

Empty words accompanied by feelings that suggest another response by the child are not setting limits, but, on the contrary, give tacit permission for the activity that is being verbally forbidden. For example, five-year-old Elsie puts her hand in the goldfish bowl. Immediately and automatically, her mother says, "No, No! Elsie, you'll kill the goldfish, and then we'll have to buy more." But as she says this, she smiles indulgently, turns to the father, and audibly whispers, "The little rascal is so cute I can't get angry with her." This has happened before. Mother says, "No, No!" but Elsie knows that her mother is also enjoying it. Elsie therefore continues unperturbed to do as she pleases.

Except during the mouth stage when the baby is dependent upon the mother for food, extreme dependency means that the dependent person is nothing more than a vassal, subservient to a master. In this state of abject humiliation and practically nonexistent self-esteem, how can the vassal love his master? Yet he needs the master for his support and livelihood. Who could say that the master who keeps another human being in such a condition loves the vassal? Such ambivalent feelings become intensified when the vassal questions the motives of his master, who in turn thinks, "Look at all I'm doing for you—the food, the clothes, my protection. You should love me. And I'm giving all this to you because I love you."

By this analogy, the reader may recognize some of the undercurrents in the relationship of Eddie and his mother.

If the vassal rebels against his master, he immediately loses all the material things he is receiving, and he realizes that it is a fight to the death with the master, who is stronger. The master, on the other hand, realizes that if he does not suppress the vassal's revolt, he, the master, will not be able to live in the style to which he is accustomed, for he also has much at stake. In the resulting struggle, each will unleash previously disguised feelings, and each will become aware that the previous amenities and professions of love really hid underlying hatred. The vassal envied his master, and the master had contempt for his slave.

This, then, is the situation between Eddie and his mother. The tears, the embraces, the clinging, and all the other signs of dependency point to the fundamental conflict between mother and son. The physical outbursts of anger—the kicking, biting, and slapping—only serve to bring this underlying conflict to the surface. Each becomes aware that this conflict exists, but this only leads to further physical outbursts. The mother and the child attempt to patch up their differences by more fervent protestations of love (and dependency). They continue to exist in this state of conflict marked by tears, clinging, and other superficial manifestations of what they consider

"love." They manage to keep their underlying conflict in check by protesting that they love each other
so much that they cannot leave each other.

THE CHILD WHO EATS TOO MUCH

Holding tightly to his mother's hand, 12-year-old
Rudy P., 5 feet-3 inches tall, weight 165 pounds, came
to the physician's office to receive his tetanus booster
shot. Rudy preferred his mother's hand to playing or
talking with other children in the waiting room. He
smiled continuously as he nibbled on a chocolate bar.
When his mother got up to answer the nurse's routine questions, Rudy went with her. When a child
cried inside the office, Rudy's mother turned to him
and said, "The doctor's not going to hurt you, Rudy;
he's just going to look at you; wait until you see the
lollypop he has for you."

Five-year-old Tim, playing on the waiting room
floor, looked up at Rudy and then turned to his
mother, "Gee, Mommy, he's a fatso." Rudy lowered
his head, looked straight ahead, blushed, and continued to munch on his chocolate bar. Mrs. P.
squeezed Rudy's hand, twisted on the couch, and
effectively interposed her body between Tim and
Rudy. Rather self-consciously she asked the nurse,
"When will Rudy have to come again for his next
shot?"

"Mommy, I got to go—I got to go. . . ." "Just a few
minutes, Rudy, and we'll be inside. . . ." "No, Mommy,
I can't wait, I can't wait." The nurse directed Mrs. P.
and Rudy to the lavatory. Mrs. P. went in with Rudy.

When they came out, the chocolate was gone, but Rudy was busy chewing his nails.

Nearby, two waiting mothers were discussing their children's repeated colds and earaches that past winter. Mrs. P. entered the conversation by proudly proclaiming that her son was in such good health that this was his first visit to the doctor since his preschool examination seven years previously. "I've never had any trouble with Rudy. He's a model child, perfectly obedient and eats everything I put in front of him." The other two mothers looked at Rudy and smiled.

Two-year-old Dianne came toddling over, stared at Rudy, and offered him her lollypop. Rudy remained impassive, but Dianne's mother pulled her away angrily, saying, "That's yours, Honey; you keep it! I'm sure his mother doesn't want him to have any more." Rudy's mother could not miss the hint of criticism and said, "I know he's a little chubby now, but all boys are fat at this age. He'll outgrow it when his glands mature!"

The nurse finally beckoned Rudy and his mother into the office. The physician looked up, "Well, what have we here? You sure are a big boy, aren't you, fellow?" Mrs. P. broke in, "I've never had any trouble with his appetite, Doctor, but, of course, as you know, it's just his glands." Rudy cried out, "Don't let the Doctor give me a shot, Mommy . . . please, Mommy, no shot!" Mrs. P. shushed Rudy and continued, this time without interruption. "Please excuse my little boy, Doctor. He's not half as good as Marge, his sister. Nothing frightens her. Why, she'd come into your office, know all your patients, play with the toys, and then take the shot without a whimper. But she's different from Rudy. She's like me that way. She's built like me too . . . slender . . . always on the go. That girl doesn't stop from morning to night. Someday she'll make some lucky man a wonderful wife and mother. The women in my family have always had good figures. People always thought Mother and I were sisters. I guess they'll make the same mistake between Marge and me."

Unable to get in a word until now, the physician asked about Rudy's father. Mrs. P. blurted, "All men are alike . . . my own father was the same way." The physician looked confused and repeated his question. "That's what I mean, Doctor; Rudy's Daddy lives for only two things—food and sleep. No ambition at all. Funny thing, after seeing Mother suffer with my father, I always promised myself it would not happen to me. I guess sometimes we marry too young.

"Take the doctor's pencil out of your mouth, Rudy. He's always got something in his mouth, Doctor. I can't stop him. He's always got to eat between meals. When I want him to talk to strangers, he clams up. But at home he never stops chattering. If I take food away from him, he sulks and says, 'You don't love me, Mommy!' "

The physician realized that Rudy's troubles were deep-rooted and that Rudy's mother was unaware of the extent of her own involvement. From her statements thus far, the physician began to suspect that she might have considerable emotional confusion toward men, which in turn might be reflected in Rudy's obesity. The physician gave Rudy the shot, and strongly urged Mrs. P. to make another appointment when there would time for a complete investigation. The physician emphasized that the problems of obesity were often due to emotional rather than physical causes. He explained that without a complete history and an examination of Rudy, and without certain laboratory procedures, he could not be more specific. He also said that sometimes the correction of the condition, physical or emotional, which causes obesity is as important as immunizing a child against a disease. Mrs. P. smiled ingratiatingly and agreed to do as the physician suggested. She promised to phone the nurse later for an appointment. But neither Rudy nor his mother were seen again.

Despite Rudy's obvious obesity, his mother brought him to the physician for an immunization, not for the obesity. Her seeming refractoriness to the problem of Rudy's obesity was actually very revealing. In fact, her response to the thinly veiled sarcasm of the other mothers and the not-so-veiled taunts of five-year-old Tim indicated that she was far more aware of the existence of the problem than her proud denial would admit. The physician, perceiving that this was a complex problem with many explosive emotional undertones, treated her sympathetically. Nevertheless, his honest and matter-of-fact approach, which was purposely gentle and superficial at this initial visit, was unable to overcome her fears of what a sincere discussion of the roots of the problem might divulge. She could only smile in seeming agreement with his suggestion, but her real reactions were apparent when she failed to return.

Mrs. P.'s oversensitiveness about Rudy's obesity was also revealed by her rambling response to the physician's greeting to her son. She immediately silenced Rudy's protests, disregarded his fears, and proceeded to talk about herself. Her reactions strongly hinted at her complete indifference to her son and his problems and her preoccupation with herself. So far as could be seen, her chief avenue of communication with Rudy was on a very immature level. Although 12 years old, Rudy always held his mother's hand, talked like a very much younger child, and responded to upsetting situations by the "mouth stage" mode of behavior: eating chocolate bars, sucking lollypops, chewing his fingernails, and gnawing on the doctor's pencil. His mother encouraged all of this.

Mrs. P. said that she loved her son. This apparently meant that she fed him, because if Rudy had been really comfortable and secure in her love, he would have had no need to resort so often to such babyish behavior. From her rambling monologue and without the complete picture, the physician received the impression that Mrs. P. was a strong-willed woman who imagined herself to be perennially young and attractive. In boastfully comparing her daughter with Rudy, Mrs. P. was really extolling her own virtues. In her brief and scattered allusions to the men and women in her family, she gave a description of the women that was highly complimentary while that of the men was derogatory. She strongly hinted at her marital dissatisfaction by her description of her husband as a placid, easy-going man of no ambition, for whom she felt neither love nor respect but only contempt. Ironically, her mother felt the same way about the latter's own husband, Mrs. P.'s father.

Beneath the facade of the mother's solicitude for Rudy, there were the facts: Rudy was fat; he would not mix with children his own age; he was completely dependent upon his mother—an extremely unhealthy situation. Her unflattering appraisals of her husband, her father, and her son pointed to her own poor adjustments with men. Her complimentary appraisals of her mother, her daughter, and herself indicated her superficial view that the facade of a good figure represents femininity. Finding himself in a family whose women were unfriendly to men and whose men could not assert themselves with women, Rudy would never know any alternative to the docile submission of men to women.

Rudy responded as might be expected. He adopted the attitudes that his mother had toward men. His own estimate of himself was contemptuous. He completely complied with his mother's wishes and needs, which required that men be kept subservient. She could not help feeling as she did; these feelings depended upon her own early upbringing. Rudy ate the food that his mother substituted for genuine affection and respect for men. This became his way of life; he became fat and remained helplessly dependent like a baby. When confronted with life's problems, Rudy showed few outward signs of emotion, nor could he attempt to solve a problem by an appropriate reaction. Faced with a problem, Rudy developed tension that needed relief. He found an outlet for his tension through his own body in the way he had first learned with his mother while a baby. He ate, and he continued to eat until the situation that caused the tension changed and his tension disappeared. The situation could be explained—as it was in Rudy's case—by the unhealthy parent-child feelings in the home, which had their tragic effect on Rudy. Since these feelings never changed, Rudy continued to eat. Placid like his father and submissive to his mother, Rudy was physically inactive. He used less energy (calories) in the physical exertions of his daily life than the amount that he ingested daily in his food. He became swathed in fat.

His mother's personal problems and self-doubts were partially resolved at the expense of Rudy's needs and growing-up; he became an obese, shy, socially backward, dependent boy with a complacent smile but no happiness. Forever doomed to eat as a means of assuaging tension and forever the brunt of jokes, Rudy was laughed at but never with.

It may seem strange that there has been no mention so far of the popularly ascribed and more palatable causes of obesity. In a large proportion of cases of obesity, however, the cause is simply eating too much for the exercise one does. "But, Doctor, everything Tommy eats turns to fat. He eats no more than Johnny, the same age, but Johnny isn't fat." When an obese child's daily intake of calories is checked by a trained dietician, it is often found that such a child ingests much more than the average.

Fat people do not generally engage in the more competitive physical activities. "Chubby" plays marbles well, but he is not wanted on the neighborhood baseball team; he is too slow. This physical inactivity, however, is quite secondary in importance to the overeating. Eating depends on hunger and on appetite. Hunger is determined by the body's actual need for growth and living. Appetite, on the other hand, indicates the pleasure of eating (as contrasted with the physical need for food). Appetite is highly variable and is determined almost solely by how one feels. When one is temporarily sick with fever, or angry, or depressed, appetite may decrease. When such feelings get out of control and persist, decreased appetite and subsequent weight loss appear. Physicians frequently see depressed patients who are slowly "wasting away." When one feels gay, satisfied with the world or well rested, he may indulge his appetite. However, there are emotionally disturbed patients who eat not less but more, as in Rudy's case. These people use eating as a means of assuaging tension just the way that children frequently revert to thumb-sucking when faced with an emotionally disturbing situation. Thus, if such people stop overeating, for any of various reasons, without changing their basic emotional structure, they may develop a serious depression with, in some instances, an accompanying risk of suicide.

Although he suspected the emotional basis of Rudy's obesity, the physician insisted on a complete examination, including necessary laboratory tests, to establish the cause. He knew that brain tumors, and infections, glandular disturbances, and certain diseases can cause body changes that may be mistaken for obesity. Such cases are rare. He also recognized that what our culture so often classifies as obesity is really a hereditary stockiness in body build. In such people the physical proportions, which may not be currently fashionable, are appropriate and healthy for that particular individual. Rudy's physician, knowing his patient's family and noting the obvious extreme overweight, recognized that Rudy's problem was more than simple hereditary stockiness. In most patients—adult or child—obesity is due to overeating; overeating depends on appetite; appetite depends on emotion.

A rare dread condition that is more serious than obesity, because life itself is jeopardized, is "anorexia nervosa" (nervous loss of appetite). This condition is evidenced in the reverse of the fundamental feeding mechanisms noted in the obese child. In such patients, there is nothing wrong with the brain, the glands, or the stomach. But the appetite is greatly decreased as a result of deeply rooted emotional conflicts that frequently go back to infancy and childhood. These patients lose all interest in their family, friends, acquaintances, home, work, dress, and so on. They lie on the bed, a depressed bag of bones, totally uninterested in the world about them. In children, most cases appear at or shortly after puberty when the preexisting parent-child conflicts become intensified.

CHARLIE—THE BOY WHO WAS AFRAID TO GO TO SCHOOL

Five-year-old Mike enthusiastically looked forward to starting kindergarten. As the great day dawned, Mike was up early, ate a good breakfast, and, with some impatience, waited for his mother to take him to school. "Hurry up, Mommy, we'll be late!" When they arrived at school, however, Mike's mood changed. He stared at all the other children, had little to say, and began sucking his thumb. Finally, when his mother introduced him to Miss Jones, his teacher, it was more than he could stand. Although Miss Jones was young, friendly, and smiling, like Mommy, she was not Mommy.

Mike held tightly to his mother's hand. As she tried to leave, the storm broke: he cried, held tightly to her, and could not even speak. His mother was sympathetic and kneeled down to speak to him, as Mike held on. "This is really very scary for you, Mikie, I know. It's no fun to meet all these strange boys and girls at one time. But you are growing up, Mikie, and all big boys and girls go to school. Even though we talked about going to school before, I know you don't like the idea that Mommy is going to leave you. But you remember it is just for this morning; I'll be back when it's time to eat. And then we can talk about what you and all your new friends did. Miss Jones, your teacher, knows how little boys feel. They don't like their Mommies to leave them and are even a little bit mad with their Mommies. But Mommies and teachers understand, Mikie. Miss Jones has lots of games, and I know it will really be fun." At this point Miss Jones sympathetically took hold of Mike's hand and gently pulled him to her as his mother just as gently but firmly disengaged herself, kissed him, and left. "Good-bye, Mikie," she smiled, "I'll see you soon."

Charlie U. also had looked forward to school as he spoke about it boastingly to his playmates. He, too, had come to school with his mother this first morning. To the casual observer, there seemed little difference between Charlie and Mike. Charlie clung to his mother, sucked his thumb, and then suddenly began to scream and howl. No words came, just piercingly loud, unintelligible screams. Charlie kicked at his mother and even at Miss Jones, who had been unable to say anything yet. Mrs. U., tears in her eyes, cradled her son in her arms as she sat on a small kindergarten chair. She cooed, "It's alright, Charlie. Don't cry. Teacher won't hurt you. Mommy wouldn't let anyone hurt you. Please Charlie, please be a good boy. When Mommy comes back, if you've been a good boy, we'll go together, you and I, and have an ice cream cone. Just you and I, no teacher and no daddy."

Charlie held on to his mother tenaciously. "No, no!. Don't leave me, Mommy. Please, Mommy! Don't leave me!" During this pandemonium, Mrs. U. looked around the room, saw the clock on the wall, and knew that it was time to leave Charlie with Miss Jones. Charlie would have none of this. Crying, sobbing, and clinging, he blindly kicked, striking his mother's shins with his shoe. "No son of mine is going to hit me!" Mrs. U.'s eyes blazed as she grasped Charlie by both shoulders, shook him violently, and struck him on the cheek with the back of her open hand. "I've got to teach you to stop hitting and biting me." Angrily shaking her finger and with her voice trembling, she continued brokenly, "Little boys who love their Mommies don't do things like that. You're acting just like a baby. You'd better be good to Miss Jones, because she'll tell me everything that happens, and when you're bad, I'll know it. You can't do in school what you do at home. You can't bite and kick other people like you do Mommy."

Apparently noticing the other mothers in the classroom for the first time, Mrs. U. said, "Charlie's never been away from home before, and this is hard on both of us." Mrs. U. got up and walked to the door, turned and looked at Charlie struggling and crying in Miss Jones' arms, and then impulsively ran back to her son. Tears in her eyes, Mrs. U. hugged Charlie, kissed him, and said, "If Mommy is a little late today, Charlie, don't worry; just stay with your teacher until I come."

Mrs. U. left. Charlie and Mike were both crying. Miss Jones was not concerned about Mike, but she knew that Charlie faced a real problem.

After three days, Mike looked forward to school and the games with his classmates and teacher. In fact, when he and his mother arrived at the classroom, he would immediately leave her and eagerly run into the room, calling to some classmate who had arrived earlier. The tears and fears of the first day were all gone.

Mike was indeed growing up. He always had received love from his mother and he gave love in return. Long ago he had learned to trust his mother's word. She meant what she said and always did what she promised to do. When she promised that she would return, she was specific. ". . . I'll be back when it's time to eat." From past experience, Mike believed her. Although only five years old, and just beginning kindergarten, Mike already had a good measure of self-reliance. His mother and father were straightforward in expressing their feelings for Mike as well as in showing each other mutual love and respect. They had no warped need to keep Mike too closely tied to themselves. Mike was able to test many things for himself and even looked forward to new situations like school. Of course he cried; he was faced with a completely new situation among strange people. But Mike's faith in his mother and his own curiosity and fledgling independence were soon able to overcome this initial fear. Mike soon settled into his new surroundings.

Mike's mother understood and respected his feelings, even to the point of admitting to him that he might be mad at her and frightened. By putting herself in his shoes and being able to accept his justified anger, Mike's mother permitted him to express himself. Mike did not strike his mother. That never had been permitted and never would be. Mike expressed his rage in response to a justifiable situation. His rage was specific and directed at his mother. It was realistic in so far as it was accepted by the mother, and limits were set to the expression of his rage. He could cry or say he was angry with his mother, but he could not resort to striking his mother or engage in any destructive acts. The rage did not get out of hand and, since the underlying feelings between mother and son were sound, there was no need to disguise their feelings by meaningless words and gestures purported to show "love."

Miss Jones' hunch about Charlie was correct. Charlie was unable to live and play happily while separated from his mother. The original scene on the first day of school was repeated daily with many variations. Charlie never really accepted his playmates—nor they him. Several times Miss Jones was called to the office of the principal, Mr. Penrod. Having met Mrs. U. himself, Mr. Penrod understood the situation and sympathized with Charlie and Miss Jones. "Charlie is really tied to his mother's apron strings, isn't he? Mrs. U. even asked me to phone her family doctor. He is well acquainted with the situation and has often tried to persuade Mrs. U. to take Charlie to the Child Guidance Center to see what can be done. As you might guess, Charlie had problems long before school began. But Mrs. U. only gets angry with the doctor and denies that any emotional problem exists. Here we have all this interest nowadays in mental hygiene . . . raising funds, setting up centers for study, magazine articles . . . but it seems that those who need help the most will not go. They just come and complain to us. It's always our fault—the teachers. We're expected to teach these kids what they should have learned at home. Certain responsibilities belong to the parents . . . not to the teacher.

Poor Charlie! He has a hard road ahead. One child like him can stir up the whole class. They'll copy him. And he'll take up too much of your time. The deserving kids will be short-changed. Well, Miss Jones, let's do what we can for him."

Mr. Penrod truly described Charlie's problem when he said that Charlie was tied to his mother's apron strings. Like Rudy, the obese boy, Charlie was really overdependent upon his parents. Although Mr. Penrod said that Charlie's problem began before school—even though the mother was now blaming the school as the cause—he did not realize how long before school the problem really first appeared. Charlie was the result of an unexpected and unplanned pregnancy. His mother and father had wanted to wait for a few years while they both worked in their new florist shop. Charlie was a feeding problem, sucked his thumb, bit his nails, and still occasionally wet the bed. Mr. and Mrs. U. felt that if Charlie had not appeared so inopportunely, they would have been in better financial condition now. Beneath this reasoning were some facts that were not discussed.

Like Rudy's mother, Mrs. U. was unable to see any connection between Charlie's problems and her own past feelings and experiences. Mrs. U.'s father had been a strong-willed man, a virtual dictator in his household. Mrs. U.'s mother had been a timid little woman with many fears and superstitions. Charlie's mother was raised in this unwholesome and unrealistic atmosphere. As a girl, she lived in the constant fear (and hatred) of her father's tyranny and the interminable harping of her mother, "Don't touch this; don't do that." The fears of Mrs. U.'s mother served as an escape valve for her own tension resulting from her unhealthy relationship with her husband. It would be hard to imagine her as having any warm feelings for a man who was so aloof and stern with his wife and daughter. Consequently, Mrs. U. and her mother depended upon each other; each fed the fears of the other. Neither was really happy; neither could exist without the other. Even when Mrs. U. went to a Girl Scout camp one summer, she was very homesick, and her mother had to be sent for. Mrs. U.'s extreme dependence upon her mother was carried forward another generation to her son Charlie's extreme dependence upon her. In each person, Mrs. U.'s mother, Mrs. U. herself, and her son Charlie, this extreme dependence was shown by the exaggerated fears of being separated from each other.

In practically all instances of school phobia, the problems are similar to those of Charlie, with many variations. The extreme anxiety resulting from any separation between the child (or grownup) and another person is founded on helpless dependency and mutual hatred as in the analogy of master and slave (see p. 113).

THOMAS—ASTHMA AND THE EMOTIONS

Dr. M. was coming out of Grandma L.'s room. This time she was complaining of a "lump" in the throat so that she could not swallow. Dr. M. had been seeing

Mrs. L. since he first began practice 30 years previously. His office record on her was voluminous. Even though no abnormalities had been found, new complaints continued to crop up. Dr. M. knew that Mrs. L.'s troubles were due to nervous tension and not the cancer she often feared. But his suggestion that Mrs. L. see a "nerve specialist" always met with angry refusals. When he discussed the problem informally one day with Dr. O., a psychiatrist, in the hospital coffee shop, Dr. O. threw up his hands and said, "Bill, I know how you feel. It's one of those cases that can use psychiatric help but can't see it. You'll just have to carry on as you have done. After all, she might be like the little boy who cried 'Wolf.' You never can tell; she might really develop cancer some day. That has happened with my patients a few times. You'll just have to watch her and check each new complaint. What an unhappy woman!"

As Dr. M. mulled over these thoughts, he passed an open door in the hallway outside Grandma's room. Through the door he saw her married daughter Adele, playfully wrestling on the bed with Adele's eleven-year-old son, Thomas. Giggling and laughing, they rolled over and over on the bed, their arms tightly clasped around each other, with Thomas trying to get a scissors hold on his mother with his legs. Neither, of course, noticed Dr. M., who shrugged his shoulders, grunted, and walked out of the house. As he drove down the street, his thoughts returned to Thomas and his mother.

"Here it is again. Adele is just like *her* mother. It's like talking to the wind: Adele, is it still necessary for you to bathe Thomas? Why haven't you moved his bed out of your own bedroom so he does not sleep in the same room with you and your husband? Why must you walk Thomas to school each morning? And now this wrestling match! And why call him Thomas? Why not Tom or Tommy?

"It's hard to believe that Thomas is eleven. With all the boys his own age in the neighborhood, why must he continue playing with the six- and eight-year-olds? Adele seems to do everything possible to keep him young. I wonder what *she* gets out of it? How pathetic it all is when he has one of his asthma attacks: Thomas in bed wheezing, puffing and gasping for air; the room reeking with vapors and menthol; Adele half-lying on the bed, hugging him to her, kissing him, and repeating, 'My poor little Thomas; Mommy will take care of you.' Thomas clasping his mother with both arms as if she were his lifeline, refusing to let her go. 'Hold me, Mommy, please don't leave me; I'm afraid.' And Nelson (the father), standing in the doorway looking helplessly on; he never says anything; he never does anything.

"What a surprise that last time. Adele used a suppository on Thomas in front of Grandma, Uncle, Father, and me. 'Why have you never used suppositories on Thomas, Doctor? That other young doctor prescribed them when you were away last summer. Thomas likes them, and they help more than the medicines you gave by mouth.' "

Dr. M. mused, "Suppositories! Perhaps for another child, but not for Thomas! Can't blame Dr. Y.; he didn't know Thomas or his family.

"During the attacks, Adele tends to Thomas' every whim. What mother wouldn't when her child is having so much trouble breathing? But there was that time when Thomas was out playing in the yard and Adele was calling from the back door, 'Thomas, get off that ladder! Get off right now! You'll hurt yourself. Thomas, listen to me!' No response from Thomas, who continued his play unconcernedly. 'Oh hell; fall off and break your neck. I don't care.' And Adele went back into the house to her television and coffee."

Dr. M. knew that Thomas had numerous allergies to house dust and many pollens, as proved by skin tests. He recalled that Grandma L.'s husband, Thomas' grandfather, had had asthma all his life and then died at eighty years of age in an auto accident. Dr. M. knew that in Thomas' case, as in many instances of asthma, there was an interplay of emotional and allergic factors causing the asthma. (Of course, there are some cases of asthma in which the emotional factor is the only cause, and other cases in which the allergic factor is the only cause.) Dr. M. also recognized that many cases of asthma are so frightening to the child and his parents that the child can become secondarily disturbed emotionally as a result of the asthma attack. But this can happen with any prolonged or severe illness in any child or adult. For Thomas, however, the emotional problems were one of the causes (in addition to the known allergies) and not the effects of the asthma.

Thomas' case was similar to that of Charlie, the boy with the fear of going to school. Thomas was too close to his mother, too dependent upon her.

Thomas had been a well-behaved baby. In fact, he rarely cried. His mother "broke him" of the thumb-sucking habit very early. There was no nail-biting, ear-pulling, or head-banging. Thomas was an obedient child—or was this only what the mother called obedience? Certainly in the ladder situation Thomas ignored his mother's command and continued to climb the ladder anyhow. His mother did the same sort of thing: she told Thomas not to climb the ladder, but then was not only incapable of putting meaning into her words but also revealed her true feelings by saying, "Oh hell; fall off and break your neck."

Adele had been bent on becoming a career woman until she married Nelson when both were 36 years old. She had never been greatly interested in marrying, because, as she said, "Marriage is not what people say it is. My father was never home. He was always on the road as a salesman. How I'd look forward to his coming home! He'd always have a real surprise for me on my birthday. But Mother . . . staying home all the time and taking care of me. With all her suffering, she never complained. Poor Mother— sick as long as I can remember."

Dr. M., who knew the family well, was sympathetic with Adele. He knew that at the time little girls are developing their later attitudes toward men through their relationships with their fathers, Adele had in effect had no father. To Adele, a father was someone who came home on rare occasions (like her birthday) for short periods and gave her presents. He never showed any genuinely fatherly interest in her.

How many times are gifts and other material things given as substitutes for love? Adele had a roomful of toys but no father. Aware of this, although not necessarily able to put it into words, Adele resented it. Her feelings and her emptiness colored her later attitudes toward men. She was left at home with a mother who often said, "I have been more fortunate than most women in marriage. Henry is a wonderful provider."

At heart, Adele's mother knew that the satisfaction of material needs could not undo the harm from the emotional vacuum in which she lived. These needs, as well as more basic ones stemming from the mother's own childhood, could not be recognized as such but masqueraded as innumerable physical complaints and fears. As a little girl, Adele greatly missed her father, and vaguely wondered if her mother's illnesses were not due to her father's absences. Adele's mother had a marriage in name only. No one cared for her, aside from Dr. M.'s predecessor who was busy even then with her many illnesses. Not having received love, she was unable to give any. Mrs. L. could not give of herself to Adele; she could only give toys, dresses, candy, and "everything a child could want." To Mrs. L., this giving of gifts and supplying material wants meant being a good mother.

No one cared for Adele as a person. No wonder Dr. M. felt so sorry for her as a child and later as a woman. What in later life could ever satisfy these early unsatisfied needs? In her adolescent dreams, Adele cherished the hope that a husband and a baby would give her what she had never had. Many well-meaning friends advised her, "What you need is to get married."

As a young career woman, Adele met many up-and-coming young men, but she was not interested in any of them. Then, when she was 30, she met Nelson. "He was such a good companion." Their courtship lasted six years. Finally one day, Adele's mother said, "You're getting older now, Adele, and Nelson is an awfully nice fellow. Why don't you get married? If you cannot find a house, you can live with me. Every girl should get married."

Nelson is a nonentity. He works, earns money, and helps around the house by making beds, scrubbing floors, doing laundry, and occasionally preparing meals. Adele has achieved her goal. She has a "model husband" who likes to stay around the house and is always at home. "My situation is so different from Mother's!"

How does all this background relate to Thomas' asthma? How do all these life experiences of his grandmother, his mother, and his father affect Thomas? Dr. M was aware that Thomas' attacks of asthma seemed to follow situations that conformed to a pattern. By careful study of what had been happening to Thomas and his family just before an attack, Dr. M. could usually find this pattern. Thomas' attacks occurred at any time of the year; therefore, they were due to something that did not vary with the pollen seasons. The attacks usually followed a situation in which Thomas was faced with separation or threat of separation or in which overtones of

the "first romance" were being handled in an unhealthy, seductive manner. During the previous
year, for example, Dr. M. had been called to treat
Thomas following a fishing trip with his father, on
the day his mother was hospitalized for a minor illness and the day after he had accompanied his father and the family dog on a squirrel hunt. The most
recent attack of asthma was most graphic. Adele had
predicted it would occur: "Thomas has never been to
camp before—has never even been away from home
before. I know if I send him to camp, he'll have one
of his attacks." He went to camp; he had an attack;
he returned home in two days.

For a child as dependent as Thomas and with all
the negative feelings that such a state implies (see p.
113), one of the most frightening things that could
happen was separation or the threat of separation
from the mother. At the price of submission to every
whim and wish of his mother, Thomas received
"love" that was equated with food, a roof over his
head, clothes, and toys. Submission also meant the
absolute denial of his angry feelings. Like Grandma,
Thomas always smiled. Other children might cry,
but not Thomas. Adele defined her love in terms of
worldly goods for Thomas, and she defined Thomas'
love for her in terms of his complete dependence on
her. Nelson was a good provider; he therefore loved.
To show her great "love" for Thomas, to herself and
to the world, Adele was extremely generous to
Thomas. In fact, she boasted of this and compared
herself with her neighbor, Mrs. Brown: "She has five
kids . . . all dressed in rags. They'll never have a

college education. I can't see how that family can always be so happy. They have nothing." Adele's relationship with her son lacked only the essential ingredients: mutual, genuine affection and respect.

In such a state of complete helplessness, Thomas was bottled up in a nearly hopeless predicament. His mother would not tolerate any signs of independence or rebellion. He would not be permitted even to cry. In children (as in adults), strong angry feelings directed toward someone almost always arouse fears of receiving similar feelings in return. Thomas' rage toward his mother led to a fear of receiving the same feelings from his mother, but with this catch: Mother was bigger, stronger, and older, and Thomas was dependent upon her. Understandably, Thomas was unhappy and even angry about being kept in such a helpless condition. He had two choices. He could give vent to his rage, in which case he would lose everything, even the warped semblance of love that he still received from his mother. Or he could show no independence or rebellion but swallow his indignation and appear entirely docile to all outward appearances. But the rage would persist, build up, and would finally have to escape. When it did, it still could not be shown against the mother who really evoked the anger. It would have to escape through an acceptable channel. In Thomas' case, it could not be directed against people (whom he feared); it could be directed only against himself, his own body. Thus, asthma appeared.

Thomas' attacks were triggered by definite situations and events in his life in which his dependent relationship with his mother was threatened. The solution was based on Thomas' approach to life. During the attacks he became totally dependent. His mother treated him like a baby. The relationship of mutual dependence between mother and child under which Thomas and his mother lived was reestablished and strengthened. A reconciliation was effected, and the asthma attack ended.

There was another aggravating factor in Thomas' asthma. Though he was 11 years of age, not only were the problems of the "first romance" unsettled but, as a result of his relationship to his parents, he was badly confused. He felt uncertain about his role as a young boy soon to enter manhood (see Chap. 3). He still slept in the same room with his parents. His problem was even more difficult, because his mother was so unnaturally close to him. The early feelings of competition with his father for his mother's affection had persisted. Whenever Thomas was separated from his mother and placed in a competitive situation with his father, he had attacks of asthma. Hunting and fishing with his father, situations with potential dangers (e.g., use of firearms, boating in deep waters) precipitated attacks of asthma. Similarly, his mother's hospitalization, with the implied danger to her life and health, precipitated an attack.

For still other reasons, Thomas was hopelessly confused in his role as a boy and a son. His mother was the boss in this family. His father did the housework. Since the father was confused concerning his role as a man, Thomas, who would imitate his father, was similarly confused. Although Adele's feelings and behavior as a mother were bizarre, they did follow a pattern that would provide a definite formulation, even if faulty, for Thomas' own feelings and behavior toward her (and other women in later life). Nelson occupied a subordinate position. In contrast with Adele's strong feelings and behavior, Nelson's were pale, drab, lifeless, and without substance. By Nelson's inability to accept his role as a father and a man, Thomas was delivered into the hands of his mother. Like all boys, he had a normal healthy tendency to imitate his father. But how could he imitate a vacuum?

Nervous eczema, or neurodermatitis, is closely related to asthma. Both nervous eczema and asthma frequently occur at the same time or at different times in the same child. Both have emotional and allergic factors. The physician frequently sees acute attacks of nervous eczema with an itchy, oozing, red rash that appears all over the body after a particularly upsetting emotional situation. Such children are on the surface often very cooperative and polite. They usually have great difficulty in expressing anger toward people. They are afraid to voice or show anger. But the anger that these children possess from their own highly disturbed relationships with their parents, in addition to the anger resulting from the usual day-to-day experiences, must seek an outlet. However, they can express their anger against themselves, through their own bodies. Following disturbing experiences with their parents or with other people, these children start scratching all over their bodies, and the skin becomes fiery red. The more red the skin becomes, the more it itches; the more it itches, the more the child scratches. This self-perpetuating cycle is initiated and fed by emotional turmoil. In many cases of nervous eczema, parent-child emotional maladjustments similar to those already described for nervous asthma are present.

5

■━━━━━━━━━━━━━━━━━━━━━━━■

Childhood Traits as Clues to Later Disturbances

Character traits that may be inocuous in the earliest stages of childhood can indicate emotional disturbances when they persist into later life. Such traits include stuttering, left-handedness, tics, temper tantrums, breath-holding, fainting, bed-wetting, sleepwalking, and sleeptalking.

STUTTERING, THE MOUTH STAGE OF EMOTIONAL DEVELOPMENT

Carol's brothers and sisters teased her mercilessly when she could not make the "K" sound in her name. As a result, Carol's self-confidence was badly shaken, and speech became an emotional issue. She grew to dread speaking. The harder she tried, the more frightened she became and the more difficult she found it to speak. As time passed, she forgot the original difficulty, as did her parents. Now she stutters whenever she tries to make the "K" sound. In addition to the word "Carol," her difficulty in making the "K" sound has spread to other words with the same sound: *cat, catch, cow, kite, come, kill.* Some of these words, such as "kill," may have more emotion attached to them than other words, such as "kite." The difficulty may therefore be greater with some words than with others. There are both specific and nonspecific causes for stuttering. Emotional tension stimulated directly by a specific word (teasing Carol as she learns to say her name) may cause stuttering with words having similar sounds.

The first definite sounds that the child makes—"Mama," "Dada," "baba"—commonly appear toward the end of the first year. With these early sounds the child begins learning speech, the mouth stage of emotional development. This speech-learning process continues throughout the rest of childhood—the bowel and the first-romance stages of emotional development—and throughout life. Any emotional conflict arising during any of these stages may be reflected in the developing ability to speak; and stuttering may develop.

The child first learns to speak at the time he is giving up the bottle, but when he is still sucking, spitting, biting, and making various new sounds with his lips, cheeks, vocal cords, and tongue. In turn, the making of these new sounds depends upon his learning breath control. He is a creature who stumbles, falls, crawls, wobbles, and toddles; but through it all he slowly learns to walk. His first few steps in talking are similarly awkward and unsure. Yet he can watch his parents walk, and they can show him how to walk. The child can easily imitate walking; he can see it. But he cannot "see" how to talk. He knows his father, mother, and other family members, including the dog; he knows what is going on about him; and he perceives and reacts to the feelings that others have toward him. But he cannot put all this into words. His thinking develops faster than he can develop control over his muscles for speaking. Control over these muscles is no further developed than his control over the muscles for walking, moving the bowels, or emptying the bladder. The awkwardness noted in walking and in faulty control of bladder and bowels is thus also present in his use of the muscles of speech—tongue, lips, cheeks, diaphragm, and vocal cords. Thus he stutters. All children stutter when they learn to talk, just as they wobble when they learn to walk.

Speech problems also include mechanical problems with little or no known emotional aspects. For example, tongue thrusting and lisping are common conditions in the early years. The speech therapist has much to offer in such situations.

If stuttering continues well beyond the learning stage, some emotional difficulty may be at fault. This difficulty is to be found in some conflict arising in the mouth stage, the bowel stage, or the first-romance stage of the child's development. In learning to talk it is the feelings behind the words and not the actual words that are important. For each of us, adult and child, certain words evoke certain feelings, based on what has happened to us or what has been taught to us before. For example, the word "cow" might evoke the feeling of quiet contentment;

it is related to the giving of milk. But if a child has been chased and frightened by a cow, he might quake in fear at the word "cow." If the situation and the consequent fear are handled well by the parents, such a reaction should be only temporary. To many people the word "snake" means a slimy, twisting, crawling creature of fear; the word itself becomes a symbol; it evokes unpleasant feelings. When a child is learning a language, the emotional values and purposes attached to the new words, based on his own experiences or what his mother and father teach him, are all important. The mere mechanics of speech—the vowels and consonants and their arrangement to form words—are unimportant to the child.

Also, without the child's being completely aware of it, certain people may remind him of unpleasant feelings that he may originally have had with some other person. The child may stutter when he talks to such people, and continue to stutter when he grows up. For example, John was usually quite fluent except when he had to speak to his boss, to a policeman, or to any group of people who represented an authoritative body to him. John still carried the original fear, or possibly even anger, that he had harbored toward his perfectionistic, demanding, bullying father. While he was learning to talk and while under the domination of his father, young John understandably had feelings of rebellion and hatred. But he dared not express angry feelings toward his father lest he be bullied more. These pent-up feelings needed an outlet, however, and the unintelligible biting, sputtering, spitting sounds of anger that John used as a baby became the stuttering of later life. When he was completely relaxed in friendly surroundings that evoked no unpleasant train of thought, John did not stutter.

How basic to mental health are the appropriate feelings attached to words is well illustrated by the oral behavior of schizophrenics. Contrast this with the behavior of a deaf mute in friendly surroundings. Although he has never heard a spoken word or spoken one himself, he may grow up into a happy, well-adjusted member of society. The late Helen Keller is a shining example.

Schizophrenia illustrates the importance that words themselves have for the individual. Some young patients with this serious disease never utter a word until they are well beyond the age at which speech usually appears; at that time they may speak a perfectly articulated and grammatically correct short sentence. Other children with schizophrenia refuse to speak at all and may be mistaken for deaf mutes. Some children with the disease speak well mechanically and always have done so, but they do not transmit feelings consistent with what they are saying. They may laugh while describing a situation that should evoke tears; they may cry when they should laugh.

Schizophrenia, a common and complex disease of young adulthood, is manifested in its extreme form by strange emotional reactions and thoughts that drift about in a "dream world" completely separate from the real world. So far as is known, schizophrenics do not have defects in intelligence or the senses. The earliest emotional roots of this disease lie in childhood, but the disease is rarely seen in children. In contrast, adult patients with schizophrenia occupy more hospital beds than patients with any other disease, mental or otherwise.

The schizophrenic patient may or may not have difficulty with words, but he does have difficulty with his emotions. For him, it is neither the words themselves nor the mechanical articulation of speech that is important; it is the feelings attached to the words that are all important. But since his feelings are disturbed, he often associates different feelings and meanings with words or phrases than a healthy individual does. For this reason, the schizophrenic patient reacts differently, feelingwise, to certain words and phrases than how the healthy person reacts, and that is why the healthy person often says that the schizophrenic patient reacts inappropriately. However, the latter's reactions are entirely appropriate if one considers the particular emotions that he attaches to his words and phrases. It is as if he speaks his own peculiar language, with sounds similar to those of the healthy person but with different meanings.

It is understood, of course, that there are causes other than schizophrenia for the late appearance of speech. One common example is the young child who can effectively and quickly make his needs known without speech. His parents understand him and respond accordingly. Such a child has little incentive to talk until later than the usual age.

LEFT-HANDEDNESS

In some cases of left-handedness where the child has been forced to use his right hand, various symptoms of emotional tension appear: nail-biting, thumb-sucking, tics, stubbornness, crankiness, and stuttering. Although this problem of forcibly changing handedness, like stuttering, may be due to the underlying emotional attitudes of the parents, there are other factors.

As a simple example of parental involvement, Jane wants to use her left hand to hold her spoon when eating. Her mother gently whacks the back of her left hand and firmly transfers the spoon to the right. Paul is very upset because his father, who is a civil engineer, insists that he use his right hand in writing because "I've never seen a left-handed engineer that was any good. You might as well learn correctly."

This is not to say that all children who are left-handed and are switched to the right hand will develop difficulties. As a matter of fact, if the switch is accomplished early enough in life by parents who are friendly and understanding, it is likely that no emotional problem will result. If the child balks or becomes harassed at the change, the parents should desist in their efforts.

Another factor in bringing about a change, in addition to the all-important underlying emotional attitude, is the question of how deeply ingrained is the child's left-handedness. Does he go up the stairs with the left foot first, aim a pop-gun with his left eye, throw a ball left-handed, or reach for the cookie jar with his left hand?

When Grandma Jones had a stroke, the right side of her body was paralyzed. She was not only unable to write, walk, or care for herself, but she also lost the power of speech, although she knew what was going on about her and what people were saying. She made many attempts to talk but did not succeed. The physician told her family that the paralysis on the right side of the body was due to the blood clot in the left side of the brain. He hoped that with time and treatment, Grandma would recover.

Since the day of the famous Greek physician Hippocrates, it has been known that damage to one side of the brain can account for the disturbed function of the opposite side of the body. Speech is impaired in a right-handed person only if the left side of the brain is damaged; and, conversely, speech is impaired in a strongly left-handed person only if the right side of the brain is damaged. If the right side of the brain is damaged in a right-handed person, one would therefore expect that the left side of the body would be paralyzed, but that the patient's speech would not be affected. It is felt, then, that making a strongly left-handed child use his right hand will clash with the existing supremacy of the right side of the brain over the left side. In the child of school age, the brain pathways are already established, and a change attempted at this time may cause trouble more readily than if the change had been attempted at an earlier age. These are physical factors with which one must reckon, in addition to the parents' emotional attitudes.

The complex interplay of these forces, emotional and anatomic, may well result in stuttering and other previously mentioned nervous traits, plus, in some cases at least, problems in reading, writing, and arithmetic. As an extreme example, one may see the child who writes beautifully and correctly except that nothing can be read unless a mirror is held to the writing; then one can read the words perfectly by looking into the mirror (mirror-writing). Another writing difficulty is the reversal of figures (e.g., "39" becomes "93"). Some of the reading difficulties are poor spelling and failure to understand the meaning of the printed word.

The relationship between right-handedness or left-handedness and these various difficulties in speech, reading, and writing is obscure. More important to the child's developing personality is not whether he is left-handed or right-handed but the basic underlying feelings exchanged between him and his parents.

TICS

In the age group of six to ten years, it is commonly observed that children feel an urge to carry out certain acts in a repetitive manner. Thus, one sees a child who must step on a crack in the sidewalk or kick a rock ahead of him as he walks along, whack each post in a fence as he passes, or count telephone poles. He may also insist that his shoes be lined up in a certain way, or he may feel the constant urge to clear his throat, blow his nose, or scratch his ears. In the presence of emotional disturbances during these ages, it is not uncommon to see this tendency to repetitive acts become intensified and localized as a rigidly fixed habit.

"Helen is always jerking her left shoulder, Doctor. She has lost so much time from school. We don't know what is wrong. I know she can control it, because when we tell her to stop, she does so. Yet the minute we turn our backs, it starts again. We wonder if it can be emotional. The jerking is worst when she meets strangers or when there is some argument at home. When her father has some words with her, Helen says nothing . . . just turns away and goes to her room. But then the jerking starts again, worse than ever, and goes on for hours."

During his examination of Helen, the physician noted that when she was relaxed and at ease with him, she appeared like any other 11-year-old girl, with no unusual movements. This was quite striking, because only a few minutes before, when her mother was describing the father's short temper with Helen, the movements were very pronounced. Helen would jerk her left shoulder upward and forward in short quick movements. The mother said that these movements had begun two years earlier when the father had playfully hit her on the left shoulder with a rubber beach ball. Examination by the resort physician, including X-ray pictures taken immediately after the injury at the parents' insistence, had failed to reveal any physical injury. But the movements had continued, and Helen's parents wanted to know if anything else could be done. After a complete examination, both physical and by special laboratory tests, the physician found no abnormalities other than the movements themselves. This was not surprising, since, after carefully observing the movements Helen's mother described and noting other slight movements that apparently had escaped the mother's notice, the physician had felt reasonably sure that Helen had a tic. His original impression was strengthened, even before the completion of the tests, by a careful review of her past and present emotional life.

His questioning of the mother revealed that Helen's story was similar to that of many other children who have tics. While the mother was carrying Helen, she followed a rigid self-prescribed schedule of diet, rest, and exercise. Everything had to be just so; this dependence upon an inflexible regimen was her way of life. As a baby, Helen was fed the exact types and amounts of food and at the precise times that the mother had read were best for a child. When Helen was learning to walk, her perfectly normal tottering was aggravated by her mother's insistence on early perfection. The same rigid and unreasonable insistence on perfection was directed to the child's bowel and bladder training. Helen grew up following to the letter her mother's example and desires for perfection. She knew no other way. But she had given in so long and so completely to her mother's unrealistic demands that the thought of asserting herself with anybody at all never occurred to her. She had feelings, but she had never been permitted to express them; she had to keep everything to herself.

Possibly as a result of this rigid upbringing, Helen grew up to be a meek child. She became a quiet follower, never a leader. She had little to say and then said it almost apologetically in a half whisper. She was high-strung and burst into tears at the slightest provocation. She was tense and restless and did not fit in well in any group of children. In addition to her shyness, and possibly contributing to it, she was clumsy in sports. For all these reasons, she was usually frozen out of most group activities. As a result, she had withdrawn more and more into herself.

The father was a bully around the house, loudly voicing his opinions and demanding immediate obedience from everybody. He was short-tempered and impatient with anybody he considered sloppy and inefficient. He never had shown any warmth toward his wife or daughter; both of them trembled at his voice or frown. Neither had ever dared to stand up to him.

However, feelings were there, building up within Helen and ready to explode in some form under the proper circumstances. Since she was forbidden to express her feelings toward any one by actual words or overt behavior, the feelings had to—and did—find their outlet through her own body. Tics appeared. The incident with the beach ball, in itself quite trivial, was all that was needed to cause the tics to appear and to determine their location. The tics really were caused by the past stormy relationships with her parents that she was forced to contain within herself.

If, for some reason, the tics disappeared, the basic

problems would remain and continue to ferment; they had to seek an outlet through other means. After a few months, Helen's tics actually did go away; itching then appeared all over her body and persisted for a few days after any particularly upsetting emotional experience.

TANTRUMS, BREATH-HOLDING, FAINTING

Other common problems that occur during the early school period are temper tantrums, breath-holding spells, and fainting.

Four-year-old Sally wants to go out to play. Since she is recovering from a cold, her mother wisely feels she should remain inside, even though the sunny street outside is alive with Sally's playmates. Instead of accepting her mother's decision and doing as other children do under similar circumstances, Sally continues to beg and stomp. Mother stands firm. Suddenly with a loud whoop, Sally is on the floor kicking, screaming, banging her head, and crying uncontrollably: "I want to go out. I want to go out!" Mother runs over and pleads, "Please stop it, Sally—stop it right now—don't bump your head on the floor, you'll only hurt yourself." Her pleas have no effect. Finally, as Sally's tantrum and her mother's alarm increase, the mother says, "Be quiet, Sally, stop it this minute. What will Mrs. Jones next door think? . . . Oh, well, I suppose it won't hurt to go out a little while." The tantrum immediately ceases, and the racking sobs fade away as the screen door slams shut. "You stay in the backyard, Sally. If you don't, you can come right back in. I've got to teach you to obey me."

Most children have had at least one temper tantrum in their lives, but the parents' immediate and correct management has prevented it from recurring. Standing firm in such cases and giving the child a spanking will show the child that she cannot use that method to get her way. But Sally has learned from experience that a temper tantrum is a good way to get what she wants. Mother is always alarmed, and if the tantrum continues long enough, she will give in. Mother's protestation, "I've got to teach you to obey me," means nothing to Sally when she does not stand firm and back up her words with action. Temper tantrums that continue do so only because they are serving a purpose for the child. When the child stops getting what she wants by having a tantrum, the tantrums will cease. The important question is not the remedy but what is at fault in the emotional relationship between parent and child that accounts for the tantrum.

Another form of temper tantrum in younger children and more frightening to the parents is breath-holding. When a child cannot get his way, he cries so violently that he holds his breath, and consequently the skin turns blue. Sometimes the child will actually become unconscious. Usually the combination of the child's turning blue and then fainting understandably alarms the parents—so much so that they give in, and the child gets what he wants. The worried parents send out an urgent call for the physician. But there is no medicine for breath-holding spells. The child's physical health is good, and such episodes will not harm him physically. There is only one answer: show him he cannot use this method to get his way.

Both breath-holding and tantrums can be prevented by parental firmness. Once established, however, these bad habits are difficult to break. Education of the parents in situations such as these is more important than education of the child.

Fainting in children is another difficult problem. There are numerous causes for fainting, some of which are more serious than others. Only the physician can determine the nature of the fainting by careful studies, which might include X-ray pictures, spinal fluid examinations, brainwave studies (electroencephalograms), and electrocardiagrams. Fainting can be a manifestation of epilepsy, low blood sugar, brain tumor, and many other diseases of the brain and of other parts of the body. Fainting can also be an expression of extreme terror. Thus, everyone knows of the child (or the adult) who faints just before receiving an injection or upon hearing bad news. This is one way in which the child can be protected from feeling all the unpleasantness associated with what is anticipated or what is happening around him.

BED-WETTING

In an overwhelming number of cases of bed-wetting, an emotional conflict between parent and child is the cause.

Whenever ten-year-old Francis wet the bed, his mother, Mrs. Y., required him to make his own bed and wash the sheets. But the punishment did not work; the bed-wetting continued. Other unsuccessful home remedies tried by Mrs. Y. were not allowing liquids after supper, making sure that Francis urinated before going to bed, and using the alarm clock to awaken both mother and son at 2:00 a.m. so that he would urinate. Finally, more in embarrassment than in desperation, Mrs. Y. and Francis appeared at the physician's office. "Doctor, I've tried everything, but Francis still wets the bed at night. What is wrong?" After a complete physical examination and a urinalysis, everything was found to be normal. From his years of experience with this particular family as well as from experience with similar problems, the physician suspected where the trouble was and he asked to see Mrs. Y. alone.

He learned more from her rush of talk. "Doctor, we had not expected that Francis would come as soon as he did. We wanted to establish our home first. He was a lot of trouble. It isn't that I haven't given him enough attention, Doctor. My husband and I never even went out until Francis was 18 months old. Even then, we worried about the baby-sitter and phoned home every hour. We gave him more toys than any other child had in the neighborhood. All in all, he's been a good son to us, never getting into trouble like other boys, quiet, likes to stay around the house and gets into no fights. I guess he's a mama's boy! He always wants to sit on my lap and kiss me. And Francis' Daddy is so very proud of him. He's already

dreaming of Francis' winning a letter in college football and then taking over the family business."

The physician then probed deeper into this situation.

"Yes, he still sleeps in the same bedroom with us.
I don't know why you ask about that. We have never
given it any thought. Francis used to be afraid of the
dark so we had him sleep with us. And I guess we
never changed. As a matter of fact, he often sleeps
with me when his father's away. We're very close. I
still don't see why you ask that. Francis is asleep by
the time we get to bed and he sleeps like a log.

"We're not prissy at our house. I can't see why you
make such a fuss about dressing and undressing in
front of children. There's nothing to be ashamed of
in the human body. And it is only when you try to
hide the body and be a prude that you stimulate the
child's interest. Francis has seen me many times, so
I suppose he knows about the differences between
boys and girls."

This unnaturally close relationship between
mother and son is often uncovered, with numerous
variations, in cases of bed-wetting in boys. Francis
slept in the same room with his parents. He could not
help but be aware of the physical aspects of marriage. It was naive to assume he was that heavy a
sleeper. Furthermore, seeing his mother and father
so close to each other in a way he could not understand would be confusing. How could she give herself to his father this way? This very upsetting
situation, that should not exist, further intensified
Francis' rivalry with his father. Thus, the boy might

well be angry with his father and wish to hurt him, or even to get rid of him altogether. "If Daddy were gone, I'd have Mommy all to myself." Such wishes are frightening to a small boy when he realizes how big and strong his father is.

While the parents believe that the child is fast asleep, he actually lies in the borderland of dreams and reality, where wishes can become true and where the events that go on around him may become twisted to conform to his desires. Fact, fantasy, desire, and half-knowledge all become hopelessly muddled in his mind. As many parents know who have watched young children play, the world of make-believe is very real to them: making sure the dolly is warm enough, feeding the teddy bear, having fun with imaginary playmates, and being afraid of the bogey-man. Fantasy can become confused with fact.

"If Daddy were gone, I'd have Mommy all to myself." Sleeping in the same room with his parents, then, Francis may fancy that his wishes against his rival are being realized; he may easily become convinced that his mother is really hurting his father. But the situation boomerangs. "If Mommy can do this to Daddy, why can't she do this to me?"

One can understand the confused mixture of love, hate, fear, and futile hope as Francis sleeps with his mother during his father's absence. This fear finds some support in fact when Francis has such recent memories of the conflict over bowel training. He remembers how his mother acted. "If you do not have a bowel movement when I ask you to, I can't love you." Francis also senses that his mother's "love," that her staying at home with him, never letting him out of her sight, her overprotection, and all the gifts of toys are not manifestations of genuine affection (see Chap. 4).

The physician knew that Francis' unplanned arrival was a hardship on the mother and the father from their point of view. He also learned other facts about the mother's own past and her own growing up. He knew that the unplanned arrival of a baby is no more than temporarily upsetting in a healthy household. As a result of this mother's own emotionally sick growing-up period (of the type already alluded to in this book), he knew that she would have had problems with her own children, planned or unplanned.

With reason to doubt his mother's love and with his fear of her, Francis entered the lion's den when he slept in his parents' bedroom. His solution to this terrifying problem was to make a complete about-face. He would be as unlike his Daddy as he could be. He would do nothing to provoke his mother. He would be timid, quiet, completely obedient to her. He could not be masculine at all, because then he would receive the same hurt that he fancied his father received from his mother. If the frightened Francis were to have shown his true feelings of resentment and rage at his mother, he would hardly have stood a chance in the ensuing conflict. It was easier to remain the quiet, conforming, submissive boy—Mama's boy. But, as has been emphasized in previous examples, pent-up feelings and tension must escape in some manner. In Francis' case, they had to escape in a manner acceptable to the mother and in keeping with his submissiveness.

Francis entered the first-romance stage (when these problems of self-identification as a male first came to the fore) shortly after he was bladder-trained in the daytime (see Chap. 3). In a boy like Francis, with a strong-willed mother, bladder training would have presented another opportunity for the mother to impress her dominance indelibly on her son. This uneven conflict would cause tension to build up in Francis as he was forced to submit, without apparent protest.

As a result of Francis' submission to his mother and his mistaken fancies of the meaning of the husband-wife relationship, he was confused between active masculinity (which he was afraid to recognize in himself) and passive femininity. There are boys in rebellion against the significant people in their environment who discharge their pent-up tensions by fighting with others, shouting, and doing what is expressly forbidden by parents and others in authority. Sometimes such boys may even wet in the daytime as another act of rebellion of which they are fully aware. However, a passive boy like Francis would be incapable of rebelling so flagrantly lest his true underlying rage (see Chap. 3) become unleashed and overwhelm him and those about him. But tension must escape. For Francis, it could do so only in a manner in accord with how his personality had been molded by his parents. He thus rebels in a passive (effeminate) way by bed-wetting at night, in the borderland between dream and reality, fact, fantasy, and desire. Only here could such a boy find refuge from the many subtle tyrannies perpetrated upon his developing personality. Interestingly enough he uses, as the means for the release of tension, that part of his anatomy that most differentiates him from a female.

It is not unusual for healthy children to masturbate sometime in their lives (see p. 96); in contrast, such behavior is unusual in children who wet the bed. This again reveals the fear such boys have in admitting their masculinity. Masturbation would arouse uncomfortable and dangerous feelings by directing the boy's attention to the genitals.

Although some parents cite their own or a sibling's early bed-wetting as examples of "a family weakness" ("and it hasn't hurt me, Doctor"), there has been no proof of a hereditary cause for this complaint. Also, there are fewer bed-wetters among girls than among boys. The fundamental causes are similar to those described for boys, but there are a few twists peculiar to the sex. The fundamental problem with girls is also frequently an emotional conflict stemming from the girl's sleeping in the same bedroom with her parents. In the girl's case, it is her father who is unnaturally close to her. She has fantasies analogous to those of the boy; but she competes with her mother for her father. Her wish to have her father for herself and to have her mother out of the picture is intensified by watching her father behave toward her mother in a way she cannot understand.

She even believes that her father is hurting her mother.

For example, 12-year-old Clara's relationship with her father had been unnaturally close. He continued to dangle her on his knee, tickle her, and walk into the bathroom to scrub her back (ostensibly to help her get clean). Clara and her father were in the habit of dashing unannounced in and out of each other's bedrooms while the other was dressing. "There is no false modesty in this house!" While carrying on with Clara in this apparently cozy manner, the father was in many other ways blatantly inconsistent. His promises to Clara meant little or nothing. The promised trip to the zoo with Clara was suddenly replaced by a golf date without explanation or apology. When Clara complained about this, she was sent to her room for the day as punishment. Inconsistency, unfair punishment, ignoring Clara when it suited his whim, all revealed the father's true feelings toward her. A father who shows "love" in the ways described does not really love. Furthermore, even if the father had remained consistent in his demonstrations of unnatural love, such unwholesome actions could hardly be called love when the effect was ruinous to the girl.

From long-standing emotional problems from his own growing-up period, this father had many tangled feelings about women: his mother, sister, teacher, wife, and daughter. During the daughter's first-romance period, seeds sown in previous generations bore fruit. The unresolved conflicts from the father's first-romance period blazed furiously in the daughter and the wife.

Returning to Clara's fear that her father was hurting her mother, she, like Francis, confused fact with fantasy. Being small and weak, she could not get rid of her mother and have her father all for herself. During the excitement of the marital relationship, Clara was jerked from a half-sleep in which fact, fantasy, and desire were merged confusingly together. In her state of highly charged emotions, she mistakenly believed that her father was hurting her mother. Sensing her father's true feelings toward her. Clara was then afraid that he could do the same thing to her that he had done to Mother. Her solution was to act differently from Mother, to deny her femininity. If she were to act like her father, no man would hurt her. Therefore, she acted like a tomboy: she became bossy, domineering, a leader, an athlete, a competitor with boys (and later men) in their own fields.

There are many variations, but the unnatural closeness of daughter to father and of son to mother is the constant theme in such instances. In some cases the physician could not elicit evidence that the child had been in the same room with the parents during the sexual act.

As with boys who wet their beds, girls who wet their beds seldom masturbate. The reason is the same in both cases. The girl who wets the bed is afraid to masturbate. That would make her perilously aware of her femininity in body and feelings and therefore vulnerable to her father (and other men).

The situations described reveal the causes of persistent bed-wetting without readily demonstrable physical disease. Boys with this problem are passive in feelings and behavior; girls are aggressive in feelings and behavior. This is true even though the boy may look big, strong, and masculine, and the girl may look small, dainty, and feminine. It is not the body build or shape but the accompanying feelings and behavior that determine how successfully the boy grows up to be a real man and the girl grows up to be a real woman. Fundamentally, the problem in boys is too much passivity while in girls the problem is one of protest against the feminine role associated with their sex in our culture. It is clear that bed-wetting, like obesity or asthma, is only one symptom of the emotionally disturbed child. Most bed-wetters have, or have had, other evidences of emotional problems: nightmares, temper tantrums, nail-biting, eating problems, soiling, and delinquency.

Many questions on the causes of this type of bed-wetting have yet to be answered. It is understandable that to some readers these concepts may be difficult to accept. However, if such patients and their parents are studied carefully and treated over many hours by collaborative technique (see Introduction), the validity of these concepts becomes apparent.

Some cases of bed-wetting are due to factors other than those described. Bed-wetting often occurs when a child is sick or has just been hospitalized and therefore has become temporarily and understandably disturbed emotionally. This symptom is also seen frequently in the young child (usually the first child) when a baby brother or sister is born (see p. 74). In such circumstances, bed-wetting is not at all uncommon, and the parents usually show no alarm, especially since the symptom soon disappears of its own accord.

Children may be bed-wetters when they are deprived of any genuine close relationship with an adult to whom they always can turn for help and advice. Such children, as a result of this extreme deprivation, may be emotionally retarded (so that they continue to function at an emotional level earlier than is consistent with their ages) and even intellectually backward (see Chap. 10). Bed-wetting from this cause is one of the commoner emotional disturbances occurring in some institutions for children, as, for example, orphanages.

Epilepsy may be another cause for wetting the bed at night. The rarest causes of bed-wetting are those due to certain specific abnormalities of the urinary tract or the nerves that stimulate it. Finally, bed-wetting may be associated with some severe degrees of mental deficiency. It should be stressed that only the physician can determine the specific cause for the child's wetting the bed at night.

SLEEPWALKING AND TALKING

Children who walk and talk while apparently still asleep are further examples of how feelings can be expressed through physical activity without the child's being aware of what he is doing.

The child may walk in his sleep to his parents' bedroom, which he associates with love; to the bathroom, which he associates with other biologically indispensable urges; or to the kitchen, which he associates with food. This remarkable feat is usually performed without the child's hurting himself. Sleepwalking illustrates well how indelibly imprinted memories can be upon the child's mind, and how they can be used to determine his actions without his being aware of the action or the processes of thought that guided the action. The next morning he cannot even remember the episode. He may even be completely surprised if his parents ask him about it.

This remarkable demonstration shows how, in health, the child's memories can direct him to satisfy his basic urges (for love, food, and elimination) without his even being aware that he acted in that manner or that he even used the memory. But, the memory was there, and it was used. This automatic, nonvolitional use of memory to determine current feelings and actions goes on all the time in everybody, child and adult, in sleep (with dreams) and in wakefulness.

Sleepwalking usually disappears gradually as the child grows older and begins to face his problems and satisfy his needs realistically in the world of wakefulness. If sleepwalking persists, the child should be seen by a physician. The child's deep-seated feelings may well be disturbed, usually from an unhealthy parent-child relationship, and these feelings may be seeking an outlet through such behavior, as sleepwalking. It is less threatening to admit to certain cravings, needs, and feelings during sleep than during wakefulness, especially when such cravings, needs, and feelings cannot be satisfied and when their existence cannot even be admitted during wakefulness. Society and parents do not hold the child responsible for what happens during sleep.

The same general principles concerning sleepwalking also apply to sleeptalking.

These fascinating conditions are akin to trancelike states that do not exist totally apart from the wakeful state. During sleep and occasionally while the patient is under narcosis or anesthesia, he can be influenced by various sensory stimuli, such as noises, speech, and even telepathy. For example, a patient shocked his surgeons and nurses by correctly reporting after recovering consciousness from general anesthesia all that had been said by the operating team during the surgical procedure. Although this is a rare example, it shows the individual's subtle awareness of environment in situations where it might be least expected.

6

Roots of Individual Juvenile Delinquency

"Boy Loses Hand in Shotgun Accident; Father Who Gave Him Shells is Arrested." "Boy Hurls Lye in Classroom; 20 Hurt, 1 May Be Blinded." "Boy, 2, Slain; Brother 13, Jealous, Held." "Boy Whose Dad Died in Chair Held in Killing of Pal's Father." "Girl, 12, Sets 11 Fires in Hotel Chase; Spry Youngster Outwits Firemen." "Girl, 9, Held; Admits to 8 Burglaries." "Mother Pleads for Son: 'He Never Had a Chance.'" "Youth Confesses: 'I Put Two Bullets in the Back of My Mother's Head . . .'"

Such newspaper headlines as these, and the interest shown by the wide variety of groups working with the problem of delinquency, make it quite clear that there are many factors other than emotional contributing to this problem. For instance, there are neighborhoods in which cultural and economic conditions are important factors contributing to antisocial behavior. In fact, such behavior is a way of life for many of the youth in these areas. According to their moral values, they see nothing wrong with stealing, vandalism, assault, rape, and promiscuity. They feel no guilt. The family—such as it is—and the neighborhood condone such conduct. These youth consider the law only as a rule to be violated without getting caught, and not as rules by which one is expected to live. And the degree to which such a "punk" succeeds in flaunting the law is a measure of his reputation in his society. Such individuals often group together in gangs to prey upon their fellows. The fact that some of these youths have experienced repeated hostility and brutality in their life situations compounds their already formidable problems, and they become more dangerous. Because such group delinquency is a conscious defect in conscience condoned by parent and community, it poses one of the most difficult problems faced by the dedicated sociologist, psychologist, social worker, and clergyman.

In such afflicted neighborhoods, however, there are many families whose children do *not* succumb to the destructive temptations of their environment. Under the consistent and affectionate guidance of their parents, limits are set; and they are taught standards of honesty, kindness, and respect for their neighbors (and themselves). They are not polluted by their demoralizing environment. Indeed, many such children become fine citizens and occasionally outstanding leaders in their communities.

Although all individuals are affected by their community environment and although there is commonly an overlap between the gang delinquent and the individual delinquent, the latter presents a basically different problem. That problem is primarily one of sick parent-child communications on an unconscious level. The delinquent who has an overlap of conscious and unconscious causes can be more dangerous. We shall focus our attention in this chapter on the roots of *individual* delinquency.

Study by collaborative technique of individual child delinquents and their parents in the physician's office has revealed that in every instance the problem can be traced back to faulty emotional adjustments of parent and child. Although popularly blamed, comics, movies, bad companions, and school teachers exert minimal influence. The healthy child and parents, who do not have to stop to analyze their actions and feelings but are secure in their mutual honesty and love, are not influenced by such extraneous factors. The disturbed child and the disturbed parent find it easier to place the blame on such factors than to recognize their own contributions to the particular delinquency.

Probing beneath the surface complaint of juvenile delinquency invariably reveals defects in conscience —both of the child and of the parent. What do we mean by a conscience defect? Indeed, what is conscience? And what role does conscience play in determining delinquency? How is the individual parent to be held responsible if the development of conscience is not subject to his conscious control? And how are parental conscience defects related to parental permissiveness? These are some of the provocative questions we shall consider in this and later chapters.

Let us look at three brief examples that illustrate how a parent unwittingly leads his child into delinquent behavior. Then we may begin to recognize the role that conscience plays and the significance of defects in conscience in breeding delinquency.

Mrs. Brown was knitting while reclining comfortably on a chair at the beach. Beyond the shade of her large umbrella, four-year-old Tommy was poking teasingly at a large, strange dog. "Tommy, honey, leave the man's dog alone." Tommy's mother yawned and resumed her knitting. . . .

Twelve-year-old George went up to his father one bright Sunday morning and said petulantly, "Dad, Mother won't let me go to the swimming hole with the scouts. She says it's dangerous. The other boys can do a lot of things I'm not allowed to do. Sometimes, she's unfair." Father hesitated, raised his eyebrows, winced, drew a few puffs on his pipe, shrugged his shoulders, "Do what your mother says." There was no conviction in his voice. George knew he had a secret ally. He could go to the swimming hole. . . .

Ten-year-old Glen obviously enjoyed telling his father, in full detail, how he threw a rotten tomato at "that crabby old janitor" and then enjoyed the thrill of being chased and hunted—unsuccessfully—by the angry and tomato-splattered janitor. Glen's father, with a broad grin and an appreciative nod, ate up every detail. His pride in Glen was obvious. When Glen finally completed his description with a loud, comradely laugh, his father felt he had to make some perfunctory statement in defense of propriety,

"You know you should never do that again, Glen." And, with his arm over his son's shoulder, they went out together chuckling. . . .

It is evident that the child derives his ideas of right and wrong from his parents. He does not inherit his parents' consciences, of course, but he learns from them—not only from what they say but from what they don't say, or what they imply by nonverbal means. The mother and the father who really mean business when they tell the child what he should and should not do have no problems in making their wishes understood and obeyed. But the child senses —and finds quickly—any loopholes in the parent's commands. The parent may say one thing but, by a half-smile, a tone of voice, or a facial expression, suggest something else. Verbal prohibitions by the parent lose their meaning, for example, when the parent shows unusual interest in a given situation, as did Glen's father.

A child's feelings are easily molded; he quickly senses and reacts to the hidden desires of his parents. He may have to contend with double-talk by the parents. Although the parent may tell the child what he cannot do, in the same breath he offers him an alternative, a loophole to the prohibition.

Mrs. G., horrified, glared at Linda, "Linda, your teacher, Miss Jones, phoned me today and told me something I never would have believed. Mommy was very hurt. To think that my own little girl would be caught taking pennies from Miss Jones' purse. I'm so ashamed of you, Linda. Why did you ever have to do a thing like that? You have everything you want.

Why couldn't you have taken pennies from Mommy's pocketbook? I always keep it by the toaster! Linda, what shall I do with you?" Linda's mother has an elastic conscience; it is not right to steal from the teacher, but it is right to take pennies from Mother's pocketbook without telling her.

Or again, a parent may grant permission for what is verbally prohibited by his own double standard of conduct. The parent himself does what he forbids the child to do.

Mrs. D. insists that June always tell the truth and stay within her weekly allowance. "After all, Daddy is not made of money!" June bit her lip and looked wistfully at the new plaid skirt that her mother bought on the installment plan only yesterday while she and June were shopping. And June recalled her mother had said. "Let's not tell Daddy now. He'd only get mad and worry about the money. And you know what the doctor said about his blood pressure!"

Or, Mr. V. sternly tells Jack not to smoke because smoking will stunt his growth. But Jack remembers his father's repeated boast that he has smoked since he was twelve and that he had his first cigarette behind the barn without his father's knowledge. Since Jack's father is six feet tall and as "strong as a horse," Jack is not likely to be deterred from smoking by this parental admonition.

To the impressionable child, there is no difference between a big lie and a little one. When a parent lies, the child learns that a person may say one thing and mean another; that he may say one thing and then deny it; that one may promise one thing and do another. To the child, the limits of honesty become very hazy. Thus, lies in one situation spread to lies in many situations. Lying can show the child how to give lip service to a command or a promise without obeying or even without having any intention of obeying. It makes a sham out of law, morals, common decency, and respect. The parent who is so concerned about his child's telling "fibs" needs first to do some honest soul-searching of himself. What the child learns he learns from his parents.

Conscience is the deep, ineradicable memory of standards of conduct learned from the parents; it is a system of values, of what is right and wrong, good and evil. It contains the seeds of the most lofty of human thoughts, feelings, and acts—and the most base. It determines how the individual will act. The learned code of ethics becomes a guidebook that tells a child what to do in meeting new situations throughout life. As in the construction of a skyscraper, one builds from the foundation up and does not start with the fiftieth story suspended in air.

Conscience develops in a growth pattern that starts at the beginning and goes on throughout life. The parent cannot temporize by saying, "We can put this off until next time. He's too young. Let's wait until he is older, and then he'll understand." It is always a question of here and now, not some place else or some other time.

Conscience is not static. It is continually resisting new pressures, changing conditions, and temptations, and it is continually being reinforced or altered by the impact of new experiences. If the parent finds that his child's conscience is defective, he should search his own conscience structure. The parent who is not consistent in his own thoughts, feelings, and actions exposes the child to his own highly flexible and inconsistent set of rules. The child's developing conscience will be like that of the parent; it will have all his defects, deficiencies, and inconsistencies. A conscience, then, built upon consistent parental actions and principles, becomes not a list of specific (and changing) rules for specific (and changing) situations but a set of consistent principles applicable to virtually all situations.

The church, the school, the home, and each new life situation contribute to the reinforcement or alteration of conscience. But it is the parents who, in their child's preschool years, lay the foundation. In this period the child is first learning the concept of time, of what tomorrow means. The child begins to think of growing up and wonders if he or she will be like the father and the mother. Beyond this faint inkling of what the future means, the child finds the concept of time too difficult to grasp. He lives mainly from day to day; he understands only what he can see, feel, and hear. He understands only what is happening to people that he knows in the place where he is. He is literal. He is totally unequipped to understand ideas or concepts presented to him as mere words.

The young child, pliable and highly receptive, is molded by what he himself experiences and knows to be true. What he is told without accompanying feelings and actions is not important. What is important is the substance, the constant interaction of feeling between child and parent. The form and the ritual are not important. The child learns by actual participation and by observation of actions and feelings. He does not learn from simply being told the correct thing to do when he observes otherwise.

"Tommy, how many times have I told you not to lie to me?" But Tommy has just heard his mother tell Mrs. Williams on the phone that she has a splitting headache and is so sorry she cannot play bridge this afternoon. Tommy knows better: Mother wants to spend the afternoon waxing the floors.

Similarly, what is read to the child or what he himself reads is of no importance if what he observes is quite different. As a matter of fact, the child may actually see the parents observe, on a superficial basis, the accepted code of ethics, but he knows that their deeper feelings are different. Sensing these undercurrents, he will make them his own, although he may actually see his parents go through the motions of acting otherwise.

Mrs. F. is a leader in church and civic organizations. She can always be counted upon as a willing and helpful volunteer for any worthy cause. She is always ready to offer neighborly help in any of the minor but numerous problems that can arise in a household. Thirteen-year-old Nancy constantly hears words of praise for her mother, Mrs. F. People cannot understand how such a wonderful and talented woman can have a child like Nancy: unfriendly, sarcastic, cynical, mistrusted by her classmates. But Nancy is tired of listening to the constant praise of her mother. She knows that her mother is really very different from what her neighbors think. But what can she say? She cannot be disloyal to her mother. And if she did tell, the neighbors never would believe her; they would only call her ungrateful and badly spoiled.

More tragic, however, is the fact that even when the child knows that the parent is definitely in the wrong, often he will not tell on the parent, but rather will take the blame on his (the child's) own shoulders. Nancy has heard her mother say at the supper table, "I don't know why I bother with all these clubs. None of those committee women know anything! They're so stupid!" . . ."You know, Henry [the husband], I don't think Mrs. M. and her husband are getting along together. I'll bet he's going around with that new secretary I've heard about. But serves Mrs. M. right. She's always such a mess. Doesn't know a thing about makeup or grooming." Or, "That Mrs. Taylor is always bragging about her son. To hear her talk, you'd think he's another Einstein. As if there could be any geniuses in that family. You know her father ran off with another woman. It's supposed to be a big secret. And that son she brags about, that little 'Einstein,' he's just an ordinary thief. Oh, I suppose I shouldn't say that. The poor boy only stole a bicycle. All the children have bikes these days. What can you expect of a father and a mother like that? In a case like theirs, I couldn't blame our Nancy if she stole a bicycle too." Not only is Mrs. F. showing her daughter her true hostile feelings toward her neighbors in a two-faced manner, but she is also telling

Nancy that, in a given situation, stealing is permissible. As if stealing in any situation and for any reason can ever be tolerated!

Mr. F., Nancy's father, is the perfect gentleman: always impeccably attired and handsomely groomed; he always knows the right thing to say for every occasion; he is a connoisseur of fine music and good food; his winning smile captivates. The women all envy Mrs. F. for having a husband with such sophisticated qualities. Again, Nancy's experience differs. When she goes shopping with her father he is always in a hurry, grabs her hand and practically drags her after him. He berates the clerks if they are at all slow or if he must wait for another customer. He finds fault with everything. He frequently makes a scene with the clerk and insists on seeing the store manager. Following one such scene, the intimidated and confused clerk gave Mr. F. his change and ran to the safety of another customer. Mr. F. counted the change and chortled as he quickly led Nancy away, "Stupid fool, serves him right. He gave me a dollar too much change. The store is making too much profit anyway."

Of course, Nancy is not convinced by her father's gallant manner. She knows that her father really enjoys making people squirm and that he is not the kind of gentleman her mother's friends think he is. Mr. F. gave Nancy another lesson in dishonesty in the incident described above.

Mr. and Mrs. F. can quote the code of ethics and the laws of religion. Nancy may be taught these same rules at home and at Sunday school. But she knows that her parents pay only lip service to the rules. They do not live up to them or believe in them. Nancy has been taught by her parents to be the perfect lady, knowing when to rise, when to smile, what to say, when to say it, and all the finer points of etiquette. Like her parents, she presents the outward appearances of conforming to the accepted rules of conduct; but when her self-interest or whims are at stake, she sets aside the rules automatically, with such skill that the infractions may not even be recognized by those about her. And Nancy herself does not realize that she is doing wrong.

Conscience is not a matter of intelligence. From the examples already given, it is apparent that many people with obvious defects in their conscience are highly intelligent. Other examples could be cited in which the intelligence was below average, and yet the conscience was sound. In these people, their conscience compensates in measure for their below-average intelligence. They can hold down jobs that require loyalty, honesty, and dependability.

An important problem during this period of the child's developing conscience is what the parent should do when the child steals for the first time. Almost every child has stolen at least once in his life. If the parent handles the problem directly and honestly the first time, the situation will not recur. What should be done?

As Mrs. R. leaves the department store with Johnny, she notices for the first time that he is carrying a toy monkey. In a natural matter-of-fact voice, she asks Johnny where he got the toy. She does not accuse him nor does she show undue excitement or interest. Finding out that Johnny took it from a counter in the store, Mrs. R. said, "You know that the toy monkey does not belong to you. You should never take what is not yours." Since this is her son's first such act, Mrs. R. realizes that he does not really know the meaning of what he has done. It is her job now to show him that what he did is wrong and naughty. Without any fuss or lengthy explanations, she returns with Johnny to the toy counter, finds the clerk and explains, in Johnny's presence, just what happened. The clerk, used to this situation with young children, fully understands and takes the toy back. Johnny is told again that he has been very naughty and must never again take anything that does not belong to him. To discourage any possible repetition, Mrs. R. withholds from Johnny some other toys or does not permit him to do something or have something that he enjoys. For example, Mrs. R. gave Johnny no desserts for one week and did not buy him any ice cream cones. Johnny's father fully supported his wife. He did not make any deals with Johnny that would undo the mother's punishment. He knew what had happened and subscribed fully to the punishment.

The value of the stolen article is unimportant. Stealing any article, expensive or inexpensive, under any conditions, is always forbidden. Permitting the stealing of any article, no matter how trifling and inexpensive, gives tacit parental approval for further stealing.

If Johnny had been permitted to keep the toy monkey and nothing had been said or done except the admonition, "You are naughty; you should never do that again!" Johnny would have enjoyed the use of the toy. In such a situation, what his mother told him would have had no meaning compared with the fact that he kept and was enjoying the toy. Such acts would be repeated. Johnny would steal. It cannot be emphasized too strongly that it is the underlying feelings, not the acts and the words, which are of paramount importance in this and any situation. The parent may make an empty ritual of words and actions in strictly following the procedure used by Johnny's mother. However, if the accompanying feelings for honesty are not present in the household, the child will never learn honesty.

The parent may show undue excitement and consternation on first discovering that the child has stolen. The parent who is overcome by fear that the child may grow up to be a thief often flies into a tirade. "You thief; you dirty little thief. Steal! Steal! You rotten thief! How can you steal! How can you do such a dirty thing? I'll break you in two! I'll show you! Steal, will you? You . . . You thief! If I ever catch you doing this again . . . !" Rather than effectively handling the stealing in a straightforward way that the child will understand, this parent only communicates his own overwhelming fear that this will be the first of many acts of stealing. The child quickly senses the parent's fear that the stealing might get out of hand and that it will be repeated. An alternative to complete future honesty has been shown. The parent's intense excitement indicates his own underlying uncertainty over the concept of honesty. Why should a parent who is basically honest and sure of his own honesty fear that his child will develop otherwise? The child learns that there really are two possible roads: one may steal or one may not steal. Johnny R., on the other hand, was given no alternative. There was only one road: he could not steal. In the instance of the parent and the emotional tirade, a thought (and therefore implied permission) was implanted in the child that the stealing would get out of hand and be repeated.

In addition to the tirade, there are other ways for the parent to communicate his distrust to the child. "Doctor, I was afraid that he'd break into somebody's house. I took the precaution of secretly following him so I'd be sure he was getting into no trouble." Such bizarre precautions only indicate how deep is the parent's distrust of his child. The child cannot help but sense this distrust even if he does not detect that his parent is following him. The distrust is communicated from parent to child in subtle ways. Without apparent reason, the parent quizzes the child: where has he been; with whom has he been; what has he done; how long was he there; is he sure; is he telling everything; is all the time accounted for; did he forget to mention something? The child knows that the parent is suspicious. With the passage of time and constant exposure to such suspicion, the child himself gradually succumbs to this malignantly distrustful attitude which he, in turn, may apply to many of his own life situations. Other subtle and treacherous ways include checking the contents of the child's pockets, smelling his handkerchief, secretly reading his notes or diary, questioning his friends about his activities, and checking by phone or actually following the child to make sure that he is actually where he said he would be. The parent often consoles himself with the thought that the child does not detect all these clandestine signs of distrust.

But, even were this true, there are other even more important ways of communicating parental feelings and deceit to the child. As the child tells the parent about his activities of the previous night, he comes to a part which might lead to something immoral or off-color. The parent leans forward with intense interest and anticipation. Momentarily, there is an expression of disapproval at what might come. But nothing out of line is mentioned. The interest rapidly wanes. The knowing smile, the dirty look, the arched eyebrow, the clucking sound with tongue, the impatient tap of fingers and foot, the disdainful blowing of smoke rings from the cigarette, the nervous whistle, the muttering of half-heard oaths, the clearing of the throat, the self-conscious inspection of ceiling or floor, the repeated nose-blowing, the ribald laughter, the inappropriate guffaws and the "come-on" expressed in the tone of voice—all these in endless variations and combinations can show a parental reaction entirely inconsistent with what the parent says. The child learns from the parent how the parent really feels—and this is parental permission.

"But, Doctor, I don't see why you keep asking me

questions about myself. And why do you keep asking about my father? That was a long time ago and has nothing to do with this situation. My Robert is a firebug because of his heredity. What can you do about that? My husband's Uncle Joe had to be sent away because of setting barns on fire. And many of Robert's friends have been no better. Robert is the only one of my five children who sets fires or does anything wrong, so the cause must be outside our home. Please, Doctor, just give me some pills for my nerves —this is very upsetting, and I don't want to discuss it any more."

Firesetting, like lying, stealing, and sexual difficulties, results from parental problems and defects in conscience concerning the specific delinquency. Bad heredity is frequently given by the parent as the reason or the excuse for delinquency: "And what can you do about heredity?" There is no scientific evidence to support this opinion. But in every case of delinquency where the parents and the child have been thoroughly studied by the collaborative technique, the physicians can always find specific emotional factors at the bottom of the delinquency.

Of course, in practically all instances the parents are unaware of their connection with the problems. Nor are they aware that they themselves have any problems. These problems are based on intangible feelings and values; they cannot be seen, touched, or heard. Though present, they cannot be grasped. What cannot be seen concretely, touched, or heard, is often difficult to understand or believe. And often, in these cases, one does not want to understand or believe, because the cause lies within oneself and not in an outside situation or in another person. Therefore, there are repeated denials and the constant search for scapegoats: placing the blame on heredity, bad companions, the school, and even acts of God. "It is not in our stars but in ourselves."

But the parent whose own feelings are shaping his child's actions and feelings was in turn molded by the feelings of his parents. It is a continuing cycle. The feelings of one generation subtly inoculate and influence the feelings and the actions of the next. These same mechanisms apply to mental health as well as to disease. Stated another way, the parent whose own disturbed feelings flowed from those of his parents before him may not be to blame (since he had no control over the process), but nevertheless he is fully responsible.

If this destructive cycle is ever to be broken, a spade must be called a spade, and responsibility for the delinquency must be firmly established. Flimsy excuses, rationalizations, vacillations, knowing smiles, deceptive winks, loopholes, and the like must be recognized for what they are. Unless the attitudes of the home and of society in general are changed, each succeeding generation will be inoculated with the destructive and unhealthy feelings of the old.

This vicious cycle can be broken only by a genuine understanding of the way the parent, through his own defective conscience and emotional problems, uses his child as a destructive outlet. It is far better that the parent in question find the outlet for his own inner tensions through himself and have some disabling emotional or psychosomatic illness than that his defects in conscience and emotional problems find an outlet by showing up in his child. Naturally, it is easier on the parent to have his child, rather than himself, disabled by these defects and problems. This poses no problem to the parent, because he often does not even know of the existence of the defect or the problem or that he is passing these on to the child. It is far simpler to take the easy way out and thus appear to be the innocent victim of tragic circumstances before an indulgent and misinformed society. The child takes the rap from society for his parents. The newspaper headlines and radio accounts unwittingly enforce and condone, with sensational headlines, the parent's defective conscience: "Mother in Tears As Son Is Sentenced for Shooting Playmate."

"If it is an emotional problem in the parents, Doctor, I can't see why all my children are not affected equally. Of all my children, only Tony steals." The same question may be phrased differently to ask why the older child, the middle child, the boy, the girl, or the adopted child is delinquent while the rest of the children are not. As we have already seen, the parent's selection of the specific delinquency by his child depends on factors in the parent's own past experiences, which he himself does not recognize. The means by which the parent fosters the specific delinquency depends upon many subtle and devious forms of unconscious communication.

These emotional problems cause a continual

buildup of emotional tension in the parent, for which he finds a suitable outlet through a specific child. This affords the parent vicarious gratification, because the child does that which he, the parent, would like to do because of his own emotional needs but which he, the parent, dares not do because of his fear of the opprobrium of society. Again let us emphasize that the parent is unaware that he even has a problem, let alone that there is a connection between his specific problem and the child's specific delinquency. The parent who vicariously finds an outlet for his pent-up emotional needs and tensions, through one child (or possibly more than one) has no need to involve the rest of his children. The parent has found a satisfactory means of relieving his inner tension; there is no need to look for other outlets.

The selection of the scapegoat child conforms to these seemingly irrational, illogical, and emotional processes of which the parent is unaware. But by full and adequate study of both parent and child the physician finds definite and specific reasons why the particular child has been made the scapegoat. This child may be the only daughter in a family whose mother's emotional problem was with her own mother. The delinquent girl's mother may have had a relatively healthy relationship with her own father, and therefore the sons escaped. The position of the child in the family, the name, a symbolically significant stage of development, the physical appearance (color of hair, shape of nose, voice), or the sex may determine which child will be the scapegoat.

For example, Robert, the firebug, was the oldest boy and looked like his Uncle Joe, the black sheep of the family who was sent away for setting barns on fire. Robert's father, who was the younger of two sons, always played second fiddle to his brother Joe. Joe got everything despite the fact that he always was in trouble. Robert's father was always blamed for Joe's many misdeeds. Joe was always praised; but his parents never said a kind word when Robert's father did well in school. He always tried to prove to his parents and himself that he was better than Joe. Despite his excellent grades in school, good behavior and running a newspaper route to earn his own spending money, his parents took him for granted. They lavished all their hopes and attentions on Joe. Robert's father resented such favoritism, but was forced to maintain silence; he had to contain his anger within himself until he finally found relief through his son's delinquency.

Young Georgie, who was in reform school for stealing, was named after his mother's brother. Uncle George, the skeleton in the family closet, was always involved in truancy in school, accidents, petty stealing, and later in molesting girls. When younger, Uncle George took delight in tormenting his sister, young Georgie's mother. Uncle George had been his own mother's pet. As a young girl, young Georgie's mother resented the favoritism shown her brother. She never could fight back. Her brother was always right; she was always wrong. Even when the brother's taunts were cruelly excessive, the parents merely stood by and smiled or told her to stop upsetting George. Her parents never offered any help. These early experiences became indelible memories of bitter resentment. Through young Georgie, his mother found an outlet for the resentment that she had been forced to contain until that time. Young Georgie's two older sisters had no problems. His mother found complete relief for her warped emotions through her son; she needed no other outlet. Young Georgie, like his uncle before him, was destined to become another family "skeleton in the closet."

From all of the foregoing it should be evident that the problem of childhood delinquency is not only the punishment of the youthful offender but, more important, the search for the cause and the establishment of responsibility at the source. Each individual case of delinquency represents a highly destructive unwitting partnership between the parent and the child.

Seldom, if ever, does one incident determine a child's character, as has been shown in these examples. Rather, it is the constant exposure to a set pattern of parental feelings and behavior manifested by these repeated everyday trivialities and undercurrents. In the aggregate, these determine a child's personality. In acquiring this personality, the child will detect and respond to his parents' true underlying feelings regardless of what may appear on the surface. In fact, observers have called the child a "natural psychiatrist," who possesses unusual skill at sensing the nuances of his parents' feelings. Yet he is forced by his dependence to deny the verdict of his senses and to accept as real the facade of excuses, outright lies, and distorted reasons that his parents may present to him. Of course, the child is confused. From repeated exposure to such distortions, his ability to test and to accept the reality of what his senses tell him becomes compromised.

7

Sick Attitudes Toward Sex

Most sexual deviations are preventable and treatable. But we must first recognize the role of parental permissiveness in establishing such sick attitudes toward sex as homosexuality, transvestitism, and promiscuity.

What does a parent do when confronted with his child's abnormal attitude toward sex? What he may do is ignore it, minimize it, disguise it, or distort it. But whatever his overt attitude, he will be upset and anxious. Though he may bring the child to the physician for some trivial reason, he is actually seeking help for the sexual disturbance. By the physician's sympathetic interest and without an attempt to sit in judgment, the parent is able to discuss the child's sexual problems.

When collaborative study of both child and parent is undertaken, there is revealed the same causative relationship between the child's sex problems and those of one or both of his parents that is apparent in the study of other forms of abnormal behavior.

Often the parents do not recognize the existence of their own sexual problems, as is true in other areas of human emotions. And even if the parents recognize that they have sex problems, they usually believe these do not affect their children, because "we never talk about such things in front of the children."

The facts say otherwise. Whenever there is an emotional problem, as we have seen, tension builds up. Finally, the tension must boil over. The release of tension affects both parent and child emotionally as well as physically. It is evident, then, that when such tension is due to parental sex problems, its spilling over affects the child's sexual feelings and attitudes.

From our earlier discussion of asthma and bed-wetting (see Chaps. 4 & 5), we may recall that in many cases the parents of such children were found to be sexually maladjusted. The excessive hugging of father and daughter and of mother and son, and the sleeping, bathing, and dressing practices described were shown not to be a true expression of parental love or modern frankness. Such practices, with hidden feelings of parental hate, only serve to keep the child very young and at a safer and less emotionally charged level of development—the mouth and the bowel stages. Thus he is kept from progressing through the barriers of the first-romance stage.

This "modern frankness" takes a further toll of such a child who, in addition to possible asthma and bed-wetting, often develops much confusion over his role as a boy, or hers as a girl. The boy may become extremely passive (a feminine attribute), and the girl extremely aggressive (a male attribute). As a result, the boy's basic role as a male is destroyed, as is the girl's role as a female. Our case studies revealed that the mother who had basic underlying conflicts with men from her own past had unwittingly revenged herself on a man; the father, with similar problems with women, had unwittingly revenged himself on a woman. What was called parental love and modern frankness had, in fact, served only to harm and to destroy.

Parents do well to realize that sexuality in the child is different from that in the adult. For the child, it means how comfortable he feels in the presence of his own sex as well as the opposite sex. It also means how successfully he has fulfilled his role as a boy or as a girl. Does the boy play football and basketball, climb trees, and in general act like a Tom Sawyer or a Huckleberry Finn? Does the girl play with dolls, have tea parties, and help her mother around the house? Does the boy act like a boy, and the girl like a girl? The difference between the two sexes, therefore, is not only an anatomic difference but also—and surely as important—the differences in attitudes, feelings, and values attached to their own and the opposite sex (see p. 88).

Very early in life the child knows the anatomic difference between boys and girls and men and women. It is during the first-romance stage that the boy and the girl first notice the physical differences in their bodies. They show their healthy curiosity by their reactions and their many questions. At this time the child really learns, by example from his parents, as well as by the behavior of other grown-ups, that boys and girls and men and women act and are treated differently. The child learns this chiefly from his parents. Barring some rare trick of nature, the boy and the girl will develop into a man and a woman with all the adult physical attributes of their sex. But how well the adult man and woman adjust to, work with, and enjoy life with members of their own and the opposite sex depends on their values and feelings in this regard, which they have learned from their parents.

These same feelings—and seldom any recognized physical disease—account for how well grown-ups function sexually as men and women. The frigid woman and the impotent man, with rare exceptions, are anatomically normal but physically disabled because of emotional problems stemming from their early childhood. Unfortunately, this problem will continue from generation to generation. Innocent children are robbed of their future as happy and healthy men and women by highly destructive household nudity and flagrant sleeping and bathing practices extending all too often into the child's pubertal or even postpubertal years.

Modern frankness is nothing less than a complete perversion of the traditional role of parent toward child. By appropriate modesty the parent will give his child healthy attitudes toward his body and later sexuality. The parent is not to use his child as an outlet for his own unresolved problems, tensions, and conscience defects. Although the parent may not be to blame for these serious problems (which stem from his or her own childhood), it is certainly his responsibility to see that he does not perpetuate this corruption.

The problems of the parent become apparent in the child while he is still a growing youngster as well as when he becomes an adult. In general, society adopts a close-mouthed, hush-hush attitude toward these problems in both the child and the adult. The superficial aspects of sex may be sensationalized in the press, movies, and television, but the underlying factors often go unmentioned. Let us take a more thorough, frank look at several cases to examine this definite and tragic relationship between parent and child.

PETER—DESTROYED AS A MALE BY HIS MOTHER'S PERVERSION

January 3

The mother of 19-year-old Peter came in for an interview. She is 49, a large aggressive woman, dressed in gay clothes and a large hat with decorative flowers. She looked at least ten years younger. She immediately took a chair close to the physician's desk and started to talk in a highly modulated, histrionic voice. She said that one of Peter's bad habits was telling wild stories. "It's a failing. His brother and sister suffer from these stories. For instance, when Johnny had his operation for a tight heart valve, Peter wrote his pals to say that his own finger was being amputated. Also, Doctor, tell me, could he have had transfusions when his teeth were extracted the other day? That's what he told me. And when he applied for a job, he built himself up to say that he was a great athlete and had set many records. The only thing he was ever great at was being a rifleman!"

[Peter tells many lies. It will be interesting to see why he does so.]

"He is very nervous and high-strung. I think the trouble is really due to a fall he had from a bicycle at the age of six. He was at the City Hospital then."

[Parents, and the patient himself, often blame behavior problems on diseases and injuries, especially head injuries, but without any justification in medical fact. This is another common scapegoat mechanism (see p. 188).]

Peter's mother then related some of the background factors surrounding his current institutionalization. Peter, she said, was a poor student in school. He always played with much younger boys. He would bring them home from school and also take them hunting or ice skating. She never suspected anything was wrong until her husband got a phone call from the police in another state. Soon thereafter, Peter returned and explained his trouble with the law by saying, "I blacked out." The mother said that while thinking his problem over she remembered that when Peter was eight years of age she had a fear that he would molest little girls by pulling their dresses up.

[A child begins life with a clean slate: no fears or

abnormal thoughts. Here, however, is a mother who has a very unusual fear concerning her son. Peter cannot help but be aware of this fear. Is she putting ideas into his mind?]

Some of the potentially dangerous homicidal elements in Peter's situation can be identified in the following: "We were called recently by the police who said Peter was keeping boys out in a cabin, that he wanted them to join a club. He claims he's never harmed them. He gave the boys an enema. He says he's afraid he's going to hurt somebody, or injure them, or strike them. He's a great one to handle guns. I thought he'd shoot someone if the little kids resisted him. I don't understand, because one of the boys said his father was a policeman."

[The significance of the enema will soon become clear. Note the mother's fear of Peter's doing violence.]

When Peter's mother was asked how she thought her son became this way, she said that he was a lone wolf as a child and that the only time he ever took a girl out was when she had insisted that he do so for the junior prom. "He always has been afraid of girls." When he was thirteen, a neighbor woman said, "Have you ever suspected Peter of molesting girls? He threatened to give them all an enema." "I questioned the girls," continued Peter's mother, "and asked them if he picked up their dresses or touched them. They said, 'No,' so I wasn't worried.

"Concerning sex, Doctor, when Peter was twelve or thirteen we talked these things over, that is about girls and where babies came from. Yet he seemed to know it all . . . When he was in the bathroom, I would go in, and he wouldn't mind. You see, Peter was never circumcised, and it bothered me. His foreskin was too tight. I always checked it until he was seven. I'd tell him to clean it out good. He was always pulling at himself. We changed doctors and the new doctor said, 'no, it wouldn't do any harm.' I thought it was bad for him to do this. When he was older, I was afraid he wouldn't take care of his foreskin. I thought that this might cause the testicles to shrink."

[In no uncertain terms the mother was communicating to her son her own preoccupation with his genitals in a frightening manner. She conveyed to him her fear that harm may be done.]

"When he was older, he had a room to himself. But even to this day, if I'm stretched out [nude] taking a nap, he'll enter my room, and I'm not ashamed of my body." She then volunteered the information that dressing was very open in her home, that she frequently walked around with only her brassière and panties on, and that it didn't make any difference to the children.

[The complete lack of modesty in this household is obviously an indication of deeper problems. The following quotations from Peter's mother are in their original sequence.]

"He always had rectal troubles, and I gave him enemas. Today I no longer worry, since I feed him plenty of vegetables and fruits that make him regular. So, when he was home, he'd say he didn't have any troubles. When he was ten, I gave him many enemas for nervousness. . . . Lately he's been affectionate again. He kisses me when leaving the house and coming home. When he was young, he never liked thunder and lightning. He'd come and sleep with us. Quite recently we went to a hotel and we shared the same bed, Peter and I. It made no difference."

[Note the mother's fixation on rectal troubles and enemas. And a nineteen-year-old boy sharing the same bed with his mother!]

Peter's mother said that, although she had explained menstruation to him, he had "never seen that. . . . He was an instrument baby and weighed over 9 pounds at birth. I cried when the doctor told me it was a boy; I had set my heart on a girl." She then described her pregnancy and how sick she was, vomiting throughout the pregnancy and how "hard put" she was in the early feeding: "breast fed him, weighed him, breast fed him again, and he'd always cry." The mother mentioned with some interest how "abnormally shaped and pointed Peter's head was at birth."

[From the mother's wandering, disconnected remarks, it is evident that Peter's troubles were determined long before the first-romance stage, even before he was born. His mother was preoccupied with his alleged abnormalities from the first day of life. Her only memories of his infancy were unpleasant ones.]

"As Peter grew older, he preferred to visit with grown-ups, because of his trouble in getting along with children his own age. I kept changing his schools. I was very concerned about his sexual development. I kept waiting for him to start having wet dreams. I would carefully look over the bed sheets and smell them to be sure. Yet, he only had one once! At that time, I noticed tissue in the wastepaper basket, and he said that he had a headache."

[Note the maternal preoccupation with sex.]

January 7

Today the physician put Peter into a deep hypnotic trance. Peter then returned to periods in his earlier childhood and relived many upsetting situations that he had since forgotten. Hypnosis enabled him to remember and describe these experiences. Information that Peter's mother supplied, as well as his own dreams, did, in fact, indicate experiences such as these. Before the trance, Peter had little to say about himself and nothing to say about his family. But under hypnosis he relived the following incidents.

1. "Dad's holding me in his arms. I kick my mother. She's going to give me an enema. There's a pillow on the floor. My dad is laying me down on my side. Getting a bad tummy ache out of it. I have a bottle, [presumably to suck on]. She's looking at me very angrily. She wants me to go on some more. I'm lying on the bed." During this period the patient jumped, kicked, and winced.

2. "I see myself buying an erector set in a store. I have to buy one. I take it home and play with it. Mother comes down and sees me. She asks me where I got it. She says Dad will have to find out about it.

She makes me sit in a corner by myself. I make up a story when Dad comes in. I try to get out of it. I'm scared that I'll get a spanking. I try to run away. Dad catches me and tells me to take my clothes off. Mother is standing in the kitchen. I ask her to help, but she says nothing. Dad calls for a big stick. Sister and brother will hear everything. He's spanking me. I break away. He catches me behind the table. He's beating me. It hurts awful." At this point Peter is crying and jerking all over. "My brother is coming upstairs with a hamburger and cake. He must feel sorry for me."

3. "I go to the park where there are young boys. I play I'm a doctor at the hospital. I tell them I want to give them a physical examination. We go up by the lake. I have one boy watching from the tree and one watching on the road. I get the other one undressed. I feel nervous and tense. I take his pulse, examine his chest and sexual organs. I check his back and rectum. Put a stick up his rectum, and he doesn't object. I check under his knees and between his toes. He says he will join my club. I initiate him with five whacks on his feet. I beat him until he cries, and he says he won't tell. I feel pins and needles all over me." At this point the patient repeatedly pulls his legs rapidly apart and together again and jerks all over.

[Peter shows the same preoccupation with the rectum and the genital organs that his mother has shown all his life. Peter does to the little boy what was done to him when his mother gave him the repeated enemas. His confusion between the organs of sex and elimination is apparent, as is his underlying hatred. Peter whips as he has been whipped.]

4. "I see Gloria; she's not old. I see her downstairs. I tell her I'll examine her. She says, 'Yes.' I undress her, look at her. I try to do the same thing Mommy and Daddy do. Gloria yells. I pull it out. It's like giving her an enema so she'll feel better. But I put it in front instead of the rectum. She doesn't mind."

[It would seem that Peter had learned his precocity by observing his parents because of their laxity and open-door policy. Even more important than actual observation is the previously discussed unbridled maternal interest in sex. Again we note the same preoccupation with and confusion between adult sexual practices and enemas.]

5. "I know I'm going to be caught, but I keep on doing these things. I can't stop myself. I have to keep on going. I'm driving to Junction City. Feel somebody is watching me. Two cops pull up in a car. First they ask me if I'm crazy. My mind is going blank. They put me in jail. I told the others [prisoners] I stole a Cadillac. I don't want them to know what I really did."

[Although Peter knows that what he does is wrong, and although he is ashamed of his abnormal actions, he cannot help himself. He must go on, even with the certainty that he will eventually be caught and punished by the law. Peter is driven on by a devil he cannot resist. But this devil is not a mysterious force; it is a sick, badly confused person of flesh and blood —his mother. Unless this problem is recognized and uprooted at its source before it can permanently cripple the growing child, the child and society must suffer. The growing child becomes the young man, who is already lost by the time he first comes to the attention of the law. Peter and his mother should have seen a physician years ago. In fact, Peter's mother should have seen a physician when she was young, long before her marriage.]

6. "The doctor is in my room giving me a shot with a big needle. Mother pulls my pajamas off. She has me by my sex organs. It hurts. She rolls me over. The needle hurts. She takes a nice long look all over me.

7. "I'm nude in the bathroom. Mother comes in with a yardstick, spanks me for filling my pants. I hate her! I could kill her! I'm going to kill her! She has given me many spankings like this. I'm mad! She has done this before! I'm mad! I'm going to kill her when I get out of here!"

[The unnaturally close relationship between Peter and his mother and her hatred for him have had their effect. This mother's life is really in danger. It is often feelings such as these that lead children later to become wanton murderers.]

8. "I'm out trying sexual intercourse with a neighbor girl. She says yes. We get off her bike and go into the woods. Feels good. She says that we should go back.

9. "I'm with Aunt Louise, Father's sister, on a trip. We're in a motel; it's bedtime. I forgot my pajamas. She says it's OK. I sleep in my shorts, and she undresses down to her bloomers and brassière. Crawl into bed together. I'm scared. I'm only 12. I'm afraid to go to sleep. I'm awake all night."

[More evidences of "modern frankness." This time it is from the father's side of the family.]

January 16

10. "I see myself and four others in jail. I'm supposed to have molested some boys in the Tennis Club. They tell me I'm going on trial. Now I'm going up to the courthouse to see the judge for the hearing. I plead innocent. They say a young boy told them I gave him a spanking and checked his pulse. I start crying, because I don't remember it, and I'm scared. The judge tells me to go home and get out of town by sundown; otherwise I'll be prosecuted. I'm brought to the railroad station. I'm scared. I didn't do it. I'm getting off the train now and meeting my dad. He's getting me to tell what happened. He's mad. I feel I've been gypped."

When pressed by the physician and told that he really could remember and that there must be complete honesty, Peter went on:

"Dad wanted me to tell him. I have a young boy in the basement of the Tennis Club. I'm giving him an enema. The manager catches me and calls the police. I've been caught red-handed. It's true! It's true all the way! I tell Dad I can't remember, 'cause I'm afraid to tell him. But he keeps trying. Finally, he gives up. He thinks it's all a big story. I never told the truth too much. Mother knows; yet she doesn't say a word. Keeps me in suspense. I'm worried about it. I wish she'd let me know. She just gives me a mean look all the time. I wonder if Mother will beat me for misbehaving at the Tennis Club. I'm scared of Mother. I don't like her any more. She never did me any good. She babied me and made me feel too young. She always sends me to the doctor, because my foreskin is too tight. The doctor said it's all right. I feel I'm not sexually all there. She says I have to pull it back. She pulls it back. Looks well pleased. It's mine and I should do what I want with it! She doesn't mind too much if I play with smaller boys. She doesn't encourage me to go with girls. I feel it from the way she acts. She doesn't want me to go with older boys. I want to run away from home. She examines my testicles. I have no will power to stop her, and I think she's doing right. My mother would say I'm lying if I ever told my Dad about this."

[Peter is terrified about what the law will do to him, but he cannot help himself. He is even more terrified of his parents, whom he cannot trust. Worse still, he realizes that his mother knows, but she says nothing. Her silence gives tacit permission for continuing such misdeeds. After all, Peter has long been aware of his mother's overwhelming interest in sex. She much prefers that Peter not go out with girls or older boys but only with younger boys. Again the mother is the motivating force. She is supposed to help the child, but in this case she is encouraging his interest in unnatural, highly destructive acts. Peter has no one he can trust. He knows that if he were to tell his father what his mother is doing, she would lie and deny it all. He stands alone, frightened and totally unable to stop his march to destruction. His mother repeatedly brings Peter to physicians not for the many obvious and serious emotional problems but only to use the medical profession as a tool of her own perversity.]

11. "I want to go to work or join the service. She's to blame for my troubles, for getting me here. I wanted revenge on young boys, the age she used to work on me all the time. She wants me to become a doctor. She always did."

Peter then told how his mother made a point of stepping out of the shower on some pretext to talk to him and that he was frightened when she so exposed herself.

"I'm afraid to go with other girls, because they'll do the same thing, undress in front of me. It makes me scared and uneasy."

January 20

Peter's father, who came to the office today, is a middle-aged businessman, tall, well-built, but passive in his demeanor. He had to be beckoned into the room three times before he entered. He has the appearance of prosperity in his sporty clothes and in his frequent allusions to business trips to California and Hawaii. He started at once to discuss what he thinks are the causative factors in Peter's illness. "Peter was the first child, an instrument baby. Perhaps a fall from the bicycle 15 years ago was responsible. Ever since that time he has had a terrific imagination." The father then expanded further on Peter's management of his finances, in which he had "many bad streaks." The father's conscience defect about money is evident in the way he counseled Peter. Peter was in trouble with several loan sharks and installment-buying agencies. But the father always bailed him out of financial trouble with fresh transfusions of money and even bought him flashy sport cars.

[By continually bailing his son out of financial difficulties, the father only encourages their repetition.]

The father continued, "I nagged him all the time about whether his fingernails were clean or not." Following one of the most recent court incidents, the father said that he reminded his son, "Now, Peter, if you feel that coming on, your weakness, let me know, so I can help you."

[With all of Peter's serious problems, his father worries about his son's keeping his fingernails clean! He does not forcefully tell Peter, "No, you must not and cannot do it." Instead there is the bland "let me know so I can help you." By not forcefully setting definite limits, the father is, in effect, giving permission for other similar acts, as he had done in the past.]

The father frequently spoke about Peter as though he were a five-year-old rather than a boy in his late teens. He described Peter's illness as "a cross of life we have to bear." His attitudes toward Peter's difficulties were well summarized by his parting remarks. "I was always scared he'd attack a child. I told him as long as I can remember, way before this, 'Always remember your actions, Peter. You know the stuff you read in the papers. I'm worried.

I'd hate to see my own children attacked.' Gee, Doc., my own son looks like a criminal!"

Despite all evidence to the contrary, the father looks upon Peter's problems as an act of God. Like the mother, he fears his son will be delinquent. Not only that, but he also has communicated these fears to Peter verbally and directly. Why should a parent, secure in his own conscience structure, fear that the child will be anything but completely normal and law-abiding? The father thinks that his son looks like a criminal! Fond parents may see in their children evidences of the future musician, physician, contractor, accountant, and so on, but to see evidences of criminality!

The same general principles described in Peter's case apply to the girl who indulges in abnormal sexual play with girls, as Peter did with boys. Such a girl becomes the woman who never makes a satisfactory emotional and sexual adjustment with men and prefers women. Rather than love, which they claim is the motivating force in their choice of behavior, hatred is the determining factor. Although not usually mentioned as frequently, this preference of woman for woman (lesbianism) is as common as the preference of man for man. In the case of the man, society formerly actively abhorred the situation—but the current trend in some quarters actively condones such behavior and is itself another symptom of society's increasingly sick and perverted values. (This is evident from the explicit contents of many current plays.) In the case of the woman, society still tolerantly closes its eyes.

SEXUAL CONFUSION—TRANSVESTITISM

Man or woman? Boy or girl? Some boys are so confused about their sexuality that they dress like girls. Boys who are passive often have feminine qualities; girls who are aggressive often have masculine qualities, as we have mentioned earlier.

Further along the scale of this disturbance are boys who are boys in an anatomic sense only. They feel like girls; they act like girls; they dress like girls; they wish they were actually girls. When they grow up, some even undergo mutilating surgery (see p. 88) in an attempt to change their genitals to fool themselves as well as the world. Parental misinformation and superstitions to the contrary, these individuals *are* boys. Remove their clothes, examine them, do laboratory tests to check their actual hormone levels, and one will find they are boys.

Transvestites are completely different from those exceedingly rare cases of disturbed physical and hormone structure in which the two sexes are truly mixed in the same body. In transvestites, the confusion concerning sex is in the emotions and not in the body structure, hormones, and fluids. How does this confusion occur?

PAT—THE BOY WHO THOUGHT HE WAS A GIRL

Fifteen-year-old Patrick is talking to the physician: "Mother and Daddy called me Tillie until I was six years old . . . and they did not cut my hair until then. Mother really wanted a girl. Then I came. I had curly yellow hair and big blue eyes. She always dressed me in girl's clothes until I was six and had to go to school. Even after that, Mother would try my sister's clothes on me. If I looked nice, she'd tell me. One day I tried on Mother's high-heeled shoes, black silk dress, lipstick, and fingernail polish. I was eight years old then. Mother came in and laughed, "Tillie, what would your father say? I don't know why you must do things like this. Don't let me ever catch you outside dressed like this. What would our neighbors think?' She then looked at me, smiled, 'Oh! come on, Patty; I can't get mad at you!' She hugged me and kissed me."

[Note that the mother never simply and firmly said, "No!" Her way of saying "no" had many loopholes. "Don't ever let me catch you outside dressed like this." Does that mean that such actions are all right in other circumstances, such as inside the home? She is more alarmed over what the neighbors will think than about what her child is doing. Her closing remarks and embraces give further permission for the repetition of such acts.]

"Another time, Mother told me what a trial it was [pregnancy and delivery] . . . she told me she had her heart set on a girl . . . I wish for Mother's sake that I were a girl to help her . . . if I were a girl I could stay home and help . . . I used to wait many hours [at night] for her to sneak in [my room], tuck me in, and kiss me good night. I was the only one she was close enough to, to sleep with . . . I like to bake, cook, make pies and cakes, and clean the kitchen . . . Mother always said I shouldn't abuse myself [masturbate], because I would become dull and lifeless. She showed me neighborhood children [who did it] . . . Mother was always open and frank; she bathed with me until last year, because she loved me and wanted to be close to me. Only a few times did she have disagreements with Father . . . he was oversexed. She told me he was too demanding . . . regardless of her physical tiredness, he forced his attentions on her."

[This mother not only slept and bathed with her son beyond pubertal years, but she also discussed with her son the secrets of her own physical relationship with her husband. It is apparent that this mother has done everything to achieve her desire to have a little girl. Unfortunately, nature gave her a boy, whom she unwittingly transformed into a girl in feelings, clothing, and actions. In doing so, she has ruined her son's future as a man. By her actions it can be seen that she not only permitted but fostered this transformation.]

"Father is a farmer and works hard all the time. Once he threw me in the creek . . . it was over my head. I was quite scared . . . we never understood each other. I felt I wasn't good enough . . . he was unfair and not understanding. I couldn't agree with him . . . when I was little, he'd beat me all the time.

"My oldest sister was closest to me. We went on trips overnight together. She tried to do the things I liked. We used to fix [castrate] the baby pigs. It would get me very nervous, because it was painful and cruel."

[This boy remained close to his mother and imitated her rather than the father he feared. A farmer's son is used to seeing pigs castrated, and, under usual circumstances, accepts this as part of farm life. Pat's overreaction to such castration might well be related to the extreme mutilation he has endured in every aspect of his sexuality except the physical.]

The mother confirmed much of her son's story. She said, "This is very embarrassing, Doctor. I was always afraid something like this might happen. And now it has really got out of hand. I know, because I've secretly followed him to see what he does when he goes outside dressed like a woman. Once I was afraid he had seen me and knew what I was doing. This is terrible. What can be done? My husband and I are really very broad-minded [this refers to family nudity, the mother dressing and bathing in front of her son, and so forth]. My son is such a good boy. If I looked nice, he'd tell me. He'd even advise me on what dress I'd look best in. Even if he doesn't say so, I can tell, because he gets that funny look in his eye. My husband isn't half as thoughtful. He wouldn't even know if I were dressed at all. I don't think he even cares."

[Here is a mother who secretly follows her son, observes his actions, and is fully aware of his unnatural interests. But she does nothing about it and says nothing to him about it. The son may even have seen his mother following him, and still she said nothing to him. This mother failed to forbid such behavior immediately and unreservedly. Indeed, her actions revealed her complete awareness and acceptance of her son's peversion. Even if the son were not aware of her spying, he would sense her true feelings by innumerable other ways already noted (see Chap. 6). Here was not only maternal permission but actual maternal fostering of bizarre behavior.

This mother delights in her son's unusual interest in what she wears and even seeks his advice in such matters. She compares her son with her husband in a manner which need not and should not be. Father and son should not compete to see who can compliment the mother best. The relationship between mother and son should be different from that between wife and husband. However, this mother is confused about the difference and thinks of her son in a way that should be reserved for her husband. This in itself would be destructive enough to her son and serve to keep him functioning emotionally at the first-romance stage of development. But she goes further and encourages his dressing and behaving like a woman, actions highly destructive to his manhood.]

The destructive nature of the mother's permissiveness in the way she reared her son was greatly clarified when she described her relationships with her own father. She went into detail about her father's violent temper and abusiveness, but spoke with few visible signs of emotion and, in fact, had a sweet smile of forebearance on her face. Her father had been abusive and had a violent, explosive temper. On one occasion, the father threw a penknife at one of his daughters, cutting her on the shoulder. During one of his nightly violent arguments with his wife, he ran through the house after his terrified, screaming wife, brandishing an andiron. Fortunately, Pat's mother knew how to get around her father. She seldom had to endure his cruelties, because she was a "goody-goody."

On special occasions her father was very affectionate to her; even into her late teens he held her on his lap, hugged her and kissed her. There was an unspoken understanding in the house that the father went out with other women. The mother knew about this, as did the daughters, and the father knew that they knew. But nobody ever said anything about it. Pat's mother vividly remembered an occasion when she was passing a tavern late at night. Looking in, she saw her father drunkenly embracing a neighbor woman. The father looked up and glared at her. Frightened, she raced home. Never since had she mentioned this incident to anyone.

Toward the end of her interview with the physician, Pat's mother said, "My own parents fought continuously. I always sought a peace that they never had. I tried my best to take myself from their world and enter another when I married. If life hadn't been so good to me in giving me such a wonderful son, I don't know what I would have done. If it were not for my son, I would not be able to continue living with my husband."

Pat's mother wanted from marriage everything that was missing in her parents' married life. However, the emotional inoculation she received as a child from her confused relationship with her sadistic, philandering father permanently affected her attitudes toward men. Not surprisingly, her own married life was therefore a failure, and her mother-son relationship became a perversion. Although life was not unbearable so far as she was concerned, and although she was making a go of her marriage, her feelings beneath the surface had robbed her son of his manhood by nearly transforming him into a woman. In fact, life was bearable, and the marriage was saved only because the mother could give vent to her hostility toward men through the destruction of her son. The vicarious gratification afforded this mother by the destruction of her son's masculinity was sweet revenge upon her father. In this way she could continue to live in an uneasy peace with her husband and with herself.

The two-faced behavior of Pat's mother and her own father was mirrored in the similar behavior between Pat and his mother. Father and daughter (and wife) were both aware of the philandering; mother and son were both aware of the transvestitism. Each knew of the other's awareness, but all concerned accepted this bizarre behavior without comment. Failure to react forthrightly when one is aware of a perverted situation constitutes frank permission for such perversion. One might wonder what sort of man Pat's father was to permit this to occur. Although little is known about him other than what has already been mentioned, his own emotional stability should be seriously questioned.

The problem of boys and men with lesser degrees of confusion regarding their sex is more prevalent than the cases of outright transvestitism. Thus, more common than boys and men who actually dress like women are boys and men who are passive and effeminate and even choose occupations usually reserved for women. By this means their confusion regarding masculinity and femininity may be constructively adapted to behavior that society will accept.

Although in transvestitism parental deviations are of extreme degree, the same causative factors, to a lesser degree, are present in the background of most passive boys and men. These factors, so easily and vividly perceived in such a gross deviation as transvestitism, make it easier to recognize the same mechanisms when they are operative to a lesser extent and in a more subtle manner. Some of the closely related factors that are important in accounting for such passivity are these: too close a relationship between mother and son; a mother's fostering femininity in her son; constant exposure to the example of a father's passivity; and the son's fear of a tyrannical father who hostilely competes with him. Among examples of such lesser degrees of passivity in men already mentioned are the fathers of the obese boy (Chap. 4) and the boy with asthma (Chap. 4). In most cases, there is a blending of these factors.

The same kind of parental confusion may also exist in the backgrounds of girls and women as in those of boys and men. The same grotesque deviations and the same differences in degree (but not in type) result. Analogous to passive boys and men, girls and women who are aggressive and masculine often have backgrounds in which there has been an unnaturally close relationship between daughter and father (see Chap. 3). These girls and women have a lurking fear of inferiority to men. They must prove that there is no inferiority by continually competing with men on their own grounds. "Anything you can do, I can do better." It is a protest against men and their presumed superiority. Women with such confusions about masculinity and femininity may tend to dress mannishly; act, walk, and talk like men; compete with men; and even show a preference for occupations usually reserved for men. This behavior should not be confused with a prevalent cultural practice today, although the two can overlap. It is now not unusual to see boys with long, flowing, curly hair; tight-fitting colorful pants, and jewelry, while girls may have a superficially boyish look.

PROMISCUITY: DELORES, THE GIRL WHO LEFT A TRAIL OF BROKEN HEARTS

The telephone rang. "Doctor, can you help my daughter? She's a nymphomaniac. I've known for a long time that she is loose with fellows. I can't stop her. I'm afraid she'll get pregnant and disgrace us all. You must help us. Please let me see you as soon as possible."

[One wonders at the sudden urgency in seeking medical help when the mother has known of her daughter's difficulties for a long time. The mother has been unable to cope with this problem, and her chief concern at the present time seems not to be the possible harm to her daughter but the possible shame to the family, including herself. She pleads,

"You must help us," not "You must help her."]

When Mrs. N. came to the physician's office the next day, she was dressed like a Hollywood starlet, although she was obviously in her late forties. Tinted hair with bangs, generous use of makeup, bright red fingernails, excessive perfume, and shoes in the most exaggerated style could not hide the fact that life had not been kind to her.

"It's Delores, my daughter, Doctor. We're worried she's going to do something foolish. She's boy-crazy, running around wild, going with bad company . . . I don't see how she can be this way . . . my husband and I have always given her everything . . . why should she be interested in boys? We might not have much, Doctor, but we are decent, moral people. She's such a beautiful girl. She has my hair and eyes. I remember my Uncle Bob telling me when Delores was only two, 'All pretty girls get into trouble.' . . . Such a shame!"

It soon became clear that at the root of the daughter's problem there were many parental factors. The consistent pattern of a series of events left little doubt about the causative factors.

"Jack's [the husband's] mother lived with us when Delores was young. Grandma was never married, and Jack never saw his father. I've always felt sorry for that, but you can't blame the child for what his mother does. But I've always wondered if this family weakness might have come out in my own child. Once Delores asked me about her grandfather. I read in a book that a mother should always tell the truth to her children. I told Delores everything I knew; I told her not to ask Daddy about it because it would upset him."

[This mother has a dangerous fear. She is afraid that Delores will follow in the path of her unwed paternal grandmother. Did she help Delores by telling her the whole truth? On the contrary, by telling her daughter about the illegitimacy she cast moral slurs upon the father, thus decreasing his stature in the child's eyes. Even more important, she was telling her daughter what could be and had been done in her own family. She was revealing an alternative to complete morality and thus was leaving a gaping hole in Delores' developing conscience. Illegitimacy because of bad heredity: another convenient scapegoat and, in this case, also permission for future similar acts by the daughter!]

"When Delores was four, I caught her out in the street without any clothes on. I was terribly upset . . . ran out into the street, grabbed her by the arm, and yanked her back into the house. I had told her never to do that. She knew that there are boys and strange men on the street, and little girls should be careful . . . if she did that then, what would she do later? I knew Grandma should never have lived with us."

[Children at that young age take great interest in their bodies and at times innocently remove their clothes in public. This behavior, handled correctly with tact and with knowledge of what it really means, disappears of its own accord with the ongoing development of the child. The child learns from the parent that such things are not done. Delores' mother was terribly upset by such behavior and feared serious consequences (". . . boys and strange men on the street, and little girls should be careful . . . if she did that then, what would she do later?"). In fact, her fears were voiced even before this incident ("I had told her never to do that"). Her specific fear was that Delores would get into the same kind of trouble as her grandmother. Why should a mother who is comfortable in her role as a woman, wife, and mother, and who loves, is loved, and has been loved, have such fears for her four-year-old daughter? May she not be putting ideas into the daughter's head and inoculating the child with her own forbidden desires, which she herself may not dare to express?]

"Delores used to play doctor with a neighbor boy, Johnny, about the same age. She was very good about it . . . played in the house where I could see what was going on. They did it for years . . . a childhood infatuation. However, one time my mother-in-law caught them together; Delores was eight then; she didn't have her periods yet, so there was nothing to worry about. Since then I've always reminded Delores of what she did and what a close call she had. Fortunately, we knew an unmarried girl with a baby; I warned Delores to be careful or she'd end up that way too. My husband says that in many ways Delores is just like me. He keeps reminding me of my past, what I did before I met him . . . I'm sorry I ever told him . . . that's just water under the bridge. I wish he'd shut up. He even brings it up in front of Delores. He knows how it upsets me. I get so angry. . . ."

[The daughter has played doctor in front of the

mother for many years. Is such obvious sexual play between children permissible only because it is done in the house under the mother's watchful eyes? Is not the mother encouraging this situation? Curiosity about their bodies is not unusual in healthy young children. In this particular instance, however, with the values attached to sex by this mother (and daughter), it would seem that such play, permitted only under the mother's eyes and persisting over a long period, had become the means for this mother to derive vicarious enjoyment from the situation. What eight-year-old Delores does is permissible (and encouraged) as long as there is no fear of pregnancy. What a distorted sense of values to instill into a child's developing conscience! This continual harping on pregnancy sounds as though the prevention of illegitimate pregnancy were the sum total of one's moral values! In the mother's mind it is not a question of forbidding promiscuity; it is only a question of not becoming pregnant.

It might be conjectured that the father and the mother are not getting along well together. The father's harping on his wife's past betrays his faulty relationship with her and his thinly disguised contempt and hostility. It not only savagely undermines his wife's self-esteem but, being done in the presence of the child, it destroys the mother in the child's eyes and gives permission for the child to do what the mother has already done. The father blames the mother for her earlier moral laxity, while the mother flaunts the loose morals associated with her husband's origin.

In order to introduce the subject of Mrs. N.'s own life, past and present, as tactfully as possible, the physician asked her what she liked to read. With an embarrassed laugh, Mrs. N. replied, "I wish I were living it and not reading it, Doctor, but since you ask, I mostly read magazines with stories about the private lives of actors and actresses, women in love . . . you know . . . the kind of things we middle-aged women read . . . ever since I was a girl I've read that kind of story. Delores does too. I guess she takes after me . . . I guess you'd say I am oversexed. I suppose I am."

Mrs. N.'s answers to the physician's further specific questioning, however, convinced him that she was, on the contrary, a frigid woman, who had an unsatisfactory physical adjustment in marriage.

[Such women obtain compensatory pleasure for their own (sexual) difficulties through encouraging sexual overtones in the play and the behavior of their children. By the parents' continued interest, permission, and encouragement, such play and behavior emerge as outright sexual promiscuity. Seeing this, the parent obtains fulfillment of his or her own deep desires, although, outwardly, to the world, he (or she) appears to be horrified. All this has been accomplished without either the parent or child realizing that they have an unwittingly engendered complicity in the matter.]

Since the father would not come to be studied separately, the physician had to be satisfied with what information he could obtain from the mother. "Doctor, our house is very small. Our bedroom, Jack's and mine, is separated from Delores' by the bathroom. We keep the doors open all the time. Naturally, we can't have much privacy in such a small house, and it doesn't bother us anyway ... Delores has seen her father taking a shower many times, and it doesn't bother them. As a matter of fact, until she was ten, she always took Sunday morning showers with her father. She was a Daddy's girl ... she never came to my bed. Always wanted to sleep with her Daddy ... go any place he went, and even do exercises with him. He's a 'bug' on physical culture ... thinks a lot of his appearance and figure. They still do it, both in their underwear. You should see them. It's really cute.

"Why do you ask me all these questions, Doctor? What do you want to know? Do you think Jack is the cause of Delores' troubles? Come to think of it, Delores has been asking me why Daddy always has to go into the bathroom when she's bathing. She said, 'He always finds some excuse, like bringing in a fresh cake of soap, clean towels, or just to fix the window.' Is that wrong, Doctor? I wonder. Maybe something is wrong with Jack. . . ."

[Again we note many examples of unhealthy and sexually charged relationships in this family, this time between father and daughter. The mother wonders whether something is wrong with her husband. The unfortunate fact is that all three, father, mother, and daughter, are deeply involved in this unfolding tragedy.]

At the conclusion of the interview, Mrs. N. looked at the doctor and said, "I don't know what all these questions have to do with Delores' looseness with boys. Frankly, I don't see how all this dressing and bathing business can have anything to do with her trouble. All my friends do it. They're all modern . . . none of this mid-Victorian prudishness."

Does the fact that something is widespread necessarily make it healthy? Cancer and heart disease are widespread, for example, but these represent disease and not health. It is agreed that the type of parent-child behavior referred to by Mrs. N. is widespread. But many well-documented studies, in some instances extending over a period of years, have shown that such behavior is entirely unhealthy.

Modern frankness often represents unsatisfied emotional needs, disguised hatreds, glaring conscience defects, denied passions, and perverted sexuality of the parents. All those warped passions and distorted forms of hate seethe malignantly beneath the surface, constantly poisoning the feelings, thoughts, and actions of the unsuspecting parent. The unfortunate parent unwittingly spews these poisons onto his child from earliest infancy. The child cannot escape. The same passions and distorted forms of hate mar the child. This is a tragedy of life. Unless interrupted, it will go on and on, infecting and dooming each successive generation with the poisons of the old. With such destructive causes and effects, how can the "modern frankness" referred to by Mrs. N. be considered healthy regardless of how widespread such behavior may be?

The physician realized that the basic problems were deep below the surface and that neither the father nor the mother was even aware of their existence. Seeing that just touching lightly on these problems aroused much tension in Mrs. N., the physician pushed things no further at this time. He asked Mrs. N. if he could see Delores. The physician was somewhat taken aback to find that Delores was a short, fat girl who took little pride in her personal appearance and who chewed gum incessantly. She wore a plain black dress that, by its tight fit, only emphasized her unattractiveness. The way her lipstick was applied made her mouth seem overlarge and crooked. Poorly applied, heavy layers of powder and rouge could not conceal facial pimples. Delores spoke in a quiet, rather shy monotone. She seemed quite indifferent when describing her many boy friends. She confirmed her promiscuity quietly and without apparent emotion. When asked why she did these things, she answered, "I don't know." Why did she get into such a jam? "I guess I was just born that way." In a dull and lifeless manner, Delores confirmed all that her mother had said. But she was not the beautiful, interesting girl her mother had led the physician to believe. She was only a frightened girl, unhappy and lonely.

By way of summary, it should be stressed that sexual problems in the child are always a reflection of sexual maladjustments in the parents. The sexual symptoms are always related to deep emotional confusions and unresolved hostilities. The seduction of the innocent child, as described in these examples, often assumes tricky and subtle forms. Although the parent is frequently unaware of his highly destructive behavior toward his child, he is responsible for his acts. His answers to the following questions will often determine whether or not his child will develop sexual problems in later life: Do the children sleep apart from their parents? Is privacy in the bedroom really observed? Is the maturing child left to bathe himself? Is wholesome modesty practiced in every home situation?

8

Permission for Violence

GWENDOLYN, THE HATE-FILLED HIPPIE

The nurse handed the doctor a message from a distraught mother: "My daughter Gwendolyn has been with a hippie movement in Greenwich Village and in San Francisco. I am alarmed about her use of drugs. She has tried LSD and everything else. She is at home now, but I don't know if she'll come to your office. She likes to sleep late!"

Gwendolyn arrived for her appointment twenty minutes late. For an 18-year-old her appearance presented many contradictions. She wore no makeup, not even lipstick. Her curly red hair was cut very short, and she wore metal-rimmed, dime-store glasses. Although she was clean and neat, she wore a mini-mini skirt and a long sweater that reached below her hips. Any beauty of face and figure, which might have been considerable, was almost totally obscured.

With an explosion of rapid-fire speech and a highly developed vocabulary that often sank to scatology, she began: "I wanted to commit suicide. What's the use of all this? I wanted to end my misery but not lose all the possibilities of happiness. I wanted to be saved and found; to make my mother squirm and feel guilty."

[Later, when the mother came alone to the physician, he found her to be a serious-faced, middle-aged woman with a trim figure. She wore a gaily colored dress and stylish hat. Her use of cosmetics was discreet but pleasing.]

Gwendolyn continued, "The priest couldn't answer my questions. I was irritated and doubted religion. I became embittered. The taboos were absurd. Therefore I indulged [in sex] at sixteen. I went to a fraternity party with girls who were much older than I. The boys were stultifying. Marriage is a capitalist institution for the propagation of the classes. All money should be abolished. No rent. Profit is corrupt. Competition is the root of all evil. I am aware of the impersonality of the university structure. I've lived in communes, I've begged for a living, I've known many men. I've had gonorrhea. I've sat on stoops in the slums and found a romantic beauty amid all the squalor. I've seen prostitutes fighting for territory. I've seen gangsters and total corruption and graft that both horrified and fascinated me. I've been a go-go girl, and a topless dancer. I've seen everything."

[In her interview the mother emphasized her conservatism, politically and religiously. She described herself as sexually very modest. In her occupation as a hair stylist, she had little opportunity to meet men.

However, she recalled her daughter's frequent arguments with a 20-year-old unmarried baby-sitter, who stayed with the family for 11 months, along with her own illegitimate baby.]

Gwendolyn boasted, "I'd walk into the worst sections of New York at one o'clock in the morning and wind up in unbelievable scrapes. But out of sheer naïveté I escaped. Once I met a group on 'speed' [methedrine] and went up to their apartment. I only owned a pocketbook and the clothes on my back. They took a collection and bought a carton of orange juice. They passed it around. It was germy since we all drank out of the same container. The group left, and I was there all alone for twenty minutes. Then three narcotics detectives arrived. There was all kinds of dope in the house. I was in the perfect scapegoat position. The man who owned the place, a fellow in his twenties, knew one of the detectives from high school days. He said, 'That girl is not an addict or a junkie.' Yet the cops harrassed me. They looked at my arms and my eyes, and I was frightened. After they left, I learned from the young man that they were paid off. The narcotics detectives themselves were addicts. I was appalled.

"Another time, when I was under LSD, I took a shower. My clothes were dirty, so I wrapped myself in the window curtains. I went outside, into the park, and played in the sand. People stared at me."

[Although Gwendolyn had been using LSD and other drugs for a few years, the mother had had to work to support her and her brother. The mother knew nothing about her daughter's drug habits. She described how long she had been a widow and her hardships. In defiance of her mother, Gwendolyn had introduced her brother to marijuana and LSD. The mother later learned indirectly how a high school English teacher had once taken the brother to a coffee shop for "teenage discussions sponsored by the Church," but where in reality he had been introduced to a teenage drug ring.]

Gwendolyn went on: "If I had a grievance I would stab and not polemicize. Violence is more admirable, although more primitive. In a pastoral sense it is much more honest [than a peaceful, due-process-of-law settlement].

"I began to hate my own upbringing—ashamed to be an American—felt guilty of being brought up in this place. Every time I saw a policeman, I'd clench my fist and get a pain in my stomach. Out of guilt I'd side with the underprivileged. I saw groups I disliked as victims of a higher order. I've lived in 'D's' [a well-known politician's] neighborhood one year. He's a white fascist.

"I became involved with an art teacher in school. He was going to introduce me to a famous underground film producer. I was going to write scripts for him. I hate menial labor like waitress work, cashiering, and such. When I arrived at the producer's office I found him on the floor in a pool of blood. He had been shot and I walked in on it."

Gwendolyn's spontaneous talk ranged from the idyllic glories of Communism to the militancy of civil rights, from sex to the unreal world of experimenting with psychedelic drugs. She said little about her family background until she was gently questioned.

[The mother revealed her daughter's affiliation with a Communist-front student organization at college and the sudden change in her thinking. Gwendolyn then began to espouse anarchistic causes, drugs, and extremism in civil rights. She flagrantly exhibited all this before her mother without shame. The mother, whose background and political orientation were entirely opposite, was helpless to cope with her daughter's defiance.]

"My father died of mouth cancer at forty [when Gwendolyn was twelve]—he smoked three packs of cigarettes a day. That's when I started. Mother was a smoker and couldn't object. She gave me my first cigarette. Since then I've lost all control. I want to stop but can't."

[The mother blamed herself for her daughter's smoking. "How could she do any better when I set such an example and when all her friends smoke?" The mother wondered about the effects of so-called advice Gwendolyn had been given during her high school years that marijuana and LSD were essentially quite similar to alcohol and should not be feared. The mother disagreed, and one of her friends, a police narcotics official, agreed with her. It was after this "advice" that Gwendolyn took her brother to a "hippie crash-in" in Greenwich Village for his initiation into LSD rites.]

"My father was conservative, but he had a penchant for glamour. He lived beyond his means— flashy foreign sports cars and imported clothes. He was a book publisher's editor and a complete teeto-taler. He was constantly separating from Mother. She told me that he had received a dishonorable dis-charge from the Navy before he met and married her. There was no hostility between him and me when I was a child. I remember having severe asthma and also blackouts whenever my parents fought.

"Mother is from a rural, pastoral background. She is very vain and won't admit her age. She's a hair-dresser. She drank heavily after Father died. That was the beginning of my contempt for her. She is a malevolent, shriveled-up disappointed woman. She had an incestuous symbiosis with my brother and me because of her disappointment in my father, which was the basis of her concern over us. It was a difficult marriage. She had an exaggerated loyalty to her sis-ters, who were dominant matriarchal types. They helped Mother with money, but Pop went from job to job and didn't make enough money for all he spent. The sisters were all insipid and henpecked their hus-bands."

[The mother denied any personal difficulties with alcohol. Her husband's job instability forced her to go to work after three months of marriage. She had to postpone having a child for five years. She at-tributed this to her husband's unreliableness. "He's been psychotic—diabolical—verbally and physically abusive—has made me black and blue. He wanted a girl and only a girl, but he made no preparations. I had to go out and earn the money and prepare. I remember Gwendolyn saying in kindergarten,

'Daddy will never get to Heaven when he dies.' I said, 'No, he's not really that bad.'"

[Through the years of separation the father never consistently supported the family. The mother lost herself in martyrdom and work. She recalled the many times that Gwendolyn and her brother used to visit the father and said, "The children talked about Tanya. He was living with her. They said she looked like a gypsy. She had black hair and eyes and long fingernails. I later learned that Tanya had a child by him, but I didn't talk to my daughter about that, and I'm sure she never understood. My husband was a very selfish man, the oldest of a large family. He and his oldest sister hated each other. There was always a terrible animosity. His family told me about it. His troubles all began when he quit his studies for the priesthood."]

Gwendolyn: "I was a tomboy in grammar school. I considered myself intellectually superior to all my girl friends. I had no coquetry, no lipstick, no makeup —I belonged to no cliques, nor did I act cute. I was left out and excluded. When I was a little older—after Mother and Father had separated—I had to be Pop's escort. He would take me to fancy meetings. I had no interest in boys my own age. My interests were sublimated in my father. I once met President Kennedy. I attended balls where there were senators and congressmen."

[Apparently the mother, who frequently referred to the poor communication between Gwendolyn and herself, had no knowledge of her daughter's role as an escort to her father's parties.]

Gwendolyn went on: "Mother's violence came out when she was drunk. There were so many episodes that I could relate. Once when I was 14 I was visiting relatives. I was sound asleep when Mother poked me in the side, and I screamed out while still half asleep, 'What the Hell do you want?' She was mortified, but she did nothing until four hours later when we got home. Then she beat me on the top of the head with the steel-tip of her shoe. There was blood all over my face. I ran down the street screaming and crying. Another time she was agitated because of the boys who called me on the phone. She would say I wasn't home. Once, when I asked her about this, she beat me on the top of my head with a cast iron frying pan. I ran out hysterical and bleeding. The police were called. I was rushed to the hospital and sewed up. She was vicious. I got A's and B's, but it did no good. I didn't even have to work for good grades.

"When she was drunk, she used to chase my brother around with a poker from the fireplace. Finally, when he was bigger than she, he'd restrain her and lock her in the closet [Gwendolyn had claustrophobia]. She's great for yelling, screaming, pinching —always hurting us when we were little. Myriad instances of her screaming hatred—her religion— overly so! The worst thing that could happen would be if you missed church [Gwendolyn was contemptuous of religion]. She's bourgeois, conventional, afraid of independent thinking, afraid of me. She accuses me of things and distrusts herself. She was educated in a convent school and is tremendously inhibited."

[The mother did not mention any of this material

despite many opportunities. Gwendolyn was desperately trying to be as unlike her mother as possible—the person she most hated, from whom she had sought love in vain. Although repeatedly given the opening to do so, the mother denied her own drunkenness and violence. Such behavior had further estranged the mother and daughter and blocked any chance of a healthy mother-daughter relationship. The mother expressed great fear over her daughter's being promiscuous, having venereal disease, and becoming pregnant.]

Gwendolyn again: "My brother, who's just turned sixteen, was sent away to relatives. He is more precocious and disturbed than I. The school stifled him and was inferior. There is too much interference from the Board of Education and the police.

"My goal? I don't know what I'll do. I can't fall asleep. I can't shut my mind off. I get headaches all the time. It's like a steel cap jammed on the head. There's tremendous pressure. Now I'm living with a boy in Spanish Harlem. It's therapeutic for me, but I don't know where it's leading. Certainly, marriage is out of the question. I'm too mixed up."

When asked about the connection between some of her fervent beliefs and some of the horrors and hardships of her home life, Gwendolyn slowed in her volubility. When some concern was shown for her, and when, with a friendly smile, she was told that judging from the record, she might have many assets and some ability as a writer, like her father, Gwendolyn smiled for the first time and seemed interested in receiving psychiatric help.

At the conclusion of her interview, the widowed mother wept, clasped her hands to her head, sighed, and pleaded for guidance and help for her daughter and herself.

SHERIDAN, THE BRUTAL MOTORCYCLIST

Seventeen-year-old Sheridan was a leading drag racer. He made the front pages by giving 13 patrol cars a chase through the city streets. Finally, he sideswiped a policeman and sent him to the hospital. As our study of Sheridan proceeded, the connections between his current motorcycle accident, arrest, and past behavior gradually came into focus. He had been arrested previously for disorderly conduct and for speeding. He bragged, "I laugh at everything. I've taken goof balls, cough medicine, and marijuana. I've even had heroin three times."

Later, his father said that Sheridan had been frightened when, within one year, two of his friends had been found dead from the effects of intravenous narcotics. Sheridan also smoked three packs of cigarettes a day.

The parents were aware of their son's flagrant violations of the law, his numerous close calls with death, and the many instances, noted below, of past erratic behavior. However, they did not really believe their son needed help and that was not the reason they had brought him to the physician. They had simply done so on his lawyer's advice. It was thought that a letter from the physician to the court, detailing the patient's problem and stating that the patient would undergo treatment, would take the boy off the hook legally. It was felt that the judge might then suspend sentence.

The threads of Sheridan's problem were not hard to unravel. As a baby he had had temper tantrums. He had always been involved in fights. He would lose his self-control and, when quite young, he had used "just [his] hands" to give neighbor children concussions. Sheridan boasted how he had sent them to the hospital with cuts and broken ribs, because he had been so "tough." Later, he had been in several auto accidents. He had cut classes and had been a truant. He had also been arrested for breaking into junk yards.

This boy's parents had never said, "Halt." They had never recognized that their son's brutality presented any problem whatever for society, for his family, or for himself. They had, in effect, done nothing.

Sheridan was a well-built, athletic-appearing, handsome young man, but his two upper front teeth were missing. He spoke in a matter-of-fact way, frequently smiled, and insolently puffed one cigarette after another. "People tell me to do things, and I walk out. I don't listen to anybody. I got a girl pregnant, and she took off. My parents found out about her. They didn't care. She stayed with me a year ago when my parents went to New Hampshire for two weeks. Again they said nothing." Sheridan showed no concern for the effects of his actions on the girl, his parents, or others. "Nobody ever seems to care about me. Why should I give a damn about them?"

He continued, "I stole things as a child and I think

my parents knew it, but they did nothing. I was babied a lot and always got what I wanted. If I saw a toy and cried, that was it. They got it for me."

[Although he still acted like an immature child, taking what he wanted without regard for the rights of others, he considered himself a "man," equating his physical prowess, his motorcycle, and his sexual escapades with masculinity.]

Sheridan's father glowed with pride, as he said, "I also was wild when young. I had a motorcycle, and my parents told me how crazy I was. One year the motorcycle club that I belonged to had ten members killed in major accidents." Sheridan knew all this and, instead of feeling remorseful, he felt cheated that he had been caught while his father had "gotten away scot free" for the same thing.

The father apologized for his wife, who couldn't come to the interview because she suffered from severe heart trouble. "She's had heart disease since Sheridan was eleven. She's been bedridden and close to death many times. She would usually be nice to the kids, but every so often she'd become a pain in the neck—cry all day and have to go to an institution to get electroshock and run up more bills."

Sheridan added to this portrait of his mother: "She had a bad temper—she'd throw and smash things. She'd drink a pint and a half of brandy a day. Dad would get mad, but he wouldn't do anything. Mother would say she could look into the future and tell what was going on in my mind—ESP. She'd accuse me of doing things whether I did them or not. She was a religious fanatic who went to Mass every day trying to save Father and me."

With virtually no awareness of his real role in life, Sheridan was a born loser. Though not immediately apparent, the mother's emotional shortcomings were more detrimental to her family's well-being than was her severe physical disability.

The father felt boxed in. From his point of view, he had an invalid wife who was totally unable, physically or emotionally, to lay down the law to their son. The father bristled and sighed, "I must do everything. She's too sick to manage the house, cook my meals, or give me clean clothes. She never goes to school conferences. I can't be father and mother too. It's breaking my back. Yet she runs to church every morning."

This family is held together only at the horrible price of Sheridan's playing with death—his own or that of innocents. The tragedy of this marriage lies in the concealed husband-wife hostilities which, instead of being communicated and resolved in a healthy manner, have been displaced by each parent onto the son. The outward signs of this displaced hostility are their parental attitudes toward their son and the parental permission for this boy's destructiveness, which make him anathema to society. Being unaware of these forces, they are unable to break the cycle. They indeed need help.

[In many cases of antisocial behavior, the child's first response on being caught is relief. Not only society but he himself may now be saved from the devil within him, for an outside force has now intervened. His fear of what he might really do is, for the moment, relieved. Paradoxically, many delinquents act out violently so that they will be caught. Such violence is an unconscious plea for help, for someone to call a halt to their actions.]

STACEY, THE VIOLENT FOLK SINGER

Stacey, a 13-year-old tomboy, had thrown a footstool at her brother. The mother also recalled, "Stacey threw a butcher knife at her sister Jean—but not a sharp one!" Once Stacey had bashed Jean with a powder box when Jean refused to lend it to her. The mother became "scared" whenever Stacey threatened to strike her. During a "terrible row" Stacey jumped on her father and scratched his face. She had also thrown a skate at her mother, pushed her, and punched her. The mother resorted to ineffectual tirades.

Stacey's father, without any appreciation of his wife's permissiveness, remembered these incidents: "I imagine that was the end of it. My wife would do nothing. That would be it."

Once, when Stacey splattered water on her mother's face, the mother lashed out, in contrast to her usual blandness. She said, "That really got me angry —my worst scene!"

Stacey had also bitten her father's hand. Once she ripped his pajama sleeve; another time she tore the shirt off his back.

Stacey elaborated on her father's reaction to her threats of violence: "He would change his tone of voice and try to sweet-talk me out of it." Once when she had smashed an electric clock against the wall, her father simply walked over, picked up the clock, and put it on the table. Stacey's acts of violence almost never elicited any parental punishments or firm and unequivocal prohibitions.

The mother further revealed her own involvement when she said, "Stacey tells me, 'Oh, shut up!' And I don't do anything, although in my day, I have been very harsh to her." From this, and other incidents, it was clear that the mother's guilt was related to her previous "harshness" toward Stacey. Such guilt prevented the mother from setting strict limits to Stacey's behavior. If the mother's past attitudes toward her daughter had been healthy, she would not have felt guilty about getting angry at her. And through firm maternal discipline, Stacey would have learned to curb her violence. But the daughter's conscience in respect to hostile aggressive behavior was blocked by the mother's own confused values.

The mother continued, "When Stacey threatened me with a tennis racquet, my instinct was to run away but I didn't. [Stacey was quite aware of her mother's fear.] I just stood there, and then I walked out of the room. Stacey kept saying, 'Sh— man! You can't tell me what to do! I have a good mind to bash you in the face with it!' I just stood there and said nothing. When she threw the knife at Jean, I went to Stacey and asked, 'Did you throw this knife at her?' She said, 'Yes!' I just stood there. I couldn't say anything. What can you say? 'Don't throw a knife at people?' What good will that do? How will that teach her to be a lady?"

After each such "explosion," Stacey would sing

and play her guitar. "She spends much of her time plunking on it . . . she uses it as an escape. It is a good way for her to let off steam."

Again, the mother's total inability to set limits to her daughter's destructive behavior is confused and rationalized with ladylike behavior. Apparently it was not ladylike for a mother to show anger and stop such outbursts. It is unfortunate that the mother's realization of Stacey's need to let off steam (guitar playing) was not matched by a firm resolve that Stacey develop self-restraint.

Insight into Stacey's problems required probing beneath the outward social status of the family. Both parents had an old New England background. The father had inherited the family business, which provided the means of enjoying "the finer things of life." The parents' almost obsequious politeness, observance of stilted etiquette, and measured use of "the King's English" in the physician's office was unmasked by Stacey: "Our home situation stinks! Everybody is fighting and yelling. You should be seeing my parents, not me! Mother gets mad a lot. She comes around and slugs me. My father has ulcers. Although he's a marshmallow to the outside world, he's hotheaded in the family. He takes my arm and yanks me when he gets mad."

RUSSELL, THE BULLY

Russell's mother laughed as she described how another boy had accidentally splashed a few drops of water on her eight-year-old son while both boys were washing their hands after a Saturday morning art class. Russell had angrily picked up a glass bottle of paint and hit the other boy on the head with it, splattering him with paint and glass. "Russell came home and told me about it. I told him how bad it was to have done that. He must have struck the boy with some force. Russell insisted on an early lunch so he could go to the movies that afternoon as he had planned. What could I do? I gave him the early lunch, and he went to the movies."

The physician wondered aloud why she, in effect, had rewarded rather than punished Russell for such dangerous behavior. "I'd just be hurting myself if I'd kept him home. I had a beauty parlor appointment, and I was planning to go out that night. And if I refused, he'd make it miserable for me. My husband came home that noon. The other boy's father had already come to my husband's office to complain about Russell. My husband almost never comes home for lunch on Saturday. He spoke firmly to Russell and spanked him hard. Then Russell went about his business laughing and playing as if nothing had happened, and then, of course, he went to the movies."

Russell, a husky, well-built boy, had been recently diagnosed by a neurologist as having "minimal nonmotor brain damage." The diagnosis was based on a history of "mixed dominance," evidences of "hyperkinetic behavioral syndrome" (characterized by hyperactivity, short attention span, low frustration threshold, impulsivity, distractability, and "aggressiveness"), and the findings, on examination, of "prominent perceptual and cerebellar deficits." The electroencephalographic tracing revealed minimal abnormalities. This boy's behavior was so disturbed during an IQ test that the psychologist felt his data insufficient for a valid appraisal. He wondered whether this boy's poor school performance was due to other factors than the lack of basic intelligence. He was aware that the IQ test alone is not a good measure of a child's social adjustability.

The mother reported that the developmental milestones had been acquired at the "normal" times. The parents had been advised to place Russell in a special class for neurologically impaired children of near-normal intelligence. But at their insistence he had been placed in a regular second grade and arrangements were made for supplementary tutoring.

As the specific details of Russell's relationship with his mother were carefully reviewed with her, her initial statement that she had been "consistent and firm" in her management of her son had to be rejected.

She smiled and laughed frequently as she talked. "Everything was perfect as long as I had complete control. He started to assert himself at two years of age. That was the end of my happy days. Then we knew this was going to be a wild child. He was very aggressive in all his actions and movements. If there was a playpen, he'd climb out. If there was a fence, he'd climb over. [The physician interjected a question.] What did I do? I just accepted it. I certainly did not throw him back in. I certainly did not hinder his development. After all, that's what you read in all the books on child development. The child must always be allowed to express himself. I just made sure he didn't hurt himself."

A young child may, by chance, do something naughty. Whether he repeats such behavior will be determined, to a large extent, by the reactions of his parents. The blithe statement that parents should not hinder a child's development can become a rationalization for continued antisocial behavior. It is important that the child does not hurt himself; it is just as important that the parents teach him to respect the rights of others and to obey the rules of society.

The mother continued, "Nothing serious happened till the time we discovered he had learning handicaps. We have watched him to be sure he wouldn't be murdered, since he can't get along with other children. [Again, she showed little concern for the safety of others.] He had no fear and would climb the highest tree. Outside of this, we've had no problem. But we had to watch him . . . he's very aggressive. He bullied the other children so much that the mothers refused to let their children play with him. [Russell's mother laughed.] He received a 'social promotion.' The teacher said that if she kept him back in the first grade, he'd be too big for the other children. He'd hurt or murder them. He was big physically, but he had not done his first grade work . . . He's argumentative. He fights you on every single thing. Anything you want him to do, he does the opposite . . ."

Russell disobeyed his parents and was spiteful to them. He would not listen to reason, and he delighted in finding ways to provoke them. For example, he would try to pull the tablecloth off the kitchen table "just to get [his mother] angry"; he would go into the den with food even though such behavior was forbidden; he would hang out the window of an upstairs room although he well knew that he was never to do so; he had marked up the walls in his room; and he had repeatedly set fires. Interestingly, the father tried to deny that Russell had actually started these fires.

The mother smiled, "It's a nightmare. I've had it. We don't know what to do, where to turn . . ."

"Last Sunday morning he wanted butter on his bread. I was busy, but gave it to him. Then he insisted on cream cheese. I was too busy. He insisted, so it was easier to give in to him. As he left, he laughed, 'Huh, I get everybody to do everything I want all the time!'" This mother recognized how her son irritated her—and the boy knew it too. The tragic effects on her always "giving in" never strengthened the bonds of affection between them. Hostility and violence were fused. They had become a way of life for Russell.

The above will suffice to show that this represented the mother's usual response to her son's self-centered, antisocial actions since his earliest childhood. Russell's destructive behavior, which could be treated, was more incapacitating to him as a social creature than was his neurological impairment.

To evaluate a relationship between minor degrees of "brain damage" and various behavioral disturbances can be difficult. It is known, for example, that electrical stimulation of some specific parts of the brain of epileptic patients with attacks of rage can provoke similar episodic violent behavior. It can be seen how there are various causes of violent behavior and that this is a very important question to resolve, and a promising area for research. It is evident that a study of the mind-brain relationship should also include a careful investigation of the child's emotional life.

There is much that the parent can do for such a child. By understanding his child's illness and the role of his own emotions, the parent can learn to say "no," to be firm when it is called for, and to use punishment judiciously. Such a parent, although confronted with some unique mind-brain features related to his child's violence, will still have to face up to the responsibility of setting healthy limits to destructive behavior.

All these cases, typical of many more, delineate defects in parent-child relationships that have been going on over a long period of time. The events recorded are warnings, all pertaining to the final perils of violence. We find the same tragic similarities: unresolved parent-child tensions, unacceptable conduct, permissiveness, and surcease through destructiveness.

9

●━●━●━●━●━●━●━●━●━●━●━●━●━●━●━●━●━●

Tensions Related to Surgery and to Handicaps

In the past few decades medicine and its many allied fields have been responsible for reducing the dangers of surgery. As a result, surgical procedures that were dangerous or that could not even have been considered a few decades ago are now commonplace in most large hospitals. This newer knowledge has made possible a hospitalization experience during which more can be done for the patient with greater safety and with milder and shorter emotional upheavals.

The technical skill of the surgeon is frequently extolled, but too often it is forgotten that it is not the surgeon who is heroic but rather the child (or the adult patient) who must undergo the surgery.

A child does not know whether an operation is a serious one or a simple one. Nor does he care. To him the whole situation is frightening. Since most operations that children undergo are not to relieve pain, the child often cannot even understand the reason for the surgery. In this category are included tonsillectomies, circumcisions, and operations on the eyes, the bones, or the joints to correct deformities with which a child may be born.

Suddenly, with little apparent reason, the child is whisked from his home into an entirely new world. He finds himself in a strange room or in a children's ward filled with noisy, crying children, many as fearful as he is. He sees children swathed in bandages, encased in plaster casts, or lying in oxygen tents. He sees other children motionless on their backs, with large tubes coming out of their noses, mouths, or bodies and attached to complicated, noisy, gurgling machines that suck out blood and fluid from the body. He sees other children being stuck with needles to take blood out of the body while adults hold the screaming child still. Other children, bound down so that they cannot move, have needles placed in their arms or legs that are attached to long tubes which lead to bottles of blood or fluids hung high above the bed. He sees white-uniformed nurses give injections to frightened, sobbing children. He sees men in white, with caps and masks hiding all but their eyes, wheeling giant stretchers on which are children who breathe noisily but lie very still. Curious new odors of antiseptics, ether, bedpans, and draining body fluids pervade the air.

But this is the children's wing of the hospital. In spite of all their new and frightening experiences, children will be children. They must explore, play, laugh, and get into mischief. Happiness, fear, curiosity, and suffering are all intermingled. Whether the child is in a private room, a semiprivate room, or an open ward, he is interested in and aware of what goes on about him.

One fact is all-important: the child has been separated from his parents and abruptly transferred from the shelter of his home to the children's wing of the hospital. He may adjust readily to the new situation. If able, he may soon be playing merrily with the others. On the other hand, his initial loneliness and fear may increase, and no amount of consoling by the nurses and the other children can help. Such a child demonstrates the same background of helpless dependency already seen in the school phobia (see Chap. 4). Even though the physician and the parents discuss the situation with the child before hospitalization, a child with excessive fear of separation from parents will usually not benefit from such discussion to the same degree as the healthy child. Such a child adapts himself less readily and less completely to the new situation.

How should the child be told of the surgery that is planned? And when should he be told? The answers depend largely on the age of the child. A young child, up to three or four years of age, has an inadequate and limited concept of time, past or future. A trip to the zoo that he took a month previously may seem to him to have occurred "yesterday." For the child, the distant future usually has no meaning; he thinks in terms of the immediate future, of hours or days. "I want what I want when I want it." He cannot keep his past and future tenses straight when he talks; his speech is usually in the present tense. He understands only the here and now.

Should the physician decide that emergency surgery is necessary, the child should be told at once. The feelings and the respect that the parents have for the physician as a healer are communicated to the child. The physician's kind and firm attitude goes a long way toward ensuring an emotionally smooth hospitalization, provided that the parents uphold him throughout. But if the parents show exaggerated concern or agitation, the child will naturally also become extremely fearful. This in turn hinders the doctors and the nurses in their care of the child.

If surgery is not to be done for some time, the physician and the parents need not discuss the situation with the child at the first visit unless he is old enough to comprehend the time element. This would apply, for example, to an operation for an uncomplicated rupture, which is certainly not an emergency. The planned surgery should not be discussed with the child until the appropriate time. This means a matter of days, not weeks or months. Of course, an older child should be prepared earlier.

If the child wishes to talk about the expected surgery, it is highly beneficial that he do so. Young children have many ideas, right, wrong, real, make-believe, and exaggerated, about what surgery will entail. This may be more evident in their play and in dreams than in anything they actually say. It is important, therefore to correct any misconceptions that the child may have picked up from his playmates—and, all too frequently, from his parents. This can be done by giving appropriate, simple information, emphasizing the good and not the frightening. It is better that such information be given in answer to the child's specific questions. The attentive parent will immediately understand what the child is trying to say.

Often the fear of surgery is so overwhelming that the child will not dare talk about it or ask about it directly. But the parents should know their child well enough to recognize any hints, indirect questions, or veiled fears, but they should not harp on the minute details of the surgery, for this does not help the child. In fact, it has nothing to do with the child's needs, but frequently is only an expression of the parents' own confusion, fear, and need to talk about the surgery. Under the guise of modern frankness and the desire to make things clear to the child, such ill-considered emphasis becomes another way by which the parents communicate their confusions and fears to the child.

What the physician and the parents tell the child should be honest and in a language the child can easily understand. Long, detailed explanations are not needed. It is not a question of "We will cut here" or "We will cut this out or that," and so on. Emphasize, rather, in general terms, the constructive and the positive: "We will fix it"; "You will be able to play with your friends again"; "We will make it better"; "The pain will go away." The child should be told honestly, however, that following the operation there will be some pain, but that after a short time it will go away.

Shortly after his admission to the hospital, the child will, as a matter of routine, have blood tests done which will require his being stuck with a needle. Often he will receive injections of various medicines, or he may receive an intravenous injection. If a child is to have a dressing or a plaster cast applied to some part of his body during surgery, he should be told of this in advance. He should be reassured that the dressing or the cast is another part of the treatment that is necessary to make him better. For example, it is a terrifying experience for a child to awaken from eye surgery and find a dressing over his eyes so that he cannot see. If he has not been prepared for this, it will be extremely difficult to allay his fright.

Equally important in preparing a child for surgery is the preparation of the child for anesthesia. He should be told that before the operation he will be given medicine to make him sleep so that he will feel no pain during the surgery. This medicine, he should be told, will make him sleep until the operation is finished. Shortly before surgery, the physician who will give the anesthesia should tell the child, in terms that he can understand, the method by which he will be put to sleep. This not only gives the child information which he needs to allay his fears but also introduces him to the physician who will anesthetize him. In this way, at the time of anesthesia, the child will not suddenly be faced with a stranger whom he may fear and mistrust.

To lie to the child is misguided kindness, plain stupidity, deceit, and even brutality. For example, he may be told that he is going to the store for a new pair of shoes; then he finds himself in the hospital getting prepared for surgery or in the doctor's office getting a "shot." Similarly, telling a child that there will be no pain in anticipated painful surgery, painful change of dressings, or getting a shot is unrealistic, stupid, and brutal.

When the child goes to the hospital, he may well be leaving his home or his parents for the first time. It is helpful to give him something to bridge the gap, a reminder of home and parents. Most young children have a favorite toy or a tattered blanket to which they are attached and with which they go to bed every night. Why should not the child take this toy or blanket with him to the hospital? In any event, the parents owe it to their child to accompany him to the ward or the room in which he will be and to introduce him to the doctors and the nurses who will be with him. The child is not just a tonsil or an appendix to be removed; he is a complete individual, however tiny, helpless, and inarticulate he may be. He has his own feelings and rights that grown-ups should respect.

The child will receive with indignation any violation of these feelings and rights, no matter how sympathetically and justifiably presented. Emotionally, the child will view any injection, insertion of a tube into his mouth or rectum, or any operation as an assault on his body. Something painful is being done to him with little or no consideration for his feelings. He will usually feel like this whether he is the "good patient" who is quiet and almost obsequiously cooperative or the noisy protesting child who fusses constantly.

Just because the child is a "good patient"—quiet, uncomplaining, and obedient—does not mean that he is escaping the emotional stresses of the situation. Often this only means that he is afraid to express himself. He is too aware of his helplessness. But the tensions are there and build up even more because he is unable to give vent to his feelings. An explosion, when it does occur, may be greater and more startling because of its unexpectedness. The proud parental statement, "He took it like a man!" may mean not that the child was brave but that the observer was stupid and insensitive to the child's feelings and needs.

If a teddy bear or a blanket means so much to a child that it is almost a part of him, other things that belong to him are equally important. Such items as a wristwatch, a pocketbook, a cowboy belt, or eyeglasses are so closely associated with the child, both in the parent's mind and in the child's mind, that they are a part of him. The child thinks of these things as not only belonging to his own person and body, but he has the same kind of affection for them that grown-ups might have for one another.

This is exactly the same feeling that the child has for his own body and its parts, his arms and legs and general appearance. In a word, he has highly personal and charged feelings for each part of his body and all the parts together—his total image. He takes these feelings for granted; he is not even aware of them. This applies as strongly for body characteristics that may be attractive as for those that may be ugly but which the child has learned to accept as an integral part of himself. For example, a child looks upon a birthmark as a part of himself, no matter how large and unsightly it is or how much it sets him apart from others. He will have mixed feelings about such an unsightly part of his body. On the one hand, the birthmark is his, to be cherished as a badge of his individuality; on the other hand, it is an unsightly blemish at which people may stare; it may even repulse some. These same feelings apply to visible scars, burns, and other longstanding acquired blemishes and disabilities that the child has learned to accept as a part of him.

The child cherishes as old intimate friends his body and all its parts, inside and outside, in health and disease. These feelings later develop into the pride that men or women take in their personal appearance, neatness, and grooming. In some individuals these normal feelings become exaggerated, and personal appearance becomes an end in itself. These people are obviously vain; they take extreme interest in every change in their bodies. They are the devotees of physical culture.

For example, a 13-year-old girl reported, "Mother is so vain that she won't wear clear eyeglasses, but she will wear prescription sun glasses. Dad and I ask her who she's fooling when she wears them so much, even in the house."

Any surgery or injury that alters the physical appearance and the function of the body or any of its parts, particularly if visible, will naturally upset the child. How well the child adjusts to these changes depends on how well he is managed by the grown-ups before, during, and after the operation or the treatment and on the importance that the child and his parents attach to the changed part.

A ten-year-old boy had suffered a severe fracture of the leg in a skiing accident and was placed in a cast from the mid-thigh to the toes. Physically, the boy was doing well. However, when it was time to teach him to use crutches so that he could return home from the hospital, he could not cooperate. He cried, from much more pain than was expected, and was privately considered a "whiner" by the nurses. Study of the problem revealed that his first attempts at walking with crutches were in the same hospital area (physical therapy) with a middle-aged woman whose leg had been amputated. From his limited observation and from overhearing the nurses, the lad had erroneously concluded that were he to bear weight on his cast-encased leg, it would "break off" completely, and he also would be an amputee. When these understandable confusions were clarified, the boy's fears (and pain) subsided, and he promptly learned to walk with crutches.

Some questions that need to be answered include: was the child tricked or told lies when he was taken to the hospital? Have the parents previously threatened the child with taking him to the physician, the dentist, or the hospital if he was not good? Does the mother fear some dire effects from surgery despite the physician's reassurances, fears that the child readily senses? Do the parents lack confidence in the physician, another feeling the child readily perceives? Have X-ray pictures, enemas, changes of dressings, and other procedures been done in the hospital without proper regard for the child's feelings?

Hospitalization for the child, as already mentioned, frequently represents his first separation from home and parents. Certainly it is one of the few times when he is placed with complete strangers. If at the time of separation there is the same mutually unbearable anxiety between parent and child that is seen in school phobias (and for the same basic reasons; see Chap. 4), such tension is likely to get out of control and become more destructive to the child than anything in the current situation. The hospital and everything connected with it becomes the scapegoat for the parents' and the child's own deep-rooted, unresolved tensions.

A common example is the mother who fears all sorts of complications and insists that she or her husband stay with the child on a day-and-night vigil. Such parents ask countless and repeated questions about the dangers of putting the child to sleep, of serious reactions to drugs and blood transfusions, of the child's chances of surviving the operation, and of the possibility of complications, mutilations, and unsightly scars. The physician's reassurances and explanations seem to fall on deaf ears.

But even more significant than the spoken fears of the parent are the underlying parental feelings that the child senses. This is clearly shown by the subsidence of the electric atmosphere in the room and the change in the child's attitude as soon as the mother leaves.

Despite the technical success of the operation and

the treatment, such parents, in the presence of the operated child and of other children, dwell at great length on the narrow escape from death that the child had, his profuse bleeding during surgery, exactly what and how much was removed, together with detailed and frightening descriptions of each phase of the treatment before and after surgery.

For reasons to be found in the family situation, the child and parents have had a great emotional upheaval. This and later emotional disturbances, to be expected in such a situation, are blamed on the surgery. Such disturbances may be precipitated by surgery, but even if the surgery were not performed another precipitating event would have to be found.

Some progressive hospitals offer "rooming in" facilities, which make it possible for a parent to sleep in the same room with the child. This is an excellent practice. Despite soaring hospital costs and limited space, it is hoped that the benefits of such facilities may increasingly be offered.

INFLUENCE OF FIRST-ROMANCE STAGE ON SURGERY

During the first-romance stage, as we have seen, the child becomes aware of the physical differences between boys and girls and men and women. Parents who watch and listen to their children know that boys and girls at this stage of development attach great importance to these differences. However, the girl may wonder *why* she is different. She may wonder whether she was made like a boy originally and something was done to her to change her. Many little girls even wish that they were like boys. In fact, some girls, because of parental confusion in this matter, never grow out of this wish and grow up to be tomboys, competing with boys at play and, later in life, with men at work (see p. 217).

Because of the significance that the child attaches to sex characteristics during the first-romance stage, he becomes especially concerned at this age with any procedure, surgical or otherwise, directed to the genitals or any other part of the body that he may unwittingly associate with this region. Everyday examples are dental work and haircuts. Equally important, if less frequent, are procedures done on the nose, the throat, and the mouth. At this age, circumcision of the boy or catheterization (insertion of a tube into the bladder) of either the boy or the girl can be especially fearsome. If such a procedure can be deferred until a later stage of development, it is advisable to do so. If it must be done during this stage, even greater emotional preparation and precautions are necessary.

A six-year-old boy who had just had surgery for a rupture in the groin proudly showed the scar to the pediatrician and confidently said, "You know, the doctor who did this must be a very good doctor. He had to be careful. If he cut too far, he could have cut this off." The boy pointed to his penis.

Boys and girls also attach special significance to particular parts of their bodies, for reasons learned from their parents. The violinist's son will be extra careful of his hands. The hairdresser's daughter is more concerned about her hair than is the case with other children. The pretty little girl, praised for her beauty by proud parents, doting relatives, and even strangers, will be very disturbed by anything that may disfigure her face. The swimming champion's son will be greatly concerned about the muscles of his arms and legs. In all such situations an injury or operation to that part of the body that has special significance to the child (and his parents) will be more upsetting emotionally than an operation or injury to another part of the body.

Parental overconcern for specific parts of the child's body is also significant. Common examples are the mother with deeply pitted facial scars from acne who is panicked by a minor pimple on her daughter's cheek, or the father with a limp from childhood polio who is terrified on discovering that his son's foot turns in slightly.

In discussing the effects of surgery, injury, and hospitalization (removal from home and parents) on the child during the first-romance stage, we must consider another important factor. During this stage, as we have seen, the boy competes with his father for his mother's affection while the girl competes with her mother for her father's affection. At times, the boy has the half-formed desire to have his mother to himself while the girl has similar feelings toward her father. But the feelings are mixed, as in many other situations where the emotions are involved. The child cannot have his cake and eat it too. Both the boy and the girl realize that these wishes of getting rid of the parent of the same sex are rather farfetched and impractical. The boy realizes that he needs his father, while the girl feels the same way toward her mother. In addition to this obvious dependency, the boy, as noted earlier, wants to grow up to be like his father, while the girl wants to be like her mother. Dependency on and desire to imitate the parent of the same sex alternate with hostile feelings toward this parent. In the emotionally healthy child, this inner contest is decided in favor of peace with the parent of the same sex. The boy loves and admires his father and desires to imitate him—"Like father, like son." The contest is resolved similarly for the girl. At this point, each is ready to progress beyond the first-romance stage.

A residue of the former conflict remains however. From time to time, differences will arise between the father and son and between the mother and daughter. The never-quite-extinguished embers of the old rivalry temporarily burst into flames again. In a healthy situation, these differences will be solved; there will be peace again.

These feelings of guilt bring with them the fear, the expectation, and sometimes even the desire for punishment to assuage the guilt. This is no less true of the child than it is of the adult. Such a child fears, expects, and sometimes may even desire punishment. Suppose he is suddenly faced with surgery, injury, or separation from his parents (hospitalization). He readily, although mistakenly, concludes that this is his punishment for his angry rivalry with the parent of the same sex. In addition to his natural or exaggerated angry rivalry and guilt, the child is angry with his parents for permitting the surgery and the separation from home.

Four-year-old Louise has just returned home from the hospital following removal of her appendix. Louise is eager to show everybody her tummy. In her play she is the nurse, and all her dolls have become patients with "sore tummies." She reveals the feelings that she must have had in the hospital by reenacting her own hospitalization. She forcefully slaps the doll down, gives it an injection with a pencil, and then gives three or four more injections. "There, now, you be quiet and be good, or I'll give you more injections. Stop crying for Mommy; I'm here. I'm a nurse, and I'll make you feel better." Louise then cuddles the doll in her arms.

Despite the excellent management of Louise by her parents, the physicians, and the nurses in this emergency, Louise has had an upsetting experience. The injections hurt, her abdomen was sore, and she missed her parents. Naturally, Louise did not like the injections. No matter how skillfully given and how kind the nurse, a "shot" is a "shot," and it hurts. Louise had understandably mixed feelings about the nurses. To her they seemed mean and they caused pain; but they were also kind and friendly when they fed her, rubbed her back, bathed her, and sympathetically cared for her many other needs. Louise revealed her mixed feelings when she handled her doll roughly and gave it repeated shots and when she said, as the nurse, "Stop crying for Mommy. I'm here. I'll make you better," and then cuddled her "patient." In playing with the doll, Louise reenacted her own operation and her upsetting emotional experience. In this way she got rid of much of the emotional tension associated with the surgery.

Louise's mother chuckled as she told the physician, "Louise did beautifully. Her only trouble was the first two nights after she came home from the hospital. She had nightmares both times. She dreamed of being chased by a big black wolf with very sharp teeth. But she's all over it now . . . and she has her heart set on becoming a children's nurse."

Here is more proof that hospitalization and surgery were upsetting: Louise is pursued by a wolf, who in the young child's mind is mean and terribly frightening. For example, we need only recall such children's stories as "Little Red Riding Hood" and "The Three Little Pigs and the Big Bad Wolf." The wolf had sharp teeth with which to cut Louise—as the surgeon had done. Her dreams are an expression of the fears she had. And by being able to express fears, even in dreams, one may relieve, at least in part, the tension engendered by these fears. The recurrent nightmares—as well as Louise's play with her dolls —acted as an escape valve for the tension built up by her recent experiences in the hospital. The triumph of good over bad in Louise's mixed feelings about the nurses is revealed by her desire to become a nurse herself.

We cannot emphasize too strongly that all adults concerned with the care of the child (parents, nurses, laboratory and X-ray technicians, and each physician on the medical team) should deal with the child with sincerity, kindness, and understanding.

When the child goes to the dentist, both the parent and the dentist need skill in handling the child's emotions. Here is a situation where the child must hold his mouth open while fully aware of what is happening. Nowhere is the child's cooperation and confidence more important. The fact that dentists can do their work under such trying circumstances shows their great skill and success in dealing with children's everyday fears.

EMOTIONAL PROBLEMS OF THE HANDICAPPED CHILD

The handicapped child sees himself as having certain differences from other children. These differences are an integral part of him. In his mind's eye his deformity or internal handicap is as much a part of him as the presence of two legs is to another child. It is difficult for the child with the weak left arm to think of himself as not having this disability as it is for the nondisabled child to think of himself as not having two good arms. Every reader will immediately recognize this basic principle in the grown-up world when he remembers how different Grandmother looked with her new eyeglasses or the new false teeth. Grandmother had learned to think of herself and see herself as she had been before. She had to adjust to her new appearance. At first she not only looked different to herself and to others but she also felt different. Part of her changed feelings were in response to the changed reactions that others may have had toward her. Similarly, the child sees himself as having a certain makeup, whether he has any disability or not, whether his deformities have been present from birth or acquired, and whether they alter his appearance externally or are internal and alter only his life habits.

Defects that alter the external appearance of the child have a great influence on his emotional life. Such defects also greatly influence the emotions of the parents. Frequently, this initial response by the parents and their resulting attitudes determine in great measure how well the child adjusts to his handicap. When a new and disturbing factor has been introduced into the family setting, not only the child but also his parents and the other children cannot help being affected. Following such a severe blow to their feelings, the parents and the other children need as much understanding and emotional support as does the child who is sick. Time spent with these distraught and frightened parents, recognizing their feelings as human beings, will help soften the blow and pave the way for a realistic and healthy adjustment to the handicap. In this way both the handicapped child and his family will be better prepared for the vicissitudes that lie ahead.

The reaction of the child to his own body is influenced in large measure by the reaction of society, his family, and his friends to his defect. A noticeable defect may seriously impair function and handicap the child physically and yet not leave him emotionally crippled. On the other hand, a child with a radical alteration in his physical appearance may have

little change in function (the parts work as well as
ever), but he may be seriously crippled emotionally.
For example, with the increased attention given in
recent years to the problem of poliomyelitis, the public in general has learned to think of polio victims as
having a disability that is unfortunately disabling
but nevertheless common and permits them to function in our society in spite of their impaired ability
to use their arms or legs as other people do. For example, their adjustment to society is made easier by
the more lenient and understanding attitudes of
their parents and the public at large. To show how
important the feelings of others are in determining
a patient's emotional adjustment, consider the case
of the child who has received a severe burn of the
face following a home accident. Unfortunately, such
a tragic accident may cause horrible scars and disfi-
gurement of his face. The child has no eyebrows; the
mouth is a thin slit; there is no nose in the usual
sense—only a hole for each nostril; the skin is a
twisted, distorted mass of white scar tissue; only the
eyes seem to be alive in the masklike, immobile, distorted face. But this is the full extent of the child's
physical handicap. His brain can function as before;
he can walk, run, grasp, and lift as before. He can
bite, chew, and swallow food as others can. But he is
an emotional cripple; he must have much medical
help (psychiatric treatment as well as plastic surgery). Society is repulsed; he in turn shuns society
because he is ashamed. If there have been emotional
disturbances in the child-parent relationship, the
child's problems become more difficult. The disabil-

ity activates any emotional disturbances that previously had only simmered beneath the surface. The parents' ability to manage the situation may be made more difficult by their memory of the circumstances surrounding the accident.

Other deformities, with varying degrees of accompanying disability and problems peculiar to the deformity and to the circumstances surrounding it, are cerebral palsy, birthmarks, amputations, clubbed foot, deafness, blindness, harelip, cleft palate, crooked teeth, chronic eczema, deformities resulting from broken bones, brain injuries following accidents, and permanent disabilities resulting from any injuries. Occasionally, permanent or temporary deformities and disabilities will result from surgery necessary to save life.

Up to this point, the emotional effects of obviously visible physical deformities have been discussed. There are many diseases occurring deep within the body with few if any obvious visible deformities, but with marked effects on the child's ability to adjust to life, physically and emotionally. For example, the patient with diabetes has a disease that is difficult even for a physician to detect without a complete examination and laboratory studies. Such a patient appears to be normal only because of diet and daily injections of insulin. By the regimen of careful dieting, daily preparation of sterile syringes and needles, daily self-injection of insulin, routine and frequent examinations of urine, and regular visits to the physician, such a person is repeatedly reminded that he is different from other people. He has been taught that the specters of insulin reaction (from too much insulin relative to diet and exercise) and diabetic coma (from too little insulin relative to diet and exercise) hang over him. He further knows that he must take extraordinary precautions to prevent and treat infections and to care for cuts and bruises no matter how trivial. He knows from long experience that infections can run rampant, wounds may heal slowly, and, in the presence of infections, the diabetes may go completely out of control and require hospitalization. This patient has learned to live with these disabilities. They are as much a part of him as the color of his hair and the shape of his nose. One may not think that the color of one's hair or the shape of one's nose is the most attractive, but they are one's own. They must be accepted for what they are.

Other diseases within the body that chiefly affect function rather than external appearance are epilepsy, tuberculosis, congenital heart disease, rheumatic heart disease, some thyroid diseases, some blood diseases, some results of brain fever, and some chronic intestinal, kidney, and liver diseases. From his own life experiences a patient with any of these diseases knows that he cannot respond to the problems of everyday living as others do. Such children are forever having to answer embarrassing questions about the reasons for their inability to do one thing or another. The classmates of the child with congenital heart disease know only that Sally looks no different from them; yet she does not go to gym class. Willie at eight years of age looks the picture of health; he "daydreams" a lot in school; He has one form of epilepsy. John is rather thin, but how many other 11-year-old boys are thin? John tires very easily and cannot keep up with the others. His parents discourage too violent play, because he has a long-standing kidney disease.

In each of these last examples the child does not appear to be different from other children. Yet he is sick with a disease that imposes severe limitations upon his activity. If in the excitement of play, work, or anger, he were to violate these limitations, his body might quickly make him aware of his transgression and rebel. Unlike the children with obvious visible deformities, who are conscious of and dependent upon the reactions of other people in general, these children, without obvious visible deformities, are much more dependent upon the fine shades of parent-child relationships and the often subtle attitudes of their parents to their disease.

Thus, children with concealed defects are particularly vulnerable to a disturbed relationship with their parents. The child's disability becomes a convenient point around which the underlying emotional tensions of the parent and the child can come to the surface. For example, at one extreme is the over-solicitous parent who insists on marked curtailment of the child's activities when such curtailment is not warranted by the degree of the child's disability. Such a child believes that he is far more crippled than he really is. At the other extreme is the overindulgent parent who permits activities of a dangerous degree not warranted by the child's disability. Neither the oversolicitous nor the overindulgent parent is acting appropriately. These parents act as they do because of basic unresolved emotional problems in themselves of which they are not aware. And, the unfortunate child's disability can become the escape hatch through which these parental feelings bubble to the surface.

JOHNNY—HANDICAPPED BY A MOTHER'S HIDDEN HOSTILITY

Johnny O. is nine years old and has epilepsy. His attacks occur only once or twice a year since the physician prescribed certain medicines years ago. But Johnny's mother, Mrs. O., is oversolicitous. He cannot play with other boys without her repeated advice to take it easy and without her repeated admonitions to go into the house and rest. At the first sneeze she puts Johnny to bed, and calls the doctor. After the doctor has examined Johnny and found nothing wrong ("He just happened to sneeze"), the mother still feels that she must keep him in bed for 24 hours and insist on glass after glass of hot lemonade. Each time Johnny sniffles, his mother is terrified: what will it do to the epilepsy? Each time the physician sees Johnny, she asks the same questions: Can the epilepsy lead to mental deficiency? Is there any sign of this in Johnny? Although the physician has told her repeatedly and emphatically that there is no evidence at all of this condition in Johnny, nor is there any reason to fear that this may occur in

Johnny's case, she remains convinced that Johnny will become mentally defective. She has heard stories, and she knows.

Because of frequent absence from classes resulting from his mother's overwhelming fear, Johnny has twice failed to be promoted in school. This has only proved to the mother that she is right, that Johnny, despite the doctor's denials, is really not bright. She goes back and forth with her son to school. Indeed, he cannot go anywhere without her tagging along. "Poor Johnny! He must suffer so! Why must he be punished this way?"

The drug treatment of Johnny's epileptic attacks has been highly successful, but Johnny has a greater, more incapacitating problem. He cannot resist the constant bombardment of his mother's fears and overprotectiveness. Johnny mirrors his mother's sick feelings and fears. Like his mother, he too is convinced that he has a shameful stigma, that he is completely different from other children, that he cannot enjoy life, and that eventually something terrible is going to happen to him. In a way, and understandably, Johnny is angry at the world and its people because this has happened to him. " Why me, and not the others?" Knowing nothing else, Johnny has no choice. He can only accept the role that his mother presents to him. She is forever keeping him young. He awaits the future with dread.

For reasons described previously, Mrs. O., Johnny's mother, had a totally unhealthy adjustment to her father and to men in general, including her husband and son. Laughingly Mrs. O. described her father as "a boarder in the house." She said he was aloof and distant. He never showed any warmth or feeling and seldom spoke to her mother or to her. He never remembered their birthdays or bought them presents. Mrs. O.'s relationship with her mother was similarly lacking in any true warmth. Late in her 'teens Mrs. O. vowed that she would marry a man who would love her and be kind to her, and she also vowed that she would love and be kind to her own children.

Never having received love, Mrs. O., in a tragedy often repeated in life, suffered severe impairment in her ability to give love. Her search for the love that she missed in childhood failed—as it so often does in such circumstances. Her concept of love was distorted by her early unhealthy relationship with her parents. She could be attracted only to someone with a similarly distorted concept. Her relationship with her own husband and son was doomed to be an outgrowth of her early unhealthy relationship with her father. She failed to find what she had missed as a child. She married a man 20 years older than herself who died shortly after Johnny's birth. When Johnny was born, Mrs. O. dedicated herself to her son. Here would be her chance to shower someone close to her with all the love and kindness that she never had a chance to show. She remembered her maiden aunt's oft-repeated advice, "All she needs is to get married and have children." The tragedy is that Mrs. O. received so little love that she had little to give in return. She could give her son only the distorted facsimile that she knew.

Her exaggerated fears represent her own confusions about her role as a mother. As a mother, she knows that she should love, and she really wants to love. Consciously, she desires to give what she missed. If one were to ask Mrs. O. about this, she would state emphatically that she wants to love her son and does so love him; and she would be telling the truth as she knows it. She is not aware of her underlying feelings of anger toward men specifically (and people in general), stemming from her own highly disturbed parent-daughter relationship. If Mrs. O. were to be told that she has deep underlying anger that is not apparent on the surface, she would be amazed, even offended. She would deny that any anger exists, on the surface or deep within. She would insist again that there is only love, and again she would be telling the truth as she knows it. But the anger, not apparent to her, is there and masquerades in a variety of forms. At times these forms are so far removed from the original anger that produced them that the connecting link between the two is completely submerged.

In an effort to deny this hostility to herself, her child, and the world, Mrs. O. substitutes a caricature of behavior that on the surface is the complete opposite of her deep-lying feelings. She shows exaggerated fears (phobias), overprotectiveness, exaggerated protestations and demonstrations of love, and obsessive preoccupation with trivialities. Although Mrs. O. does not fully understand her deeply hidden hostile feelings, she is dimly aware of them, and they affect her every action and emotion in a way that she does not even recognize. Her vague stirrings of angry emotions cannot rise to the surface without the danger of her being shattered by the unleashed rage.

The parent with such deep feelings of hate develops certain symptoms that barricade her from an awareness of these seething emotions. Her symptoms are absolutely necessary to check her rage and preserve some sort of emotional balance. The symptoms are overprotectiveness and inappropriate concern for the child. She keeps her hatreds concealed from the world and herself by extreme protestations of love, concern, and protection. These sick ideas and her exaggerated behavior serve to stunt and warp her son's emotional growth. He is enslaved in a state of abject dependency on his mother, with all the same irrational and exaggerated fears that have barred her from happiness. Her methods of containing her anger have become the instruments of her hate, and of the destruction of her son. The symptoms that conceal her anger have become in fact the means of venting her hate. This is a boomerang: the mother's symptoms that cripple her son fly back upon herself. And neither victim, mother or son, understands the role that each plays in this tragedy.

Naturally, the mother who has this deep underlying hate also has deep underlying feelings of guilt. Her impaired ability to love, when she knows she should but cannot, only increases her guilt. Normal common-sense precautions become exaggerated into a reign of terror. Were the child to be hurt or develop a disability accidentally or otherwise, and were the mother at fault or not, it would only bring her intense feelings of guilt to the surface. The mother who already feels guilty will become highly disturbed out of all the proportion to the situation. But, an emotionally healthy mother, who is comfortable in her feelings of love toward her child, does not show these extreme reactions; nor does she show the exaggerated fears and overprotectiveness displayed by the disturbed mother. The healthy mother handles the situation with her child without extreme emotional outbursts—she has no need to prove to herself, to her son, or to the world that she loves—she knows she does; nor does she have any feelings of guilt that she must assuage.

A final reason for the disturbed mother's overprotectiveness and exaggerated fears of harm coming to her son is her fear of the sheer destructiveness of her feelings. In fact, many people who are so sweet and love everyone and see everything through rose-colored glasses have many of these same feelings. They protest too much; they overreact. In the injury or illness of her son, the mother would see the realization of her underlying feelings of hate, which would thus be brought closer to the surface and to painful recognition. She must do her utmost to prevent all injury and all illness. The fears and overprotective attitudes are necessary to her to keep the hostile feelings submerged, and thus keep her destructive feelings from becoming unleashed and overwhelming her and her son. The mere thought of such underlying forces produces panic in her.

MARY—HANDICAPPED BY PARENTAL LAXNESS

Mary is ten years old and has rheumatic heart disease. Her illness has permanently damaged her heart so that she is physically unable to lead the sort of life that other children do. Since her most recent attack of acute rheumatic fever, her physician has strongly and repeatedly advised Mary's parents to make her rest in bed at least two hours each morning and two hours each afternoon. He has also forbidden Mary to run and play and climb with the neighborhood children, although she often feels good and says that she can do these activities without getting tired and out of breath. Her already damaged heart would be further weakened (and her life expectancy shortened) by any more attacks of acute rheumatic fever.

The mother has been instructed to give Mary an antibiotic medicine by mouth daily to prevent any further attacks. But Mary's parents do not obey these specific instructions. Mary's mother always gives in to her tearful entreaties to go out and play with her friends. She excuses this serious violation with the remark, "I'm just too soft-hearted" and "I want her to grow up as normally as possible." There are other violations. Mary does not always get her daytime bed rest, for she must first make her bed and dry the dishes. The mother frequently goes out to play bridge. "Now be sure you go to bed this afternoon, you hear? I don't want to catch you playing outside when I get back. Let your friends come to see you. If I'm not home in time for supper, you'll find some leftovers in the refrigerator. And don't forget your vitamins."

Mary's mother and father do a lot of entertaining for business reasons. The father always brings the guests up to Mary's room to meet his "sweet little daughter" (and incidentally interrupt her sleep and rest at any hour of the night). The father remarks to his wife, "Mary is so sweet that these people cannot help but love and feel sorry for her. I hope some of this rubs off on the boss when he makes out the promotion recommendations." Mary never remembers to take her antibiotic pills. When the mother speaks to the physician, she is very upset: "I cannot do a thing with Mary. She won't listen . . . forgets her pills, won't rest . . . wants to play all the time. I'm at my wits' end. Please speak to her, Doctor, and tell her how important it is for her to do what she is told."

Mary's disability is so serious that inadequate care will shorten her life. Although the parents have had the importance of such care emphasized by the physician, they are completely failing to give it: no antibiotic pills, no rest, no vitamins, no undisturbed sleep. The father interrupts his daughter's sleep as a means of advancing his own career. The mother blames Mary for not doing what she, the mother, is responsible for seeing done. The mother tries to pass on her little remaining responsibility, "Please speak to her, Doctor. . . ." The complaint, "I cannot do a thing with Mary," is all too frequently heard. But it should be evident that this is as much a problem of the mother as of the child. What is there in a mother's feelings toward her child that causes this laxness? The specific answer varies with the case.

The same galaxy of disturbed parent-child emotional relationships can exist for the child who was born with a handicap. Examples of this are various forms of cerebral palsy, blindness, deafness, or possibly disfiguring congenital port-wine stains of the skin. If the handicap appeared late enough in life, the parents and the child can often remember better times. In both cases, however, an *emotionally healthy* parent and child will find the rehabilitation much smoother and easier, and the emotional storms engendered by the disability will subside more quickly and completely than in the already emotionally disturbed parent and child.

10

Emotional Aspects of Mental Deficiency

Mental deficiency varies in degree from the minimally defective child who will eventually (granting no severe emotional disturbances) make a fair adjustment in society to the extremely defective child who will need constant care and protection for the rest of his life. The former will be able to support himself in society in tasks commensurate with his abilities; the latter will always need complete support by society. Someone with a mild intellectual impairment and a relatively healthy emotional background may well make a better adjustment in society than someone with a superior intellect and a completely disturbed emotional background.

PHYSICAL BASIS FOR MENTAL DEFICIENCY

Many forms of mental deficiency are hereditary. It is important that such forms of deficiency be identified and their hereditary nature explained to the parents.

Certain cases of mental deficiency have been found to be associated with chromosomal abnormalities (e.g., mongolism) or biochemical defects (e.g., phenylketonuria, or "PKU"). As in all such instances, careful clinical and laboratory studies are essential in order to establish the diagnosis—and to suggest treatment when it is available. Research in this field holds much promise for the future.

It is now known that during the first three months of pregnancy the different parts of the unborn infant's body take on much of their later form. From this point on through the rest of the pregnancy, the infant continues mainly to increase in size. Thus these first three months of pregnancy are the most critical period during which factors that affect the mother can cause incomplete or faulty development of various parts of the infant's body. One such factor is the notorious disease called German measles (rubella), which has been shown to be capable of causing mental deficiency and other defects in the unborn child. Another such factor, newly researched, is the effects of drugs, such as thalidomide and LSD, taken during early pregnancy. Prevention or modification of disease in the mother during the first three months of pregnancy may aid in preventing many birth defects. Even so, medical science has not yet found a direct causative relationship between maternal illness and most cases of mental deficiency.

In a large number of mentally defective children, the origins of the defect can be traced to diseases contracted early in infancy and childhood. This varied group includes birth injury to the brain, meningitis, encephalitis ("brain fever"), brain and head injuries; kernicterus (a disease resulting from Rh-blood reactions between mother and child), and repeated severe insulin reactions in the diabetic child.

There are other kinds of mental deficiency which, when recognized early by the physician, respond well to treatment. Cretinism is of this type. In this disease, a child is born with the inability to form sufficient amounts of thyroid hormone. But if this disease is diagnosed and treated early, the child will become healthy.

In many instances, mental deficiency is the child's only defect. In others, it is associated with physical abnormalities—internal, external, or both. Some examples are mongolism, incomplete formation of the brain, various malformations of the brain, hydrocephalus ("water on the brain," "large head"), microcephaly ("pinhead"), gargoylism, and brain cysts.

EMOTIONAL BASES FOR MENTAL DEFICIENCY

Today the mentally deficient child is beginning to emerge from the false stigma of shame and the concealment inflicted by the hush-hush attitudes of the past. In recent years, medical research has been slowly discovering the causes of mental deficiency, and the medical profession has pioneered in the treatment of those so handicapped.

Despite such commendable advances, however, many such children go undiscovered and untreated, partly because of parental attitudes. All too often the parents' sense of shame, and fear that their worst suspicions will be confirmed, cause them to delay seeking medical advice. And, unfortunately, these same attitudes frequently lead them to deny the diagnosis once it has been made.

Mental deficiency has many causes. In some cases the child will respond well to treatment; in others he will not. Distinguishing between mental deficiency which is physically based and that which is emotionally caused is essential to the determination of what treatment should be undertaken. Only a thorough medical evaluation can reveal this.

Regardless of the cause or the degree of his impairment, the mentally defective child has emotional needs that must be satisfied. These needs often can be satisfied better in an institution than at home, provided that adequate institutional care is available.

PARENTAL EMOTIONS AND INSTITUTIONALIZATION

In the face of the tragic implications of a diagnosis of mental deficiency for their child, parents may refuse institutionalization of the child when this is recommended. They do so for emotional reasons of their own. The question of placing a child in an institution is indeed one of the touchiest and most difficult problems facing both parents and physicians. The decision is a highly personal one that in the final analysis, only the parents can make. But before arriving at a reasonable decision, they need to consider the whole situation.

Other children in the family must be considered. These healthy children must be helped to become useful members of society, which means, among other things, that their emotional needs must be satisfied. These children should not be left to shift for themselves while the parents spend all their time, their care, and their financial resources on the mentally defective child. To live with a mentally defective brother or sister can be highly disturbing to the emotional development of the healthy children in the family. They have to expect the taunts of other children, the side glances of adult neighbors, and even the open remarks of total strangers. As they grow older, they may be afraid and ashamed to bring their friends home. They must always offer apologies and excuses. Moreover, the family finances can become depleted from fruitless expenditures for the handicapped child: dental care to improve appearance; dancing and piano lessons that cannot be appreciated; private tutors; nurses and maids; repeated medical consultations with specialist after specialist; and occasional expensive flirtations with the rosy promises of quacks. The family's ability to give their normal children the care and the cultural and educational opportunities they deserve is thus impaired.

Parents sometimes comment, "My other children all love poor Jimmy. They would hate to have him go away. Why, when the other kids make fun of Jimmy, his brothers and sisters always put up a fight." Such parents need to answer the disturbing question whether their other children are fighting only for their mentally deficient brother or whether they are defending their own wounded pride against a cruel society. In their own feelings, the stigma of shame that society puts on their brother seems to extend to them. A healthy child has a right to grow up in as peaceful and wholesome an atmosphere as possible. It is unfair to expose him to repeated emotional trauma merely to satisfy the parents' own understandably wounded pride.

The parents who resist institutionalization and who overemphasize their love for the handicapped child and his need for them—who, in other words, sacrifice their lives for their child—again protest too much. They overreact. For reasons already discussed (see pp. 46 and 279), these overreactions may signify only the parents' own mixed feelings toward their disabled child.

EMOTIONAL DISTURBANCES AS FACTORS IN APPARENT MENTAL DEFICIENCY

With the increased study in recent years of mentally defective children and their backgrounds, it has become startlingly apparent that at least some such cases are due to emotional causes.

Some members of this group might have previously suffered some damage to the brain from injury or disease. Their problems include various disturbances in walking, talking, writing, balance, coordination, sight, hearing, touch, and bowel and bladder control. In view of these handicaps, an untrained observer might make the unwarranted generalization that the child is also mentally deficient. But careful study of these children and their parents uncovers evidence of severe emotional disturbance. Collaborative studies by physicians reveal that long before such a child was injured, his parents had had the same highly disturbed underlying emotions as those seen in the parents of the physically handicapped child already discussed. With the tacit understanding and outright sympathy of a highly misinformed and superstitious society, it was all too easy for the emotionally disturbed parent to find in his apparently "brain damaged" child the escape hatch for his own overwhelming and disturbing emotions. By using his child as the object through which were revealed his own submerged destructive feelings, the parent found surcease from his own warped passions. By finding such release for his own tension the parent saved himself, but did so at the price of his child's mental integrity.

These destructive feelings and the mechanism for their release from the parent were completely hidden and were revealed only by the most painstakingly careful examination of the emotional life of both child and parent. Despite the fact that these hostile feelings were so subtly and completely hidden behind the facade that the parent presented to society and to himself, their destructive effects were far-reaching and tragic, namely, a mentally defective child. The causes were hidden; the effect, obvious.

For example, the apparent calm of an unhealthy parent-child relationship may be suddenly and violently disrupted by disease or injury to the child's brain. The seeds of hate, never quite asleep, lie within the sick parent, forever threatening to erupt and destroy the parent or someone near to him. The child cannot escape this inoculation of hate. It may affect him sufficiently (mental deficiency and schizophrenia) to make him unable to function effectively in society. Or he may be inoculated and affected as his parents were before him (for example, sexual deviations, various phobias, and delinquency), and thus be unable to have a healthy relationship with those close to him. One or the other possibility will occur unless medical help is sought. Which possibility will occur depends on the total life situations in each case.

When such a parent is confronted with the unexpected and overwhelming event of a disease or an injury to the child's brain, the underlying emotions of hate are touched off. The event is too close to the destructive feelings, however deep and hidden such feelings may be to the parent and to those about him. In the emergency of the injury, the accompanying guilt, as already described with the handicapped child, swells and rises closer to the surface. The parent will blame himself in an attempt to assuage his guilt. He resists well-meaning efforts at consolation.

At this point the physician may mention mental deficiency as a possible complication. The parent may overhear a chance remark by a nurse, a hospital orderly, or a relative, without being aware of his role.

For the first time since the child's birth, the parent now finds an acceptable outlet for his own underlying, forbidden, destructive feelings. The parent, whose own pent-up emotions have been straining for release, has suddenly and fortuitously found the means of showing his hate toward his child in a manner that both he and society will accept. "The poor boy is a hopeless idiot; the brain injury made him that way."

As the parent's unconscious hostility finds a suitable object—the brain-injured child—to act upon, the parent's former panic is partially relieved.

Now the confused and thoroughly frightened child can also find relief from his own pent-up tensions and fear of his parent's destructiveness by a retreat to earlier modes of behavior (see p. 36). By engaging in infantile forms of behavior at an age when such behavior should be long past, he gives the superficial appearance of being mentally deficient. He will wallow helplessly in a permanent stage of babyhood. Depending on his previous life experiences, either he will have intemperate outbursts of biting, screaming, kicking, and soiling, or he will show a complacent stage of acceptance of everything in a dull, listless, vegetative existence.

This destructive parent-child adjustment will have to be continued to prevent the recurrence of the previous panic of parent and child. Thus, unless detected and interrupted, this succession of events will continue unalterably until the death of the child. The only hope for—and the final proof of—this tragic parent-child relationship is the marked improvement and response of the afflicted child to appropriate medical treatment for both child and parent.

What if the child resists being the scapegoat in this manner? What if the child had never suffered this sudden injury or illness, and the parent had never chanced upon this solution to his difficulties? Depending on his own specific life experiences and on other poorly understood factors, the parent must find an outlet for his tensions as they build up beyond a certain critical level. When he cannot find an outlet through his child (mental deficiency, delinquency, childhood sexual problems, and other problems already discussed), it is not unusual to see these unrequited factors operating to a greater or lesser degree in certain diseases in the parent. Examples are acute depression, alcoholism, anxiety states, hyperthyroidism, peptic ulcer, chronic ulcerative colitis, nervous heart, hypertension, migraine, and neurodermatitis ("nervous eczema"). Or, when the parent cannot find an outlet through either his child or himself, he will release these tensions in disturbed relationships with his fellow human beings: divorce action, or inability to hold a job or to establish and maintain genuine friendships.

In some cases of mental deficiency present from birth, the child's handicap also serves as an outlet for his parents' disturbed emotions. The same parental problems and needs are present, but the parent has found the necessary outlet much earlier in the child's life. He may even have conjured it up in his fears before the child's birth or at his birth. One mother said, "When I was carrying Billy, he was so active I was afraid he would be like my husband's mentally defective sister who runs wild all over the house, beats her head against the wall, and smashes things."

DICKIE—RELEASED FROM REGRESSION

Dickie's story may help to clarify the role of parents' sick emotions in producing apparent mental deficiency. Many of the principles learned by collaborative therapy on this case have been found to apply, in varying degrees, to other cases of mental deficiency, regardless of the cause.

Dickie, a husky, handsome, brown-haired five-year-old, was brought to the physician by his mother because of "mental retardation." In the waiting room, he sat quietly in his chair, seemingly oblivious of his surroundings. He showed no response to the other children, the ringing telephones, the nurse's greeting, or even to his mother when she called him. She had to lead him into the doctor's office like a baby.

Complete studies of the boy revealed no known physical cause for the apparent deficiency, and no physical abnormalities. All the studies on the spinal fluid, the blood, and the urine were normal. Examination of the nervous system, including the reflexes, was normal. Xrays of the head, a brainwave (electroencephalogram), and special hearing tests were similarly normal.

The only abnormality found during extensive study was the I.Q., which showed Dickie to be grossly deficient. But from his questioning the physician found that Dickie had reached for and grasped objects, sat up alone, walked with and then without support, held a spoon, learned bowel and bladder control, and begun to talk, all at the normally expected ages. In fact, he had developed normally until he was three years old, when his sister was born. Since that time he had apparently lost his vocabulary and said only one thing over and over all day long. "Make Dickie a good boy. Make Dickie a good boy."

From the age of three Dickie had shown marked abnormalities in behavior, although until then his behavior had been like that of other children his age.

Aside from occasionally pushing and kicking his two-year-old sister, Dickie had no contact with the world around him. He did not play with other children; he showed no interest in participating in the usual family activities. When eating, he noisily gorged his food "like an animal." He would pick up food with his hands, stuff it in his mouth, and bolt it down. He soiled himself on occasion and had lost his previous bladder control both in the daytime and at night. Dickie's mother was amused because he sat down to urinate, although formerly he used to stand up.

Dickie constantly interrupted the examination by shrill cries and screams. He made no effort to wipe away the saliva that drooled from his mouth. He whirled and darted about the room without apparent purpose. He hopped about and flapped his arms like a bird.

In summary, Dickie's behavior was very different from that of a healthy five-year-old. He had progressed normally with his learning until three years of age. After that, there was not only lack of progress but actual loss of what had already been learned. Was he actually mentally deficient? Why the sudden deterioration at three years of age? It should be noted that there was no injury or illness at that time —only the birth of his sister.

As part of the complete study of the emotional backgrounds of Dickie and his parents, the physician questioned the mother about her past life. One day he spent two hours with the mother, asking questions and listening to her. He could not get any coherent story. He never received a direct answer to a question. In fact, it was almost impossible to communicate with her. An avalanche of words, a kaleidoscope of disjointed thought engulfed him. Throughout all this verbiage, some of which referred to tragic events in her past, Dickie's mother maintained the same wooden smile. Her chain smoking clouded her apparent calm. But her flow of words suggested a severe disturbance. Only after seeing the mother a number of times could the physician begin to discern a pattern to her disturbance.

The smile never faded; the smoking never ceased. Even when she interrupted her apparently meaningless chatter to describe a tragic event in her past life, she showed no noticeable emotion in either her voice or her manner.

Dickie's mother, Mrs. B., described how her own father had abandoned her mother and her brother a few months before her own birth. The father had refused to contribute to the support of the family until legal action was taken by welfare agencies. Immediately after completing her description of this tragedy, she said, with the same fixed smile, "I always loved Daddy." As the interview progressed, this phrase became her motto, accompanying every reference to her father. All these references revealed her father's glaring and complete lack of affection for his family. But "I always loved Daddy."

During her childhood, Mrs. B. never saw her father, but she received Christmas cards from him, with a quarter enclosed as a present. The Christmas card and the quarter were repeated annually until she was married. This was the full extent of the father's gifts to his daughter who said she loved him. He did not attend her wedding or send her a gift. In spite of the court order, he never gave one cent to his wife for the support of his family. His wife did nothing to insist that the court order for the support of herself and her children be enforced.

Through the years, the father never wrote to his wife or daughter. On rare occasions he did write a long letter to his own mother, who lived only a short subway ride away. When Dickie's mother was a young girl she often visited her grandmother and avidly read the long letters her father wrote his own mother. She thirsted for any information about her father. "I always loved Daddy." Her own mother never said anything.

Through these letters, Mrs. B. learned (and later confirmed) that her father had become a millionaire whose yearly income was fabulous. He traveled around Europe as a business tycoon and lavished great sums of money on "wine, women and song." Although he sent nothing, except the Christmas quarter, to either his wife or daughter, it was his custom to enclose $3 with his annual Easter card to his mother. When the brother was in high school, the father began sending him $25 a week for his personal use. The father always sent this money through the boy's paternal grandmother. The father also offered to pay for his son's education if he wished to go to business school. But he offered nothing to his daughter (Mrs. B.) or his wife.

Despite Mrs. B.'s wooden smile and repeated protestations of love for her father, one must wonder. She protests too much. The father's behavior was too bizarre to elicit any reaction but hate.

After Mrs. B.'s marriage, her father occasionally visited her and her new family. He would pop in unannounced, remain for a few days to a few weeks, and, without a word, leave. She never knew when he was coming. During these visits he never contributed any money to his daughter and her struggling family. He never suggested that his daughter or any member of her family accompany him to the opera, the symphony, or the Broadway hit shows. His main topic of conversation consisted of business discussions and detailed analyses of past and current financial trends.

He would spend most of his time in the house, absorbed in reading the financial journals and the stock market quotations. He rarely paid any attention to his daughter, her husband, or her children. He never asked how they were doing. In the face of their poverty, his only other conversational topic was his travels, what he had seen and what he had done. He delighted in describing how he held his own with the "great brains" of the world. In a continuous monologue, he repeated verbatim his conversations with intellectuals he knew, discussing all the fine shades of economic and philosophic thought. He was truly a man of the world to whom no doors of academic and intellectual pursuits were closed. But the family to whom he described all this were plain people without the background to understand. They listened respectfully without interrupting as he droned on and on. There was no common meeting ground. The family accepted the situation and saw nothing unusual in it. The father never showed the slightest interest in Dickie's problem.

The father's previous cold and self-centered attitude persisted. The daughter continued to "love Daddy." What type of woman would accept the situation imposed on her by a man of this type?

Only after many difficult hours of painstaking sifting of words and feelings that held together like sand did the physician obtain from Mrs. B. a clearer picture of Dickie's maternal grandmother. A welfare agency and not the grandmother had instituted legal action to obtain financial support from the father who had abandoned his family. Also, despite her needs and the support of the court action, she chose to struggle as best she could on her own and did nothing to insist that the court order be enforced. By her failure to take a firm stand in this matter she was giving permission and actually fostering her husband's means of showing his hostility to his family.

The differences between husband and wife that accounted for the separation can only be conjectured. As the physician assembled the shredded pieces of Mrs. B.'s life story, he repeatedly saw the parallelism of the underlying hostility between Mrs. B.'s father and mother and between Mrs. B. and her father. He also began to perceive similar feelings between Dickie and his mother.

Dickie's grandmother was strict and suspicious. Deserted by her husband during her pregnancy, refused support by him when he was well able to give it, she chose to accept in silence the role of the wronged woman. She did not struggle. She dedicated herself completely to her family and devoted all her energies to a little dress shop. But her poorly contained rage gushed out on her daughter, Dickie's mother. With the same wooden smile with which she described her father, Mrs. B. said that her mother "beat me every day of my life. My [older] brother was the favorite and always got off scot-free." Sam, her brother, was four years older. He had gone to college, knew three languages, and could hold his own in discussions with his father. In her conversation with the physician, with its myriad unconnected thoughts, she tended to belittle the intellectual achievements of her husband and herself in comparison with those of her father and brother. "My husband and I were lucky to get through high school; my Daddy and brother have many college degrees."

The daily beatings from her mother were administered until her teens without reason and often with the pious admonition, "This will make you a good girl." As a girl, Mrs. B. had to work each afternoon and evening, weekends included, in her mother's dress shop while her brother came and went as he chose (as his father did). She consistently shied away from any discussion of her mother and her own feelings toward her. However, she did mention one bizarre incident. With the same fixed smile she vividly described her mother's reaction when she, Dickie's mother, narrowly escaped death. While she had been dining in a restaurant on a teen-age date, there was a sudden explosion in the kitchen. Within minutes flames and terror spread through the restaurant. She and her date escaped with only minor cuts. When she arrived home, terrified, exhausted, and disheveled, her mother, instead of trying to find out what had happened and comforting her terrified daughter, immediately flew into an uncontrollable rage and started screaming and violently slapping her daughter's face with her open hand. "What have you done? What have you done?"

From all this it is apparent that Dickie's mother had grave emotional problems with her mother as well as with her father. She could not give any more information about her mother in spite of many hours of interview. It would be naïve to assume that the maternal grandmother's hostility and rage resulted from, and solely from, her unhappy marriage. Blaming emotional disturbances on "marital incompatibility," "mental cruelty," divorce, and separation is like placing the cart before the horse. An over-whelming number of cases of marital incompatibil-ity and related legal actions stem from preexisting emotional problems in both partners. It is these preexisting problems that adversely affect the child's developing conscience and emotional make-up. Legal solutions do nothing to change the funda-mental emotional maladjustments of the parents. These maladjustments may become less obvious as the superficial environmental factors which brought them to the surface are removed by the divorce or the separation. But, although submerged, the causes of these maladjustments remain to affect both par-ents and growing children. Dickie's mother was pre-sumably so terrified by her hostile feelings toward her own mother and father that she was unable to discuss her feelings toward them at all.

It was also clear that Mrs. B. had hostile feelings toward her brother. She could not hide her rare out-bursts of resentment at the different manner in which her parents treated her and her brother. Such seething hatred had to find an outlet. Such an outlet was provided when Dickie's young sister was born. Here was a situation which closely resembled the earlier situation between Mrs. B. and her own older brother. The memories of old injustices and present resentments against her brother still rankled. Dickie, who in the new family situation held a posi-tion similar to that of his uncle in the older family became the object against which she directed all her pent-up hatreds. Here is another example of why one particular child becomes the scapegoat for a parent's emotional disturbances while another child escapes relatively unscathed (see p. 188).

An additional ironic twist to this tragic situation is that Dickie apparently lacked that quality most admired by this family: a superior intellect. Or would not this apparent mental deficiency of the grandson and nephew be the sweetest possible revenge against a father and brother who revered above all else a superior intellect?

In later sessions with the physician the relationship between this background information and the mother's problem with Dickie became slowly apparent. The mother behaved in a bizarre and hostile way toward her son. One day in the physician's waiting room, Dickie vomited all over himself. The mother looked up completely unperturbed and then returned to her magazine. On another occasion, Dickie spilled over his head a bottle of red paint by the children's drawing board. The mother shrugged her shoulders; then, without any change in facial expression, she wordlessly brought Dickie to the sink and turned on the faucet so that the water poured over his head.

When the mother was interviewed separately, she described Dickie's upbringing. Every day from 10:00 until 11:30 A.M. she would strap five-year-old Dickie to a high chair and then, on a blackboard placed in front of him, slowly trace out the letters of the alphabet while repeating them verbally. She felt certain that all this time spent with the child in this way would cure him of his mental deficiency and make him as smart as his (maternal) grandfather and his uncle. Every day between 1:00 and 2:00 P.M., the alarm clock would ring and Dickie's mother would say, "Go make wee-wee." She was very proud of Dickie's ability to urinate when told to do so. She laughingly added that her son always sat down to urinate. Mrs. B. had another strange habit; she kept all the cereal boxes half full "so he wouldn't have an accident and mess everything up. I should follow him around the house more than I do. The way he runs around the house and jumps on the bed worries me. He's already ruined two mattresses. And our wedding dishes—they're practically all smashed. I'm afraid he'll get badly hurt some day."

There was no warmth toward her son, only an insistence on strict adherence to a schedule which she imagined was the proper thing to do. Her attempt to make her son smart like the father and brother whom she held in awe was similarly rigid, cold, and bizarre. It should be noted that one of the few times that she showed any spark of feeling was when she described how her son urinated like a woman. Her exaggerated precautions against an accident and her complete failure to set limits to her son's destructive actions around the house are more indications of her submerged rage (see p. 276) and her permissiveness. She cannot say, "No"! The hate and the deprivation to which she had been exposed as a child determined her relationship to her son. Having never gained love, she was unable to give any. The problems of one generation have been passed on to the next.

Dickie's father, as one would expect from the fact that he did marry and remained presumably comfortably married to such a woman, also had bizarre reactions. He was a nonentity who spent all his time at home in the garage tinkering with his car. He religiously overhauled the motor of his car, taking it apart and putting it together again, every weekend. Since the motor was taken apart over weekends, the car never could be used for family jaunts.

Faced with the unconscious hostility of his mother and receiving neither warmth nor emotional support from his father, Dickie had been terrified. He had sought escape by retreating to earlier modes of behavior, by acting much younger than his age (see p. 36). He tried to retreat to a previous mode of behavior during which life had been more comfortable. By behaving as though he were much younger than his true age, Dickie appeared to be mentally retarded.

This mother's seething hate almost found a revenge possibly greater than death itself. Death happens and is finished. Mental deficiency goes on and on.

The mother was seen three times a week for one hour at a time over a period of many months, while the son was seen by another physician at the same time. Weekly the two physicians conferred and exchanged information. This scattered fragmentary information was slowly pieced together to reveal the interrelationships between mother and son. As new and specific feelings of either mother or son came to the surface, the effect of such feelings upon the other person was noted. The feelings and the reactions of one always dovetailed with the feelings and the reactions of the other. As the physicians began to know their patients better, they could often predict with amazing accuracy how one would react to the feelings and the behavior of the other. Deep feelings were slowly and painfully brought to the surface of hazy awareness. The mother slowly began to realize that she had problems—serious problems—that had a direct bearing on her son's illness. Although she had ostensibly been seen for her son's sake, she gradually became aware of her own needs. During this long and difficult period of gently uncovering her underlying rage and hate from the deprivation of love, she began to show some emotion. Although her wooden smile persisted, her eyes would fill with tears when she mentioned either her mother or her father.

In the meantime, as she found herself able for the first time in her life to relate her true feelings to someone without fear of punishment, her underlying need to let some of her pent-up hatred out through her son slowly receded. While Dickie was being seen by the other physician and the mother's hatred toward her son slowly ebbed away, a change in Dickie's behavior slowly became discernible. The physician was warm and kind to Dickie; he brought his little patient candy, potato chips, and soda pop before each interview. More important, he showed his warmth and kindness by his feelings toward Dickie. Dickie was slowly and painfully learning that people could have feelings other than hate toward him and that he could live comfortably in the present without needing to retreat to early stages of behavior. The physician played games with Dickie.

When, during play, Dickie was faced with an event that caused rage (as when the blocks fell down), the physician restrained him from throwing a block at the closed window. The physician told him that he understood how angry Dickie could be but that certain things just are not done. The physician set definite limits to the destructiveness of Dickie's rage, something his mother, in her guilt, had been unable to do. The physician also showed Dickie by example that rage was acceptable as long as it was not destructive. It was now becoming safe for Dickie to return to a mode of behavior consistent with that of his age. He began to speak again, looked forward to seeing his doctor (with whom he had established a close and comfortable relationship), and began to act his age.

In short, the proof of the pudding was Dickie's slow but definite return from apparent mental deficiency to emotional and intellectual health.

▬▬▬▬▬▬▬▬▬▬▬▬▬▬▬▬▬▬▬▬▬▬▬▬

CHAPTER 11

Effects of Losing a Parent: Death, Divorce, Adoption

To the growing child the birth of a brother or a sister is less a mystery than the death of a parent. The arrival of a brother or a sister is easier for the child to understand. The child can see, hear, and feel the new infant. Although he may envy and resent the new arrival, he has, mixed with these feelings, curiosity and pride. The baby gives ever-present tangible reminders of its presence. The concept of death, however, is much more difficult for the young child to grasp. What is death? "Daddy, where is Mommy?" "Daddy, when is Mommy coming back?" "Why did Mommy leave?" "Doesn't Mommy love me any more?" "Did she leave me because I was naughty?"

At the time of a death, the adults are all wrapped up in their own feelings. Some weep without restraint. Some sit in stony silence. Others reminisce endlessly. The death becomes the occasion for a rare family reunion. While the funeral arrangements are being made, the children are frequently left to shift for themselves or are sent away to be cared for by relatives or neighbors during this period of upheaval. As much as possible is done to shield the child from the shock of death. Often the adults feel that the child is too young to understand the tragedy that has just occurred. When the child does show any feelings, the adults display a naïve confidence in the child's emotional resiliency, his ability to bounce back. "He'll get over it. All children do." When the adults do think of the child's loss, they frequently think only of the immediate loss. "Who will feed him?" "Who will buy his clothes and dress him?" Or, if the father has died, "Now the mother must go to work." "She'll be all alone." "Will the company's pension plan be enough?" "Did he have enough insurance?" "How can they take care of the mortgage?" "What can the relatives contribute to tide the family over the present?"

With the shock of bereavement still fresh, relatives and friends make well-meaning and sympathetic promises of help to the family, promises that may never be kept. There is much understandable concern for the surviving parent. "The poor mother (or the poor father)! What will she do now with all these children?" Again the thought recurs that the child will get over the loss, will bounce back. The hard truth is that the surviving parent probably will return to emotional equilibrium and will adjust to the new situation while the child may carry scars throughout life.

The child is extremely dependent upon the parent for his needs. The specific needs and the extent of this dependency vary as the child grows older. As an infant, he is totally dependent upon his parents. He must be carried about, fed, clothed, taught, loved, and protected from all danger. Without such parental protection, he will die. In short, he must be cared for emotionally and materially. As the child grows older, he develops new needs, and old needs change. But the child's need to know that there is someone near on whom he can depend continues, and this need persists through all of life.

The child's most important need is that of love. It is either there or it is not. By the mutual exchange of feelings between himself and his parent, the child must know that he is loved. Empty tokens of love, unaccompanied by feelings of love, do not satisfy this fundamental need. The lollypop or the new bicycle, used as a sop, and unaccompanied by feelings of love, does not satisfy this need. As the child grows up, he becomes able to provide some of his own material needs. But his emotional needs continue. We have already discussed how the manner in which these emotional needs are gratified does much to determine emotional health and disease.

We cannot emphasize too strongly that emotional and material needs are not separate entities to be considered entirely apart from each other. Rather, they are inextricably blended. This blending is apparent in the helpless child for whom the provision of the food, shelter, and clothing are tangible tokens of his being cared for and loved. This blending of emotional and material needs is less apparent in the older child and adult, but just as genuine. The lollypop is hardly necessary for life, but it serves as a reminder and token of the fact that the child's parents care for him. In later life the box of candy or the dozen roses serve the same purpose. However, for both child and adult, the accompanying feelings determine whether the lollypop, the box of candy, or the roses are symbols of love or are actually bribes, a means of assuaging guilt or forestalling anticipated expressions of anger.

We have already discussed the dire effects of a parent's inoculating the child with sick emotions, maliciously disguised and presented as love, while at the same time providing adequate food, clothing, and shelter. An extreme example is found in infants in some foundling homes who show a disturbingly higher rate of death and emotional and physical diseases than do infants in other foundling homes. In both types of institution, the same standards of food, clothing, shelter, and prevention of infection prevail. However, in the home with the alarming disease and death rate, there is less exchange of feelings between the helpless, lonely babies and the nurses and the matrons, who rush from baby to baby, holding them only long enough to complete routine care. Even when they do go through the motions of cuddling and cooing over the child, it is all done as a part of the necessary routine. There is little feeling; their thoughts frequently lie elsewhere. The children's need for love remains ungratified. Many become ill or die.

By unwitting and subtle communications and by purposeful teaching and imitation, the child learns and acquires the superficial and also the deep emotional values and quirks of his parents. He becomes strongly attached by example and memory to the parent who gratifies his needs and whose own feelings and actions the child imitates. The child is born with both the need and the potential for emotion. He is not born with any specific emotion. He is not born with love or hate or any of their many variations. These specific emotions and the values attached to them are learned entirely from those upon whom he depends and whom he imitates. It should be obvious, then, that the parent is the most important part of the child's environment.

The child (and the adult) needs to know that there is someone near on whom he can depend for the gratification of his needs. When death removes the one who provides these needs, an immediate tension is created in the child. The props have been removed. All the feelings and memories that united child to parent have been severed. The young child cannot comprehend the meaning of death, why there is death, and what follows death. Why and where has the departed parent gone? All that the child can understand is that the one who loved him and gratified his needs has departed. He feels that the loved one has abandoned him. He is confused and angry at being left alone. But he must keep these feelings to himself. He cannot show anger. No one can show anger in the presence of death. Only sorrow is permitted. "Speak kindly of the dead."

Unable to pour his feelings out on the world about him, these feelings become bottled up within the child. In this way, these feelings of anger become that part of his emotional life which lies submerged beneath the surface. This does not mean, as already noted, that it lies passively dormant. It continues to affect the attitudes and the reactions of the individual to the people and the events about him. Unless the vacuum created by the death of the parent is filled (see the following section on adoption) and unless the tensions created by the death are relieved, the process of imitation of the departed parent will be unfinished and possibly blighted, and anger will persist.

These submerged feelings of anger are present in any young child who loves and loses a parent. The surviving parent or the responsible relatives or guardians should recognize the fact that the child has mixed feelings at such a time. With genuine feeling and sympathy, the responsible adult should permit the child to express his feelings and ask his questions. The adult should recognize that here is another human being, albeit small and inarticulate, who also has feelings and questions. The child's feelings may not follow the adult pattern of grief and loss, but they are nevertheless real and must be recognized. While showing concern for the grief-stricken adults, it is unfair to the child to neglect his feelings. "He is too small to know." "Let us shield him from all this." Although the general confusion at the time of death and the child's quiet manner may belie his underlying turmoil, his true feelings seep out later in questions, play, and dreams. He may frequently ask, "Where has Daddy gone?" "Where is heaven?" "Why did Daddy leave me?" "Doesn't

Daddy love me?" "Did I do something wrong?"

The child will play hospital or doctor or nurse to reenact the disturbing events. In his play, toy automobiles will crash, dolls will be injured, operations will take place, and buildings and piles of blocks will tumble. Airplanes and rocket ships will soar almost to heaven. Toy child dolls will be naughty, and therefore toy parent dolls will leave them. Games with toy weapons of destruction will either be avoided entirely or will be played again and again, depending on the child's specific feelings toward the death. In dreams, departed parents will return to the child with love and gifts, children will play happily at favorite games, or nightmares of death and destruction will recur.

Even the emotionally healthy child, who can show and talk about his mixed feelings and have them sympathetically understood by the grown-ups around him, will have the same reactions. But they will not be so severe and will last only a limited time. For the most part, the child's grief will slowly disappear and be replaced by acceptance of the new situation. He will remember his father or mother as a truly fine person. He will strive to continue to imitate his idealized concept of that parent. The scars of the former turmoil will remain, but they are not deep and incapacitating.

But if the child becomes unduly disturbed or withdrawn following the death of a parent, and if this persists, many factors may be responsible. The relations of the child with the departed parent may have been upsetting. The relations of the child with the surviving parent may be faulty. The actual death and its surrounding circumstances and feelings may have been upsetting to the child and poorly handled by the adults. For example, a pain-laden and lingering death or a death preceded by amputation or other obviously mutilating surgery or disease may affect the child adversely. The brutal admonition, "Be quiet, or you'll kill your poor Mommy," is a fearsome memory for the child to recall following the death. The frequent reminder, "Your Mommy died giving birth to you," is similarly cruel and unwarranted. Making the child feel responsible for the death of a parent may brutally undermine the child's ability to develop warm relationships with other people of the same sex as the departed parent. The barbaric custom of having the child kiss the dead parent becomes the cause of many haunting and frightening memories. A death ushered in gradually by a prolonged illness is met differently by the child (and the adults) than a death which comes abruptly and unexpectedly.

Seven-year-old Danny's father died after heart surgery. Danny had loved his father very much. Everyone at the funeral commented on the remarkable composure of both Danny and his mother. The mother knew otherwise. Shortly thereafter she sought help for her own emotional problems. During treatment she worked through some very touchy areas in her own past life and noted, as an unexpected by-product, that in contrast to her former impassivity, she began to show tears and other evidences of sorrow under appropriate circumstances. At the same time, she observed that Danny had developed the ability to show his own similar feelings and to commiserate with others.

The death of a parent during the child's first-romance stage will influence the many feelings that exist between the child and his mother or father during this stage of his development. If the rivalries of the first-romance stage have been poorly handled by the parents, the bereaved child will be more disturbed by his parent's death. Should the parent of the same sex die during the height of this stage of development (and during the height of the healthy or exaggerated rivalry of this stage), the feelings of anger and guilt generated by this rivalry and by the subsequent death will echo through all the child's future feelings and actions. His future may be permanently tainted because he has not had a chance to settle the mixed feelings of love and hate that accompany this rivalry. The parent dies before the conflict can be settled satisfactorily, as it often is at the end of the first-romance stage.

"Speak kindly of the dead." Such sentiments are confusing to the child who realizes from past experiences that the feelings and actions of the departed parent could leave few pleasant memories. It is hypocrisy to expect the child to hold reverent memories of someone he actually detested or who he knows detested him. Under such circumstances it is confusing and unrealistic for the child to listen to the surviving parent credit the departed one with virtues the child knows he never had. "Your poor father, Mary, was the most considerate and loving husband and father anyone could ever have." Actually, the father had been an old roué and was drunk much of the time. Mary knew it; so did the rest of the family and the children in the neighborhood.

If the child is told lies about the departed parent, and he knows they are lies, he will not imitate the false, though ideal, behavior attributed to the departed parent, nor will he learn to tell the truth himself. By refusing to admit that the departed parent had evil qualities (when the child remembers otherwise), the surviving parent has never once censured those evil feelings and actions which the child knows existed. By refusing to censure such evil and by speaking only good of the dead father the mother is creating a loophole. The child is learning, by example, that his mother does not censure evil. This leads the child to expect that should he similarly do evil, his mother will cover up for him too. In this way she fosters in the child the evil that she tries to deny in the dead parent.

In addition, this child must contend with other emotional forces. If the departed parent was mean and cruel to the child during life, the child will have additional reasons to harbor feelings of anger against the departed parent. The desire to punish the evil parent appears with the anger. In the death of the parent the child sees his parent punished, but it is a horrible punishment, complete and final. The child had wished to punish; the parent is punished; the parent is dead. It is more than the child bargained for. Could his own wishes to punish the parent be responsible for this horrible event? He begins to feel guilty. What will happen in the future if he were to show anger toward other people? He becomes terror-stricken at the thought of ever again showing or even admitting to feelings of anger. His previous anger against the departed parent, which had no opportunity to be resolved, remains seething within him. By her denial of the facts, the mother permits the child no way of ridding himself of all this pent-up anger and guilt. He must keep all this turmoil within himself. Along with the guilt are sown the seeds for future brooding melancholy or other forms of depressed feelings and, sometimes, the complete and final solution to depressed states— self-destruction.

These same feelings of anger and guilt occur in the child whose parent has just committed suicide. Again, these feelings are intensified if the previous child-parent relationship was unhealthy. Such a tragic event has severe effects upon the child. Any one who commits suicide has been in a state of emotional turmoil in the period immediately preceding, and often for long periods before. While in such a disturbed state, the parent could not help but inoculate his child with at least some of those highly destructive feelings which led to the suicide. Another factor is the child's knowledge that the parent, with his own hand and of his own will, left him. "Didn't Daddy love me?" "Why did he leave?" "Was I naughty?" The highly impressionable child will always carry the memory of his father's solution to life's problems. The suicide has shown the child an example of inability and refusal to face life's problems. In the future, when faced with a serious problem, he may see in his parent's example permission similarly to refuse to face his own problems. With such a background, it is not at all uncommon to see alcoholism, desertion, and suicide appear. Basically, it is in the previous hostile parent-child relationships and not in heredity that one should look for the causes of suicide.

What should the surviving parent tell the child when a suicide has occurred? The answer to this question is difficult and is probably answered best by the feelings of the surviving parent. As in all cases of death of a parent, the surviving parent's reaction to the death and his own feelings toward the deceased and toward the children will determine how he will handle this problem. It is probably better to tell the truth at once (without giving any unnecessary details) than risk having the child inadvertently learn the truth later in life and have his illusions shattered. As part of the truth, the child should be told that the departed parent was very sick and that taking his own life was foolish and wrong. The child should definitely be made to understand that there can be no excuse for such an act. As in all instances of a parent's death, but even more necessary in the case of suicide, the child should be permitted and encouraged to express himself. When he asks questions about the deceased parent, the surviving parent should emphasize only the happy, good, and healthy times they all shared before the events that led to the suicide—provided, of course, that happy, good, and healthy times were actually shared.

Although the surviving parent should tell the truth, this does not mean that he should constantly bring up and repeatedly emphasize all that was wrong (and nothing that was good) with the departed one. This is as cruel and destructive to the child as the fabrication of false virtues. In both instances the child becomes the whipping boy for the hatred of the surviving parent for his spouse. By dwelling at length, without the child's asking, on the vices of the departed parent, the surviving one reveals his own intense interest and preoccupation with these vices. In this way he encourages in the child those vices which he deplored in the deceased.

What, then, should the surviving parent say? When the child asks, briefly tell the truth in response to his specific questions. Details which are not requested need not and should not be given. Long-winded harangues only emphasize to the child the parent's own interest in the vices being discussed or his own marital problems with the deceased. Simply tell the child that such vices are wrong. Do not tell him, "Don't let me ever catch you doing that yourself." Such a statement only opens up to the child new vistas for his own future actions. It tells him that the parent expects the child, at some future time, to develop the same vices. Why should a parent who is certain of his own and his child's morality fear that the child can or will go wrong?

The surviving parent must not, under any circumstances and for any excuse, tell the child any of the departed parent's vices of which the child is not aware. He must not lie to the child about what the child already knows, but he must not give the child new fuel for thought. The parent does not have to use the child to gratify his own emotional needs or as an escape hatch to vent his own angry feelings toward the departed one. The child himself gives the cue, and the parent who loves and understands his child will recognize his needs without the necessity of going verbally into most of this material. The parent and the child with a healthy underlying exchange of feelings know what the situation is without the need for much discussion. Under such circumstances little need be discussed verbally. It is often in the mutual honest exchange of healthy feelings that the above points are made by parent to child.

These same principles apply to the feelings of the child toward the death of a brother or a sister or any close relative or friend. For instance, if the surviving child had been in a stage of intense competition with the departed brother or sister, albeit the competition was well disguised, the fact is that the surviving child has lost a brother or a sister during a period of rivalry. All brothers and sisters go through periods of healthy rivalry, competing for many things but especially for their parents' affections. But in this instance, the loss occurred before the mutual feelings of anger could be resolved with time and through healthy parent-child and child-child relationships. As in the case of the child who loses the parent of the same sex during the first-romance stage, this anger persists unresolved and becomes submerged with other underlying but important feelings. If the competition was extreme, the death of one child can have a shattering effect upon the other. In his confused mental state he feels that his unbridled anger contributed to the death of his rival. He feels responsible for the death. He blames himself and has undue guilt and depression. The feelings associated with this experience may color his future attitudes in competitive situations.

Throughout this book we have noted that emotional problems have their origins in emotional disturbances already present in the family group. In the case of death, especially the death of a parent, the young child is robbed of a need essential to his development. The blighting and far-reaching emotional effects of death on the young child present one of the few situations in which a totally new factor comes into play and can completely upset the existing parent-child relationships. A parent-child relationship heretofore emotionally healthy can succumb to the unleashed and unsatisfied angers and needs created by this tragedy.

The same general principles apply when dealing with a child who has been deserted by a parent or whose parents have been divorced or separated. It is imperative that we do not deny the facts with which the child is already acquainted. Nor should we dwell at length upon the vices. Adults should not bring up the subject spontaneously without questions from the child. It is sufficient to emphasize, without lengthy discussion, that the vices were wrong. Above all, under no circumstances and for no reason whatever should the child be blamed for the fact that the other parent left. Children do not break up marriages which are emotionally healthy. The causes of marital conflict usually lie within the marital partners themselves.

Hardly a day went by since the divorce that Mrs. D. did not tell her two young children, "Your daddy left us because he didn't love us anymore." This constant refrain was drummed into her children at the slightest provocation and often gratuitously injected into her conversation. Mrs. D. was an attractive young woman who received many invitations to parties and many requests for dates. But she clung tenaciously to her self-imposed role of the lonely, self-sacrificing divorcee. With much ado and even in the presence of her children, she often refused these invitations because "I would really love to go very much. It gets so lonesome at times. But I must stay home and take care of my two children. . . ." Her mother's repeated offers to babysit were always refused, "I can't ask you to do that for me, Mother. You've already done too much." On the rare occasions that Mrs. D. accepted an invitation she spent the evening telling her escort about her loneliness, the enormous amount of time spent in the care of her children, her previous married life, her divorce, and the selfishness and irresponsibility of her former husband. Such evenings became occasions for Mrs. D. to unburden her pent-up feelings.

The children's father sent each of them a Christmas present. The presents arrived through the mail with all the festive wrappings and the usual warnings, "Do not open until Christmas." Mrs. D., without the knowledge of her children, opened the packages, examined the contents, and rewrapped the presents.

She then went out and bought for each child a gift that she knew the child wanted more than the gift that had been sent by the father. "Your Daddy . . . didn't love us any more."

The two children had numerous emotional problems stemming from the emotional disturbances of the father and the mother that long antedated the marriage and the divorce. Obviously, the divorce did not solve this problem. Mrs. D.'s stormy marriage and the subsequent divorce only provided her with someone to blame for her own inability to adjust and behave in a mature manner.

In attempting to resolve the parents' conflict over who would receive custody of the children, the court had decided that the two children would spend six months of the year with each parent. The situation with the mother was repeated, with a few variations, during the children's stay with the father. The children were caught in a deadly cross fire from which there was no escape. Each parent, without being aware of the destructiveness of such behavior, used the children as a means for relieving his and her pent-up hatreds. It should be stressed again that in most divorces both marital partners are emotionally disturbed; both are responsible for the dissolution of the marriage. And the children seldom escape this family tragedy unscathed.

PITFALLS AND OPPORTUNITIES IN ADOPTION

Although married for ten years, Mr. and Mrs. Jones were unable to have a baby of their own though they wanted one very much. Their family physician referred them to a reputable adoption agency sponsored by their church. In his letter of introduction to the agency, the physician included a report of the medical history and the excellent physical condition of both Mr. and Mrs. Jones. At the agency they were asked many questions and filled out innumerable forms so that as much information as possible could be obtained about their backgrounds—religious, social, and economic. Then they were asked to see a physician with specialized knowledge in the emotional aspects of adoption. He routinely screened potential adoptive parents for the agency to find out their emotional backgrounds, which the agency knew from experience were even more important to the successful rearing of a child than religious, social, and economic factors.

In a friendly and relaxed atmosphere the physician asked them many questions about their own parents, brothers and sisters, their own childhood, adolescence, courtship and marriage. By having them describe themselves and others close to them, their hopes for their own and the child's future and by asking them to describe their dreams, the physician obtained a clear picture of the emotional values they attached to the prospective child. He knew that people often want to adopt children for reasons stemming from their own sick emotions. He also knew the tragic aftermath of adopting children for such reasons.

The physician found that Mr. and Mrs. Jones would be happy to receive, love, and care for either a boy or a girl. They pictured their child growing up to be a happy, healthy person. Having had good relationships with their own parents and with each other, no other possibility for the child's future occurred to them. The physician knew they would accept and love the child for what he was: a healthy, intelligent child with no hereditary diseases and with the potential for growing up to be a fine person. He knew that warped emotions, exaggerated fears, hatreds, delinquency, perverted sexuality, inability to get along with people, wrecked marriages, and other evidences of serious emotional maladjustments are not inherited from one's parents. They are acquired from the parents after birth. A child's virtues or vices are determined by the parents' feelings and actions, apparent or concealed. Therefore, the physician was not at all interested in these aspects of the baby's natural parents. But he was interested in, and had as nearly complete information as could be obtained about the existence of any hereditary diseases in the baby's natural parents.

Finally, after carefully assembling all the information on Mr. and Mrs. Jones, the physician asked them what they would tell the child when he asked them about where he came from. Mr. and Mrs. Jones looked uncertainly at each other; then Mrs. Jones leaned forward impulsively and said, "I'd tell him that we were not his real Mommy and Daddy; that his real Mommy and Daddy were very fine people who loved him very much. But they got sick and died and went to heaven. Daddy and I were not able to have a baby of our own, and we wanted a baby to love and to have for our very own. We went to the place where they take care of babies who have lost their Mommies and Daddies. We looked at many babies and when we saw you, we saw how nice you were. We wanted you above all the other babies. We were the happiest people in the world to find such a wonderful baby as you." The physician was not surprised. He had expected such an answer. He knew that Mr. and Mrs. Jones would make fine parents for either a little boy or girl.

Mr. and Mrs. Smith brought their seven-year-old son, Harry, to the physician's office because they did not know where to turn next. Mr. Smith was a handsome, athletic-looking, well-tailored man in his early forties, distinguished in appearance, bearing, and self-assurance. He was urbane and cordial to the nurse who escorted the trio into the physician's office. Mrs. Smith, despite her chic clothes and faultlessly applied makeup, did not compare in any sense with her husband. Her facial expression was alert and intelligent, but she was not beautiful. Harry was a handsome child, with short, curly hair, freckles, and finely chiseled features. But he was quiet and shy and remained close to his parents. Harry had set fires in wastepaper baskets at school. The principal had called in the parents and insisted that something be done. He had refused to permit Harry to return to school until he was seen by a physician. Further questioning revealed that this particular act of delinquency had occurred three times before and that there had been repeated interviews between the parents, the teachers, and the principal.

As part of his complete review of the patient, the

physician found that Harry had always had problems suggestive of basic emotional disturbances: breath-holding spells, temper tantrums, fussy eating habits, and the most recent, fire-setting. In general, Harry was evidence of his disturbed home and family relationships. The physician found ample indication that the parents were using Harry as a scapegoat for their own long-standing, unresolved emotional problems. But what distinguished Harry from the cases we have mentioned previously was the excuse that the parents used: Harry was an adopted child. As such, he was in a particularly vulnerable position. He, as any child might, served as the receptacle and the buffer for all his parent's forbidden destructive feelings and desires. And as an adopted child, he offered his parents a ready-made excuse. They could blame the specter of Harry's heredity.

After many years of childless marriage, constant bickering, philandering, and trial separations, Mr. and Mrs. Smith's marriage was on the brink of divorce. In desperation, they decided to seek the advice of the man whose intelligence they respected the most, Mr. Smith's employer. He surprised them both by revealing that his only son was adopted, and that his own marriage had been similarly tottering until the adoption brought him and his wife together. The Smiths had casually discussed the possibility of adoption before, but the boss's story convinced them. From this point on, they did not waste any time. Through his numerous personal connections and business know-how, Mr. Smith slashed through all the red tape. They insisted upon a boy, and although they had to wait two extra weeks they got a boy. The particular social worker assigned to them was poorly prepared. She gave the Smiths only a brief verbal summary of the boy's family background. The boy's father was married and a successful businessman whose small plant had burned down many years before. The insurance from this had given him his start in a subsequently successful business enterprise. It was rumored, but never proved, that he had set fire to his own plant in order to collect the insurance. The boy's mother was unmarried, healthy, young, attractive, of Anglo-Saxon background who had come to the city with hopes of becoming an actress.

The Smiths adopted the baby in order to salvage their marriage, which was collapsing because of their mutually faulty emotional relationship. They had not wanted a baby for his own sake. If they had, the sex of the child would have made little difference. They also should have sought the best available medical advice, through a reputable adoption agency, rather than turning to Mr. Smith's employer.

No constructive purpose was served by the representative of the agency telling the Smiths about the baby's natural parents. The statement that the baby was healthy and that there were no hereditary diseases in the background should have been sufficient.

From the first, Mrs. Smith feared that Harry would develop some of the moral laxities of his natural parents. At the time they adopted him, she told her husband—and the phrase always remained in her mind—"All these pretty women seem to get into trouble." Then she commented, "What a terrible thing for her parents. If they only knew ... let's hope Harry never does that to us." She frequently discussed these fears with Mr. Smith. In an attempt to forestall these anticipated problems, Mr. and Mrs. Smith decided to tell Harry the whole truth, as far as they knew it, when he was only two and a half years old. As Mr. Smith said, "There's no sense beating around the bush. The sooner he knows what his parents really were, the better. He might as well face up to the facts. Then he'll appreciate what we're doing for him."

These highly disturbed parents were poor candidates for adoption in the first place. From a study of their lives and feelings, the physician realized that the previous threat of divorce was only another sign of their long-standing emotional problems. Without medical help, the chances of these parents raising an emotionally healthy and well-adjusted child were practically nil. Their own emotional disturbances, which were being discharged upon each other (and leading to divorce), united to find an outlet through their adopted child.

A child of such parents, adopted or otherwise, was destined for trouble. The only question was, "How would this come about?" In an adopted child, the excuse of poor heredity is too readily available to the adoptive parents, who can easily escape their own responsibility for the child's difficulties. And society, in its lack of knowledge, is too ready to accept such an excuse as plausible. This excuse can be used by the adoptive parents (and accepted by society) whether or not the backgrounds of the natural parents are known. In Harry's case, however, an added excuse was handed to them gratuitously when the adoptive parents were told about the natural parents. Although these parents would have been ready enough to invoke heredity as an explanation for Harry's problems, the agency representative made it easier for them to do so. "Look at Harry's parents. It was rumored that his father got his start in business from insurance on a fire he set himself. His mother was just a young actress. And Harry was illegitimate. What can you expect?"

The sympathy of Mrs. Smith for Harry's natural mother (and therefore for Harry) was not enhanced by her knowledge that Harry's mother was a beautiful young woman while she herself was plain and middle-aged. Furthermore, Mrs. Smith was unable to bear children and therefore might have been unsure of her own femininity in this respect; Harry's mother had already shown herself capable of bearing a child. In all these comparisons with Harry's natural mother, Mrs. Smith always came out second best. Any anger that she already had from her own life experiences could only be fortified by such comparisons. It would be easy for this anger to flare out in a highly destructive manner against her adopted son during one of the innumerable petty emotional outbursts that often occur between any mother and child.

For example, during some childish fit of rage, the

child who knows he is adopted, might burst out, "You don't love me! You're not my real mother anyway! My own mother would love me!" Here is a ready-made opportunity for the adoptive mother to show her true feelings for the child. If the adoptive mother were sure of herself, she would be able to take the child's temporary angry outburst without needing to retaliate. She would be sure of her love for her adopted son and of his love for her. She would know that nothing serious was meant by the remark or the outburst that led to it. By her actions and feelings as well as by words she would agree that his mother loved him very much, but she would assure him that she also loved him very much. But Mrs. Smith's own underlying anger and guilt toward other people, toward her adopted son's natural mother, and toward her adopted son would cause her to see some frightening truth in her son's accusation. As a matter of fact, Mrs. Smith actually lashed back, "Your mother! For your information, your mother was a little no-good tramp! If she loved you, she would have kept you. You should be grateful you have your Daddy and me to love you and take care of you."

Any child feels more secure if he knows he is loved. Telling him that his natural parents left him because they did not love him is very destructive. Any child, also tends to imitate his parents, natural or adoptive. Any child, adopted or not, likes to be proud of his parents. What had Harry to gain by learning all these destructive things about his natural parents? And what had Harry's foster parents to gain by learning all these destructive things about

Harry's natural parents? All they gained was an excuse for the gratification, through Harry, of their own destructive emotions.

There are some cases, such as Harry's, in which the natural parents did not love the child and in which the natural parents had no traits or accomplishments of which the child could be proud or which the child could imitate constructively. How much better would such a child be served if the adoption agency made an iron-clad rule to divulge no information on any child's background, other than reassuring the prospective parents that there are no hereditary diseases in the child's background. This should be done even if the prospective parents insist on learning all the details possible about the child's natural parents (and such insistence raises questions about the qualifications of such people to adopt children).

If the child is to develop in an emotionally healthy manner, he must think well of his natural parents. And if he is to think well of them when they have no traits or accomplishments of which the child can be proud, it is to the child's best interests that such knowledge be withheld entirely from both the child and his adoptive parents. How much better it would be if the adoption agency were to assume this responsibility in all cases and leave no possible loopholes in the future relationships between the child and his adoptive parents.

In Harry's case, the threatened dissolution of his adoptive parents' marriage was averted. Harry had served the purpose for which he was adopted. But this was achieved at the terrible price of his nearly complete emotional destruction. The energies of the terrible emotional conflicts of the parents, which had threatened to destroy the marriage, were shunted from the marriage onto the unfortunate child. And this pattern is all too tragically common.

Related to this problem of the adopted child is the problem of the child who is shifted from foster home to foster home. He never stays long enough with any family group to identify himself with it and to imitate its grown-ups. And above all and through all is the terrible knowledge that no one loves him and no one cares to keep him.

CHAPTER **12**

━━━━━━━━━━━━━━━━━━━━━━━━━━━━━━━

Stemming the Tide—The Remedy

All that we have presented in this book paints a grim picture of the contamination of successive generations by emotional illness and the corrosive influence of permissiveness. Yet there is much reason for optimism, as we shall see.

But first the hard facts must be understood and accepted. They are not only shocking but they involve all of us at one time or another in such an intimate way that we feel threatened by them. It is tempting, therefore, to deny or grossly underrate the facts presented in this book. To do so would only whitewash the role of parent-child relationships in today's upheaval, thus blocking any rational approach to the prevention and treatment of these problems.

One reason for optimism is that these parent-child tensions, in their various manifestations of emotional illness, are treatable; the negative process can be reversed. While it is true that these highly individualized emotional illnesses pose a tremendous challenge for successful treatment and further research, they nevertheless do yield to proper diagnosis and treatment. Such diagnosis and treatment, of course, is a technical matter and should be undertaken only by those professionally equipped through special training, skills, and aptitudes.

If the reader who has come thus far in this book is a parent, he may still be able to give his child the most precious gift of all: emotional health. More can be accomplished by prevention than by treatment. In other words, the well-intentioned parent, by being knowledgeable about such matters, can become not only forewarned but forearmed. Insofar as matters are susceptible to his conscious control, such a parent will not act out through his child his own tensions and unresolved yearnings for nonconformity. When indicated, such a parent will seek help for his own problems—and in time.

But what if the parent does not feel impelled from within to do these things? Then, through the insights offered in this book, other responsible adults—teachers, social workers, and the like—will become aware that the parent is most certainly involved when they must deal with a child having any of the problems we have discussed. By increased knowledge of how the unconscious mind acts and reacts in parent-child relationships, such a concerned individual will recognize that the parents of a disturbed child are under the influence of hidden (unconscious) forces stemming from problems and experiences that they have had with their own parents.

But this all happened in the past and is over. The parent could not control what his parents were; he could not choose his ancestors. Therefore society will strive to understand such a parent, and will not blame him for such feelings and behavior. Though nothing can be gained by moralizing, we must realistically recognize the role of such a parent in the disturbed feelings and behavior of his child. Social pressures could then be brought to bear on the parent.

The crux of the matter is what can the parent do about all this? He must find other outlets for his disturbed feelings: various psychosomatic reactions of his own body; his own overt mental illness, disruptions and turmoil in his own marital, sexual, and social relations. He must seek treatment for himself. If he is fortunate, he may, instead, gain healthy sublimations. His child will then have been spared the fatal inoculation of emotional illness, and the vicious cycle of each generation's contamination of the next will have been broken. These reflections apply when a child, a minor, is still properly under the care of and influenced by his parents.

In any case, when the delinquent is incorrigible and involved in repeated serious antisocial behavior, society must then protect itself, while well aware of the parental role in such behavior. But recognition of the parent's role in a delinquent's antisocial (psychopathic) behavior must not be used as licence for the delinquent to abdicate his personal responsibility.

Bribes, excuses, or sympathy for the hardcore repeater are useless. Society must insist that such a lawbreaker—the delinquent who has now become a criminal—be isolated. He will then no longer be in a position to harm his fellow men by committing further crimes. Such separation must be strictly maintained until he accepts treatment and responds to it. Any restraint less than this is not fair to the law-abiding majority of our citizens.

In summary, the emotional health of the child is dependent upon his relationship with his parents. This relationship, the keystone of the family and our hope for the future of civilized humanity, should be safeguarded by planned parenthood. Let parents have only as many children as they are capable of raising. And "raising" should most emphatically include not only the material needs of the children but also their emotional needs. Current measures for birth control and continued research in this area should enable the responsible and loving parent to control the size of his family. This will help not only the parent and his child but society at large. It is hoped that these benefits of family planning can be diffused to those parts of our population where the needs are just as great but the awareness of birth control is limited.

The gain to society at large from the strengthened mental health of its people is incalculable—materially, morally—every way. One step toward that shining goal is the dissolving of tensions between parent and child and the nurturing of healthier two-way communication between them. In this way, the emotional well-being of the child will be improved and his tendency to act out his tensions against his fellowmen will be lessened.

Knowledge is power to correct abuses and to see the need for treatment. Self-knowledge comes with experience and practice. It fathers self-confidence. It can give helpful insights into the causes and remedies of parent-child tensions. Then there will be every reason for hope and optimism.

INDEX